The Complete Henry Root Letters

I WISH to protest most
strongly about everything.
—Henry Root, Park Walk,
West Brompton.

EVENING STANDARD, WEDNESDAY, AUGUST 15, 1979

The Complete Henry Root Letters

Henry Root

Akadine

THE COMPLETE HENRY ROOT LETTERS

First published in Great Britain in 1992 as a paper-
back original by Mandarin Paperbacks, an imprint of
Reed Consumer Books Limited.

The Henry Root Letters first published in Great
Britain in 1980 by Weidenfeld & Nicolson Ltd. *The
Further Letters of Henry Root* first published in
Great Britain in 1980 by Weidenfeld & Nicolson Ltd.

ISBN 1-888173-00-9

To Mrs Root and Mrs Thatcher: two ordinary mothers.

The Henry Root Letters

139 Elm Park Mansions
Park Walk
London, S.W.10.

Sir David McNee,
New Scotland Yard
London, S.W.1.

21st March 1979.

Dear Sir David,

Hang on! Ignore the media! Ordinary folk are with you all the way in your campaign for greater police powers.

Better that ten innocent men be convicted than that one guilty man goes free! That's what the lounge-room revolutionaries fail to understand.

Don't be depressed by the fact that your 'image' isn't too clever just yet. We have to face it that you come across a wee bit charmless. So what? Do we want this once great country to be policed by the likes of Mr Victor Sassoon the barber and cosmetics expert from Los Angeles?

Your predecessor, Sir Robert Mark, was an accomplished PR man, so it was easy for him. And he had a lot of luck with the 'Spaghetti House Siege Situation'. The public really liked that. What a pity the recent 'Gunman Holed Up In Village Pub Shot Dead By 392 Policemen Situation' didn't happen on your patch! That would have been just the break you needed. As it was, the Chief Constable of Essex was able to pick up the apples on that one. Never mind. Your chance will come.

Here's a pound. Use it to enforce Law and Order.

So - you're doing your poor best, but what can we, the ordinary folk, do? We need you to tell us. The politicians (with the exception of Mrs Thatcher) aren't giving us a lead.

Could you oblige with a photo? I'd like to stick it up in my boy Henry Jr's room in lieu of one of a popular crooning group entitled The Boomtown Rats. The lad's 15, but he's not shaping up. He idles around in his room all day, sewing sequins onto his disco pumps and worse. When I put a photo of Sir Robert Mark on his wall, it was down within seconds and up went the Boomtown crooners again. I'm not usually an advocate of unauthorised violence, but if he takes your picture down I'll knock the wee blighter senseless, that's for sure.

Keep hammering 'em!

Support Mrs Thatcher!

Yours for greater police powers!

Henry Root

Henry Root.

**COMMISSIONER OF POLICE
OF THE METROPOLIS**

NEW SCOTLAND YARD
BROADWAY LONDON SW1H OBG

29 March 1979

Sir David McNee QPM

Dear Mr Root

The Commissioner has asked me to write and thank you
for your letter of 21 March; your kind comments are
appreciated.

As requested, I enclose a signed photograph of
Sir David. Perhaps I should warn you, however, that
the Commissioner keeps a close watch on crime reports
and will be keeping a particular eye on them to
ensure that you do not do what you propose to do
should your son take the photograph off his wall!

I regret that police are not permitted to accept
money for the purpose you propose; although the
thought is acknowledged I have to return your
donation herewith.

Yours sincerely

Brian Gittins
Private Secretary

Mr Henry Root
139 Elm Park Mansions
Park Walk
LONDON SW10

139 Elm Park Mansions
Park Walk
London, S.W.10.

Mrs Margaret Thatcher,   23rd March 1979.
The House of Commons,
London, S.W.1.

Dear Leader!
        So they said a woman couldn't do it! They were forgetting
Joan d'Arc, the maid of Orleans! She put it over the French with
their bidets and so-called soixante-neuf and so will you!
        Never give up!
        This is what we've got to do. With the help of the Scot
Nats we can bring down Mr Callaghan and his ramshackle crew of
wooly-minded lightweights. At the first suitable opportunity
we must table a motion of no confidence in the Government. I'll
have to leave this to you. As long as you get your sums right
Jim'll be back feeding his pigs and you'll be measuring for new
curtains at No 10!
        Throughout the coming battle I'll keep you in touch with
door-step opinion.
        Avarice is patriotic! Here's a pound.
        Your man on the door-step,

        Henry Root

        Henry Root.
PS.   Freedom to do as we're told under the law! Let's go!

139 Elm Park Mansions
Park Walk
London, S.W.10.

Mrs Margaret Thatcher,
The House of Commons,
London, S.W.1.

29th March 1979.

Dear Leader!

Congratulations! You took my advice, you went for the vote
of no confidence and now you can start thinking about new colour
schemes for No 10!

I believe 'Sunny Jim' is collecting his cards from Her
Majesty today. How nice for her to know it's the last she'll
be seeing of <u>him</u> for a while! She must be looking forward to
cosy tea-time chats with another woman such as yourself. Two
mothers.

Now, with great respect, a word of advice from an old
campaigner. It's been my experience that the weaker sex (God
bless 'em!) sometimes hesitate to go for the kill. I'm sure
this doesn't apply to you, but now is <u>not</u> the time to back off.
You've shaken up 'Sunny Jim' with a stiff left hook and now
you've got to dump him on his backside with a solid right cross.
The old one-two. That's a boxing term. Get your husband, Mr
Thatcher, to explain it to you. I read an article about him in
'The Evening Standard' the other day. He sounds like a nice old
stick and I think we'd get on well together. The article said
he's a simple man who believes in calling a spade a spade. So
do I.

Talking about spades, I gather you have one in your Shadow
Cabinet - the ex-Gurkha, Mr John Nott. Okay. Fair enough. Nothing
wrong with that. Trying to trick in some of the immigrant vote
by having one of our Asian friends in your inner circle is a
shrewd move on your part. But don't carry the concept too far.
Once you've won the election, ditch him.

Another word of advice. In the coming campaign, <u>don't
worry about your voice</u>. Don't listen to people who say you
sound like a suburban estate agent's wife. What's wrong with
suburban estate agents? They have a vote!

One last thing. Mrs Root and I have recently formed 'The
Ordinary Folk Against Porn Society'. We meet once a week with
some of our friends (Dr Littlewinkle and his good lady, the
Smithsons, Major Dewdrop and Fred and Rita Snipe, who live opposite, form the hard-core nucleus) to discuss sex, drugs, nudity
and violence. While I know these are all subjects that interest
you, I expect you'll be too busy at the moment, what with one
thing and another, to address us yourself. Don't worry. We
understand. However, a signed photograph and message of encouragement would mean a lot to our members.

Don't forget the old one-two!

Your Man on the Door-step!

Henry Root.

The Rt. Hon. Mrs. Margaret Thatcher, M.P.

HOUSE OF COMMONS
LONDON SWIA 0AA
4th April 1979

Dear Mr Root,

Mrs Thatcher has asked me to thank you for your
two recent letters of 23rd and 29th March.

She has asked me to say how grateful she is to
you for your kind donation and your very kind
words of support. As you request I am sending
a photograph of Mrs Thatcher, which she has
signed for you.

As far as your request for a message is concerned,
I am afraid because of the forthcoming campaign
Mrs Thatcher has so many pressures on her time
that it is not possible for her to write one
personally.

She hopes you will understand the reasons
for this reluctant refusal, and asked me to
pass on her best wishes.

Yours sincerely,

Richard Ryder
Private Office

Henry Root Esq

139 Elm Park Mansions
Park Walk
London, S.W.10.

The Chairman,
Faber & Faber Ltd,   23rd March 1979.
London, W.C.1.

Dear Sir,
          Subject to certain stipulations, I'd be prepared to accept
the post of commissioning editor, as advertised in 'The Spectator'
this week.
          I had my people check you out thoroughly and I have to tell
you they ran into a lot of negative feedback. The word on the
literary scene is that the once respected name of Faber and Faber
isn't too sweet just now.
          Never mind. I can stop the rot. Books aren't my business,
but that's neither here nor there these days. Basic commercial
principles are the same whether you're selling poetry or wet fish
(my dodge, as it happens.) Don't get me wrong. I rub along all
right with books. In fact I quite like them. The trouble is
they don't like me. Still, who reads books? You've got to div-
ersify, up-date the product, smarten up the image - or go to the
wall.
          Who's selling really BIG now? Writers? Not a chance! The
punters are buying Ustinov, Niven, Betty Bacall, Diana Dors, Dr
J.P.R. Williams, Sir Robert Mark, Lady Antonia Fraser as was, Ted
Heath, Shirley Conran (the cook) and the vet from the Midlands.
          Have you the faintest idea how many copies of David Niven's
books have sold world-wide to date? 9½ million! That means there's
a hell of a lot of mugs out there, and we've got to reach them!
          I can show you how. Of course we'll run into a lot of
trouble with the grey-beards on your board and I'm afraid they'll
have to go. Leave this to me. As I say, my background is business systems and wet fish and I'm happy to be the goon with the
big hatchet.
          I've a lot of solid contacts abroad - particularly in Ice-
land, South Africa, Rhodesia, Turkey and Chile - and a stack of
valid ideas which could put you back on the literary map.
          As luck would have it I'll be in your neck of the woods
on Tuesday 3rd April, so unless I hear that it would be inconvenient for you I'll hop through your door at about 12.30.
          We can tie up the details (salary, expenses etc) then.
          Yours faithfully,

          Henry Root

          Henry Root.

Charles Monteith, Chairman. Matthew Evans, Managing Director.

T. E. Faber. A. T. G. Pocock.

Rosemary Goad. Giles de la Mare. G. W. Taylor.

Secretary: J. D. F. Nichols

FABER AND FABER LTD

PUBLISHERS

3 Queen Square, London WC1N 3AU   Fabbaf London WC1   01-278 6881

Telex: 299633 (FABER G)

HMS

28th March, 1979

Henry Root, Esq.,
139 Elm Park Mansions,
Park Walk,
London, S.W.10.

Dear Mr. Root,

We are grateful to you for having answered our advertisement about the editorial vacancy here. We had a very large number of replies and we have now compiled a short list of those people whom we would like to interview. I very much regret to have to let you know that, after having considered your application very carefully, we have decided not to include your name on this list.

Do please let me say again how grateful we are to you for having written to us.

Yours sincerely,

Henrietta Smyth

Henrietta Smyth
Secretary to the Chairman

P.S. The Chairman has asked me to add that there would be no point in your calling in here on Tuesday morning, though he is grateful to you for your offer to do so.

Registered Office as above.   Registered in England.   No. 944703

139 Elm Park Mansions
Park Walk
London, S.W.10.

Mr James Anderton,
The Chief Constable,
Greater Manchester,
Manchester.

23rd March 1979.

Dear Chief Constable,

Your stand against the porno merchants of Manchester is an inspiration to ordinary folk down here in the soft south. Our own Sir David McNee is doing his poor best, but the odds are against him. He's a fine man, but the Hampstead pansies have got him by the tail.

We have to keep asserting that people commit crimes not because they come from so-called deprived backgrounds, but because they're _wicked_. The statistics showing that only .000137% of all crimes of senseless violence are carried out by stockbrokers living in Sunningdale prove only that such folk are stockbrokers because they've got a sense of right and wrong - not vice versa.

Since it's always been my opinion that the fight against evil shouldn't be left entirely to intellectuals like yourself, but that the man in the street should play his part too, Mrs Root and I recently formed 'The Ordinary Folk Against The Rising Tide Of Filth In Our Society Situation Society' (TOFATRTOFIOSSS for short). We meet once a week for a lively, no-holds-barred discussion over wine and cheese and a guest intellectual delivers a short paper.

We have extended invites to most of the top turns in the struggle against filth, many of whom will be familiar to you from joint porn-monitoring talk-ins. I'm referring, of course, to Lord Longford, Mary Kenny, Mrs Whitehouse, Mr Philip Wrack, the Dowager Lady Birdwood, Mr Richard West and Sir Emile Littler (or Prince Littler, as he now is, having inherited the title from his brother.) So far we've drawn a complete blank, alas. It's the old story. Intellectuals are very handy with words; less handy, in my experience, when it comes to a bit of direct action.

I realise that cracking down on the porno merchants in Manchester must take up a lot of your time, but is there any chance that you might read us a paper? We would, of course, pay your travelling expenses from Manchester and back.

Keep hitting 'em where it hurts!

'What Manchester thinks today, Hampstead will think in ten years time!' (Richard West.)

Your pal in the soft south,

Henry Root

Henry Root.

C James Anderton Q.P.M., F.B.I.M.
Chief Constable

Chief Constable's Office
P O Box 22 (S.West PDO)
Chester House
Boyer Street
Manchester M16 0RE
Telephone 061-872 5050

27th March 1979.

Dear Mr. Root,

Thank you for your very kind letter of support which I was most pleased to receive.

Much as I would like to support you and your friends in your worthwhile cause, I regret it will not be possible for me in the foreseeable future to give any address in London or, indeed, elsewhere. My diary of speaking engagements is practically full until the end of 1980.

Thank you for writing to me.

Yours sincerely,

Chief Constable.

H.Root, Esq.,
139 Elm Park Mansions,
Park Walk,
London.S.W.10.

139 Elm Park Mansions
Park Walk
London, S.W.10.

Sir Robert Mark,
c/o William Collins & Sons Ltd,
14 St James's Place,
London, S.W.1.

26th March 1979.

Dear Sir Robert,

It was with a deep sense of shock and outrage that I read in 'The Daily Telegraph' recently that you are now driving a breakdown van for the AA and selling life assurance in the evening.

Surely your book, 'In the Office of Constable', didn't sell that badly? I thought it was good! It could have done with a few more anecdotes, perhaps, along the lines of the amusing incident early in your career when you had at a fellow in the waterworks and then broke his leg. That's the sort of stuff the public likes. Shows the boys in blue to be human like the rest of us. Perhaps it was an isolated incident. I dare say that sort of excitement is just the glamorous side of a policeman's job.

Anyway, here's a pound. Not much, I'm afraid, but if ordinary folk everywhere donated a pound to public servants on their retirement they wouldn't be reduced in their declining years to patrolling the M4 in a yellow van and selling life-assurance door-to-door.

Yours for a better deal for our distressed old folk!

Henry Root

Henry Root.

139 Elm Park Mansions
Park Walk
London, S.W.10.

The Rt Hon William Whitelaw,
The House of Commons,   28th March 1979.
London, S.W.1.

Dear Mr Whitelaw,
        As an ordinary father, I have been much disturbed by two
recent remarks by men in public life.
        First, in an interview in 'The Evening News', Sir Robert
Mark said that he would not be against the decriminalisation of
of cannabis as long as he could be convinced that the substance
had no harmful effects!
        Secondly, ex-Chief Superintendant so-called 'Nipper' Reed
said in the course of a TV interview with Mr Ludovic Kennedy
that when he was a serving officer it had been impossible to
investigate serious crimes from Scotland Yard due to the fact
that more criminals ran their affairs from there than did up-
holders of law and order! To catch the so-called Krays he had
been compelled to do all his phoning from a kiosk on the corner!
        With regard to Sir Robert's amazing observation, small
wonder this once great country continues to career down-hill
like a greased pig if ex-public servants can openly advocate
the decriminalisation of a pleasure for no better reason than
that it's harmless!
        And the alarming significance of Mr Reed's remark seems
to have gone unnoticed. Is it not on all fours with saying that
the last place at which one can safely mail a letter is the
Post Office?
        Can you give me your assurance, Sir, as our future Home
Secretary, that cannabis will not be legalised <u>however harmless</u>
<u>it turns out to be</u> and that under your firm stewardship the
police will once again have as much time to investigate crime
as they now have to investigate each other?
        Support Mrs Thatcher!
        Yours Against the Decriminalisation of Harmless Pleasures!

        Henry Root

        Henry Root.

From: The Rt. Hon. William Whitelaw, C.H., M.C., M.P.

HOUSE OF COMMONS
LONDON SWIA OAA

2nd April, 1979

Dear Mr. Root,

Thank you for your letter of 28th March
and your very kind good wishes to our Party and
to Margaret Thatcher.

There is no question of any future Conservative
Government legalising cannabis. We also intend to
build up the strength and the quality of the Police
to give them a better oppo tunity to investigate
and prevent crime.

Yours sincerely,

H. Root, Esq.,
139 Elm Park Mansions,
Park Walk,
London S.W.10.

139 Elm Park Mansions
Park Walk
London, S.W.10.

Ms Esther Rantzen,
BBC Television,
London, W.12.

26th March 1979.

Dear Esther,

Congratulations on anther great show last night! The main 'How to get your knickers off' item was hilarious! Both Mrs Root and I chuckled all the way through it.

You've got the formula just right. If only more people in TV (television) realised that it's possible to be healthily vulgar without descending to schoolboy smut.

I enclose some humorous definitions and a comical poem for Cyril. I hope you can use them. On the assumption that you can, I'm invoicing the BBC separately.

Humorous Definitions.

Falsies: An enhancer to a maiden's pair!
The Vatican: House of pill refute!
The three ages of man: Tri-weekly, try weekly and try weakly!
Graffiti in Gents' W.C.: Squatters' writes!

Comical Poem.

While Titian was mixing rose-madder,
His model posed nude on a ladder.
Her position to Titian
Suggested coition,
So he climbed up the ladder and had 'er!

Just one slight criticism of the show last night. I thought your dress was rather revealing for what is essentially family viewing. One could see your legs quite clearly. I hope you won't mind my saying this. One doesn't want to see women's legs in one's lounge-room at a time when youngsters are still up and about.

Could you possibly oblige with a photo?

Yours for A Comical Definition!

Henry Root

Henry Root.

Henry Root.
139 Elm Park Mansions
Park Walk
London, S.W.10.

The Accounts Department
The BBC
Broadcasting House
Portland Place
London, W.1.

26th March 1979.

INVOICE

To four humorous definitions and one comical poem for
THAT'S LIFE..£12.95.

Kindly remit and oblige.

BRITISH BROADCASTING CORPORATION

BBC TV

KENSINGTON HOUSE RICHMOND WAY LONDON W14 0AX
TELEPHONE 01-743 1272   TELEX: 265781
TELEGRAMS AND CABLES: TELECASTS LONDON TELEX

REF: SLER

22/4/79

Dear Mr. Root,

Thank you very much indeed for taking the trouble to
write to me. Hearing from viewers like yourself is a
tremendous morale boost for us all - it really makes a
great difference to me to know that you find our work
enjoyable and worthwhile. May I send you my best wishes,
and thank you again for your letter.

Yours sincerely,

[signature]

pp Esther Rantzen

The Accounts Department
The BBC
Broadcasting House
Portland Place
London, W.1.

139 Elm Park Mansi[...]
Park Walk
London, S.W.10.

9th April 1979.

Dear Sir,

On 26th March I sent you an invoice for £12.95 for some
humorous definitions and a comical poem I submitted to 'That's
Life'.

I have not received the money and I must tell you that unl[...]
I get satisfaction by return of post I will be compelled to put
the matter in the hands of my solicitor.

Yours faithfully,

Henry Root

Henry Root.

BBC TV
BRITISH BROADCASTING CORPORATION
KENSINGTON HOUSE   RICHMOND WAY   LONDON W14 0AX
TELEPHONE 01-743 1272   TELEX: 265781
TELEGRAMS AND CABLES: TELECASTS LONDON TELEX

Mr H Root
139 Elm Park Mansions
Park Walk
London   SW10

22nd April 1979

Dear Mr Root

Your letter of the 9th April 1979 has been forwarded
to me by the BBC Accounts Department.

The That's Life programme does not pay fees for
uncommissioned material that is not transmitted.

Yours sincerely

Henry Murray

Henry Murray
Producer, That's Life

Esther Rantzen

139 Elm Park Mansions
Park Walk
London, S.W.10.

Ms Esther Rantzen,
'That's Life',
Television Centre,
London, W.12.

23rd April 1979.

Dear Esther,

You're a fat idiot and your show's a disgrace.

Yours sincerely,

Henry Root

Henry Root.

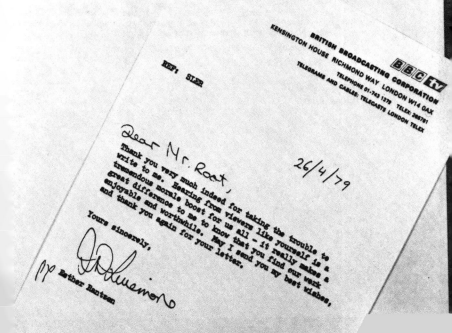

BRITISH BROADCASTING CORPORATION
KENSINGTON HOUSE RICHMOND WAY LONDON W14 0AX
TELEPHONE 01-743 1272   TELEX: 265781
TELEGRAMS AND CABLES: TELECASTS LONDON TELEX

REF: SL/ER

Dear Mr. Root,

Thank you very much indeed for taking the trouble to
write to me. Hearing from viewers like yourself is a
tremendous morale boost for us all – it really makes a
great difference to me to know that you find our work
enjoyable and worthwhile. May I send you my best wishes,
and thank you again for your letter.

26/4/79

Yours sincerely,

Esther Rantzen

139 Elm Park Mansions
Park Walk
London, S.W.10.

Ray Cooney Esq,
The Whitehall Theatre,
London, S.W.1.

29th March 1979.

Dear Cooney,

Mrs Root and I saw your show 'Ipi Tombi' last night. Better
late than never! We both thoroughly enjoyed it and the nudity, being
ethnic, was for once entirely inoffensive. I hope you won't mind
my saying this. I assume from your name that you yourself are one
of our coloured friends. Nothing wrong with that. Good luck to you!

Anyway, it struck me that a hit show must make quite a handy
profit. Do you look for outside investors – fairies, I think you
call them?

The fact is I've been in fish all my life, I've worked hard,
saved hard and now I reckon I could afford a small flutter without
breaking the bank. I'm talking about just a few thousand, spread
over several shows to minimise the risk. I believe the accident rate
is quite high in your business.

I hope you won't mind my asking. I'd really appreciate the
opportunity to invest if it's at all possible, and I'd like to encourage someone from your part of the world.

I look forward to hearing from you.

Yours sincerely,

Henry Root

Henry Root.

139 Elm Park Mansions
Park Walk
London, S.W.10.

Michael Edwardes Esq,
British Leyland Ltd,
Marylebone Road,
London, N.W.1.

31st March 1979.

Dear Mr Edwardes,

As a patriot, I am becoming increasingly distressed by the fact
that the mere mention of 'British Leyland' by a music-hall comedian
gives rise to gales of ignorant laughter, rather as the conjoined
notions of Her Royal Highness Princess Anne and a horse are liable
to take the roof off the London Palladium if mentioned from the stage
in the course of one of Lord Delfont's Royal Variety Shows.

I would remind you, Sir, that every time someone laughs at
'British Leyland' they are laughing at Great Britain.

In the circumstances I would earnestly suggest that you change
the name of the company either to 'Japanese Leyland' or to 'Jamaican
Leyland'.

The only jokes ever made about the Japanese concentrate round the
fact that they tend to be extremely small (like yourself - nothing
wrong with that) and that they are clever little monkeys who work too
hard.

Jokes along these lines would only be good for your company's
image. And if jokes were made about 'Jamaican Leyland' you could
prosecute the offenders under the Race Discrimination Act.

I look forward to hearing your reaction to this suggestion.

Yours sincerely,

Henry Root

Henry Root. Patriot!

139 Elm Park Mansions
Park Walk
London, S.W.10.

D. Dudley Morgan Esq,
Theodore Goddard & Co,   7th April 1979.
16 St Martin-le-Grand,
London, E.C.1.

Dear Mr Morgan,

Your firm has been recommended to me as being one with some experience of the law. I address myself to you personally as the senior partner since I have litigation of some import to prosecute and I don't wish to find myself in the hands of the office-boy.

As the enclosed documents will show, I wrote to Mr Michael Edwardes of British Leyland on 31st March with the viable suggestion that the name of the company be changed to 'Japanese Leyland'.

As you will imagine, it was with a sense of outrage that I discovered on 4th April that my concept was already in the pipeline. By 5th April the matter had become public knowledge, as the enclosed cartoon will adequately demonstrate.

Mr Edwardes has not favoured me with the courtesy of a reply to my letter and I am now persuaded that he is of a mind to 'borrow' my notion without acknowledgement or payment.

You will agree that in the circumstances damages of unusual consequence would come my way in the High Court.

I look forward to hearing that you will act for me in this matter. I am in a position to put further work your way pursuant to a satisfactory assessment of your performance hereunder.

Yours faithfully,

Henry Root

Henry Root.

THEODORE GODDARD & CO.

D. DUDLEY MORGAN
PETER A. J. MORLEY
J. N. FISHER
R. DEREK FOX
BLANCHE H. M. A. LUCAS
MARE N. STACEY
MICHAEL Q. WALTERS
F. J. CALDERAN
R. K. SHUTE
M. J. W. TOD
EDWIN A. JONES
WILLIAM S. ROGERS
M. A. CROFT BAKER
M. J. HARRIS

ANTONY HEALD
CHRISTOPHER CLOGG
W. H. STUART MAY
ANDREW BINGHAM
MARTIN G. CHESTER
P. GRAFTON GREEN
DIANA GUY
DAVID S. WILKINSON
R. M. PRESTON
DEREK W. LEWIS
SIMON STUBBINGS
MARTIN KRAMER
GUY I. F. LEIGH

R. DEREK WISE C.B.E. (RESIDENT IN PARIS)
EDWARD WILTSHIRE (RESIDENT IN MADRID)

CONSULTANT
DEREK F. S. CLOGG

E. A. CLARKE
A. R. W. CARRINGTON
C. J. J. MAPLES

ASSOCIATES

DIANA SNEEZUM
NICHOLAS WHITMEY

16 ST. MARTIN'S-LE-GRAND
LONDON EC1A 4EJ

Telephone: 01-606 8855
Cables: Assumpsit London E.C.1
Telex: 884678
Telegrams: Assumpsit London Telex
Telecopier Extension 208
L.D.E. and C.D.E. Box Number 47
Stock Exchange Number STX 2346

Associate Offices:

167 RUE DE L'UNIVERSITE
PARIS 75007
Telephone (010 331) 705 89 45
Telex: 250661

LAGASCA 106
MADRID 6
Telephone: (010 34 1) 275 03 24
Telegrams: Interlex

17 BOND STREET
ST. HELIER, JERSEY C I
Telephone: (0534) 36676
Telex: 41589

Your Ref

Our Ref   21

H. Root, Esq.,
139 Elm Park Mansions,
Park Walk,
London, S.W.10.

12th April, 1979.

Dear Sir,

Thank you for your letter of 7th April with enclosures concerning your possible complaint against Mr. Michael Edwards of British Leyland. I do not think I would necessarily agree with the penultimate paragraph of your letter that in the circumstances considerable damages would be awarded to you in the High Court.

In the circumstances this would not be a case which this firm would be prepared to undertake, and had we been prepared to do so we would have required very substantial sums on account before we accepted any instructions. If you still wish to proceed I suggest you seek some other firm who will be prepared to accept your instructions.

Yours faithfully,

D. DUDLEY MORGAN

139 Elm Park Mansions
Park Walk
London, S.W.10.

Eric Levine Esq,
Eric Levine & Co,
63 Lincoln's Inn Fields,
London, W.C.2.

17th April 1979.

Dear Mr Levine,

I would like to instruct you in two pertinent matters.

As the enclosed letter will show, I wrote to Mr Michael
Edwardes of British Leyland on 31st March suggesting that the
name of the company be changed to 'Japanese Leyland'. It was
with a deep sense of outrage that I discovered through 'the
media' on 4th April that my concept had been taken up and acted
on. By 5th April the matter had become public knowledge and a
source of humour in popular newspapers.

Mr Edwardes has not favoured me with the courtesy of a
reply to my various letters of protest (indeed he appears to
have gone to ground - as well he might!) and it now seems
certain that he intends to appropriate my idea without payment.

I think you will agree that in the circumstances punitive
damages would be awarded to me in the High Court.

The other matter is somewhat more trivial. As the enclosed
documents will show, I recently submitted four comical definitions
and a humorous poem to Esther Rantzen's excellent TV Show 'That's
Life'. I have chased up the BBC's accounts department, but so
far no money has been forthcoming and I judge that now is the time
to sue them.

I look forward to hearing that you can act for me with your
customary vigour in these two matters.

Yours sincerely,

Henry Root

Henry Root.

ERIC LEVINE & CO.

Eric Levine Keith Fletcher Kevin Gillon Tilly Halliwell John Wood Caroline Janzen

63 LINCOLN'S INN FIELDS LONDON WC2A 3LW TELEPHONE 01-405 7855
TELEX 28988 TELEGRAMS ELJURIS LONDON

24th April 1979

H. Root, Esq.,
139 Elm Park Mansions,
Park Walk,
London SW 10

Dear Mr. Root,

I thank you for your letter of 17th April addressed to Mr. Levine.

Mr. Levine is presently abroad and will be travelling significantly over the next several weeks. I will of course pass your letter to him when he is next in London. It may be that you would wish to pass your letters to somebody who will have a greater amount of time available to deal with the matter.

Yours sincerely,

KAY TALBOT
Secretary to:
ERIC LEVINE

/KAT

Amsterdam Office: Herengracht 518 Amsterdam-C Telephone 226446 Telex 15569 Eljur NL

Ms Kay Talbot, Co,
Eric Levine & Co,
63 Lincoln's Inn Fields,
London, W.C.2.

139 Elm Park Mansions
Park Walk
London, S.W.10.

26th April 1979.

Dear Ms Talbot,

Thank you for your letter of 24th April with regard to the matter between British Leyland and myself.

I'm sorry to hear that Mr Levine is abroad and travelling 'significantly' over the next several weeks. Nothing amiss, I hope?

I'm particularly eager to prosecute this bit of litigation with all due haste and since I have heard such excellent things about your firm I am wondering whether one of the other partners might handle the dodge for me?

I see the name of Mr Keith Fletcher at the top of your writing paper. Would this by any chance be the Keith Fletcher (known aff-ectionately to his team-mates as 'The Gnome') who skippers Essex at cricket? If so, I would be more than happy for him to handle the caper for me. He's a wily skipper who reads the game well and although I've seen him drop a couple of sitters in the slips in my time, I'm sure he won't be a butter-fingers with this one!

It so happens that I'll be in your part of the world next Friday 4th May, so unless I hear that it would be inconvenient I'll drop by at 12.30 for an initial conference with 'The Gnome'.

Yours sincerely,

Henry Root

Henry Root.

ERIC LEVINE & CO.

Eric Levine Keith Fletcher Kevin Gillon Tilly Halliwell John Wood Caroline Janzen
63 LINCOLN'S INN FIELDS LONDON WC2A 3LW TELEPHONE 01-405 7655
TELEX 28988 TELEGRAMS ELIURIS LONDON

27th April 1979

H. Root, Esq.,
139 Elm Park Mansions,
Park Walk,
London SW 10

Dear Mr. Root,

I thank you for your letter of 26th April the content of which together with your earlier letter I have now had the opportunity of discussing with Mr. Levine.

Mr. Levine regrets that he is not able to act for you in this matter since it is not the type of matter that the firm deals with.

Yours sincerely,

KAY TALBOT
Secretary to:
ERIC LEVINE

139 Elm Park Mansions
Park Walk
London, S.W.10.

Mr 'Larry' Lamb,
The Sun,
30 Bouverie Street,
London, E.C.4.   31st March 1979.

Dear Mr Lamb,

As a 'Sun' reader for many years (Mrs Root chaffs me that I
only take it for the pretty girls - but what's wrong with a pretty
girl!!?), may I say how shocked I was this morning to read the following story on your TV page?

'Fun-loving Ian McShane could not resist the temptation to
send-up the Last Supper while 'Jesus of Nazareth' was being filmed.
McShane, 36, who plays Judas, says: "I had to sneak out of the door
with evil in my heart, to betray Christ. I sneaked out all right - th
then I stuck my head back round the door and said: 'I have got it
right, haven't I? Five hake, two rock salmon, five plaice and twelve
chips?' They all fell about!" It was just one of the many zany
things that happened during the making of 'Jesus of Nazareth' (ITV,
Sunday 6.30) in Morocco.....'

It's one thing for some prancing mime to act the goat at a
poignant moment in Our Lord's story; quite another for a family newspaper such as yours to report his oafish antics with apparent approval.

Don't misunderstand me. I'm no 'Disgusting of Tunbridge Wells'.
I've knocked around the world and so has Mrs Root. We like a bit of
harmless fun as much as the next couple (Fred and Rita Snipe in 138).
Nudity (and yours is always tasteful) is all right in its place;
blasphemy, on the other hand, is below the belt.

I look forward to receiving your explanation for this deplorable
lapse and to your confirmation that the journalist responsible, Chris
Kenworthy, has been relieved of his position.

Yours sincerely,

Henry Root

Henry Root.

Copies to: The Press Council.
            Lord Grade.
            Mrs Whitehouse.
            Lord Goodman.
            Mary Kenny.

Lord Grade,
ATV,
17 Great Cumberland Place,
London, W.1.

139 Elm Park Mansions
Park Walk
London, S.W.10.

31st March 1979.

Dear Lord Grade,

Since I have always assumed that you are a religious man in the widest sense of the word (albeit of a different faith to that of myself, Mrs Root and Mary Kenny) as well as being a man with an eye for a profit (and what's wrong with that?), I thought you would be interested in the enclosed letter which I have sent this morning to Mr 'Larry' Lamb, Editor-in-Chief of Sun Newspapers.

I assume that you would not wish your fine and always tasteful TV film 'Jesus of Nazareth' to be the occasion of cheap jokes by unthinking actors.

Yours sincerely,

Henry Root.

Henry Root.

P.S. When are we to have the pleasure of Miss Shirley McLaine on our screens again? Now there's a <u>thinking</u> actress, who appeals to the whole family.

NEWS GROUP NEWSPAPERS LTD
A Subsidiary of News International Ltd

Registered No. 679215 England
Telex Sunnews 267827
Telephone 01-353 3030
EDITOR'S OFFICE

Registered Office:

30 Bouverie Street, Fleet Street, London, EC4Y 8DE.

April 3rd, 1979.

AL/MD

Henry Root, Esq.,
139, Elm Park Mansions,
Park Walk,
London, SW10.

Dear MR Root—

Thank you for your letter.

I am sorry you were offended by the McShane story. It is never any part of our purpose to offend.

I agree, on reflection, that the story may well strike some people as being in dubious taste. But we didn't invent it, nor did we necessarily approve. We just reported.

And I really don't think I can sack Mr. Kenworthy for what was, at worst, a relatively minor misjudgment.

Now that <u>would</u> be below the belt!

With best wishes,

Yours sincerely,

Larry Lamb,
EDITOR.

**Associated
Communications
Corporation
Limited**

ATV House
17 Great Cumberland Place
London W1A 1AG
telephone 01-262 8040
cables and telegrams
Ayteevee London W1
telex 23762

Directors
Lord Grade Chairman
and Chief Executive
Jack G-- OBE Deputy Chairman
and Deputy Chief Executive
Louis Benjamin Deputy Chie Inc
Sir Max Aitken Bt CSD DFC
K S d n
Norman Collins
Alexander Jarrett F C A
Vincent McIntosh
---- R Gerards

From the office of Lord Grade

11th April, 1979.

Dear Mr. Root,

Thank you for your note of
March 31st with the attached correspondence.

I know that all the actors in
our "JESUS OF NAZARETH" production worked
extremely hard over a long period and many
of them said afterwards how being involved
in the production helped to renew their
faith in their particular religious beliefs.
Young actors working in difficult
circumstances may be forgiven moments of
high spirits and I feel the newspapers may
have exaggerated this out of all proportion.

I am sorry if you found the
particular incident disturbing, but knowing
Ian McShane, I am confident that this has
been related out of context.

Yours sincerely

(Lord Grade)

Mr. Henry Root

Registered Office : ATV House 17 Great Cumberland Place London W1A 1AG
Registered in England No. 644144

139 Elm Park Mansions
Park Walk
London, S.W.10.

Her Majesty the Queen (and Duke of Normandy!)
Buckingham Palace,
London, S.W.1.

9th April 1979.

Your Majesty,

    With the greatest respect, I take leave to surmise that as
a mother you will be no less concerned than Mrs Root is about this
once great nation's collapse in terms of moral leadership.

    I appreciate that under the constitution you cannot poke
your nose into things too directly, but I do have a small suggestion to make.

    You're always opening things: hospitals, schools, theatres,
factories, fly-overs, play-grounds etc.

    Why don't you <u>close</u> a few things?

    I have in mind such blemishes on the face of our society as
The National Liberal Club, BBC 2, Soho's 'foreign' cinemas and
so-called massage parlours, the National Council for Civil Liberties, subversive periodicals such as 'The New Statesman' and
'Time Out', which are devoted to the undermining of family life
and our British institutions, and the new white tile universities,
which see it as their function to stuff the impressionable young
students with half-baked left-wing notions.

    With great respect, Ma'am, I shouldn't have to remind you
how gratified your late grandmother, Queen Victoria, would have
been to see you give the nation a moral lead in these matters.

Support Mrs Thatcher!

Royalists demand the return of the rope!

Your humble subject,

Henry Root

Henry Root.

BUCKINGHAM PALACE.

The Private Secretary is
commanded by Her Majesty The Queen
to thank Mr. H. Root
for his letter of 9th April.

12th April. 1979

139 Elm Park Mansions
Park Walk
London, S.W.10.

Miss Angela Rippon,
BBC News,
Television Centre,
London, W.12.

9th April 1979.

Dear Miss Rippon,

I and many millions of your admirers must have been disappointed to read in the paper yesterday that you plan to sue the Mirror Group for calling you the 'Iron Maiden'.

What is insulting or damaging about such a cognomen? Is not our future Leader, Mrs Thatcher, known as 'The Iron Lady'? What could be a greater honour than to be associated in the public consciousness with such a fine woman?

I gather that you think the name suggests that you are some sort of lemon-faced puritan. What's wrong with that? Surely a liberated woman such as yourself doesn't want to be thought of as a scatter-brained sex-symbol, subjected each night to the insulting stares of frustrated men who think women are for one thing only? Your admirers like you just the way you are.

Could you possibly send me a photograph of Anna Ford? I'd write to her myself, but as I'm already writing to you it seems silly to waste a stamp.

Yours sincerely,

Henry Root.

P.S. In case you intend to pursue your mistaken action for damages, I enclose a pound to help with the costs. I don't approve of what you are doing, but I'd like to support you all the same. I also enclose the postage for Anna Ford's photograph. Thank you.

BBC tv

BRITISH BROADCASTING CORPORATION
TELEVISION CENTRE WOOD LANE LONDON W12 7RJ
TELEPHONE 01-743 8000   TELEX: 265781
TELEGRAMS AND CABLES: TELECASTS LONDON TELEX

Dear Mr Poat

What an extraordinary letter!

I have sued the Mirror Group — not for calling me an "Iron maiden" but for a 2 page article in Reveille which contained numerous accusations and slanderous comments.

You are obviously a man of intelligence — why then reach such a conclusion from a paraphrased note when you would have been able to make an informed observation (and an accurate one) by reading the full article.

As I have won the case I have no costs, so I return your contribution with thanks.

Yours sincerely
Angela Rippon.

139 Elm Park Mansions
Park Walk
London, S.W.10.

The Lucie Clayton Model Agency,
168 Brompton Road,
London, S.W.1.   9th April 1979.

Dear Sir or Madame,

Once a year the officers and men of the Rifle Brigade meet
to discuss old times in the course of a knees-up. Yours truly is
the Organising Secretary of this year's get-together which is to
be held in a private suite at the Savoy Hotel on Friday 25th May.

I'd like you to supply the cabaret. What we have in mind
are a dozen or so 'models' to jump out of a cake and 'mingle' with
the guests.

I naturally don't want to be too explicit in a letter, but
perhaps I should emphasise that the 'models' should be top types
and would be expected to 'go a bit', if you follow me.

We would be prepared to pay each girl a minimum of £100 for
the evening's work, and no girl would be required to 'go with' more
than six officers or two men.

I look forward to doing business with you.

Yours sincerely,

Henry Root

Henry Root.

168 Brompton Road London SW3 1HW   01-581 0024

LUCIE CLAYTON

4th May 1979

Henry Root Esq
139 Elm Park Mansions
LONDON SW10

Dear Mr Root

Neither the Savoy Hotel, nor the adjutant
of your former regiment, confirm your statement about the 25th May and certainly you
are writing to the wrong agency. I have,
however, been on to the Provost-Marshal's
department who will be sending some men
to see what it is that you really need.

Yours sincerely

S Neill
REGISTRAR

50 Years

LUCIE CLAYTON LIMITED   FOUNDED 1928

Directors: Lucie Clayton   Ann Bridger   Cecilia Lumley   Leslie Kark MA Oxon , FRSA Chairman

The Registrar,
Lucie Clayton Ltd,
168 Brompton Road,
London, S.W.3.

139 Elm Park Mansions
Park Walk
London, S.W.10.

5th May 1979.

Dear Miss Neill,
        I don't understand. It was the Provost Marshal who recommended
you in the first place.
        Yours sincerely,

Henry Root.

139 Elm Park Mansions
Park Walk
London, S.W.10.

Miss Mary Kenny,
The Sunday Telegraph,
Fleet Street,
London, E.C.4.

12th April 1979.

Dear Miss Kenny,

May I say how much I appreciate your articles in 'The Sunday
Telegraph' with their emphasis on the need at this time to affirm
the importance of family life?

They are an inspiration in these days of sexual pleasure off
the leash.

I wonder if I could ask your advice on a matter of dispute
between Mrs Root and myself? I hold that oral contraception is
only necessary if you indulge in oral sex, but Mrs Root argues
otherwise.

I would stress that this has nothing to do with the personal
life of myself and Mrs Root. I did my duty by her many years ago -
we have two grand youngsters, Doreen (19) and Henry Jr (15) - and
of course oral sex never came into it in those days. No, the
matter has arisen because Doreen plans to go on holiday this
summer with a male student from Essex University. Mrs Root thinks
she should have a word in her ear about 'precautions', however
unpleasant this may be for both of them.

I write to you because you seem like a valid, caring person.
I expect you get literally millions of letters a week from confused
ordinary folk, so I enclose the return postage to facilitate the
convenience of your advice.

I read somewhere that you're writing a book about the meaning
of God. That's one to look forward to! Well done!

Yours for the Family!

Henry Root

Henry Root.

139 Elm Park Mansions
Park Walk
London, S.W.10.

The London Theatre Organiser,
British Actors Equity,
8 Harley Street,
London, W.1.

17th April 1979.

Dear Sir or Madam,

This is to inform you that Root Touring Productions Ltd will
be holding open auditions for its next attraction – 'The English
Way of Doing Things' by Henry Root – on the evening of Tuesday 24th
April, at 9.30 at the above address.

Artistes will be required to disrobe frontally and show themselves available in all positions to undertake acts of simulated
intercourse for the benefit of myself (choreographer) and Mr and
Mrs Snipe (investors) who live next-door.

It is my understanding that an Official Equity Observer likes
to be present at such times, and who shall blame him? Nice work
if you can get it!

I look forward to meeting your representative on 24th April
at 9.30.

Yours for Family Entertainment!

Henry Root

Henry Root.

T
889077 PO FD G
299992 PO TS G

J172 1734 LONDON T SW 18

HENRY ROOT 139 ELM PARK MANSIONS PARK WALK
LONDONSW10

CONTACT EQUITY URGENT .
MIKE CHATTIN OR CATHY ALLEN

139 10 .

889077 PO FD G
299992 PO TS G

139 Elm Park Mansions
Park Walk
London, S.W.10.

Sir Aubrey Melford Stevenson,
Truncheons,
Winchelsea,
East Sussex.   16th April 1979.

M'Lud,

        So - this is a sad day for Law and Order! A sad day too
for the ordinary man in the street who asks nothing more of life
than that his women-folk should be able to go about their business without having first to be rigged out with an 'Anti-Rape
System' or 'Personal Protection Kit' now being marketted by the
excellent firm of Personal Hazard Protection Ltd, of 69 Silver-
town Way, London E.16 (Tel No 01-476-5648, should you want to
give them a ring.)

        Equally, it's a day of celebration for softies, sapphists,
kid-glove pansies, liberals and sodomites.

        Here's a pound. Not much, I'm afraid, but if ordinary folk
everywhere gave a pound to great public servants on their retirement they wouldn't be reduced, like that fine man Sir Robert
Mark, to driving breakdown vans for the AA, selling life assurance
door-to-door, working as masseurs in so-called 'health farms' and,
most humiliating of all, perhaps, appearing in deodorant ads on TV.

        God bless you, M'Lud!

        Yours for Law and Order!

        Henry Root

Henry Root.

Truncheons
Winchelsea
Sussex

18th April 1979

Dear Mr Rooke

Thank you so much for your letter and all the kind things you say. I much appreciate them.

As to the pound you so generously sent I have thought it right to hand it over to the Sussex Police Welfare fund which I know does valuable work in helping gallant Police and their families when they need it. I am sure you will agree with this course as I am precluded from receiving personal gifts.

I enclose the receipt. You may get a further acknowledgment from the Headquarters.

Yours v. sincerely
Melford Stevenson

139 Elm Park Mansions
Park Walk
London, S.W.10.

Mr Richard Ryder,
Conservative Party H.Q.,
32 Smith Square,
London, S.W.1.   17th April 1979.

Dear Ryder,

Sorry I haven't been in touch since 29th March! I've been up to my eyebrows in it. I expect you have too. I'm now catching up with my correspondence and am resolved not to fall so badly behind again. Please convey my apologies to Mrs Thatcher.

I am addressing myself to you and have marked this letter 'Private and Confidential' since I want to touch on a rather delicate matter concerning our Leader's health and one which I judge to be best discussed between men. (No doubt Mrs Thatcher, in her courageous way, would deny that anything was wrong.)

The fact is I read in my paper the other day that a Dr Patrick Cosgrave is a constant and close attendant on her. Wishing to discover the precise nature of her complaint, I took advantage of a consultation with my own doctor (dont worry! - just my annual blood pressure read-out) to persuade him to check out Dr Cosgrave's speciality in the BMA register of practitioners.

Imagine our sense of mystification when we found no one of this name qualified to practise medicine in the British Isles!

Eventually my doctor surmised that Dr Cosgrave must be a chiropodist, explaining that practitioners of this trade often attach the prefix 'Dr' to their names, though not officially encouraged so to do.

Does our Leader suffer from corns? These can be the very devil, as Mrs Root would be the first to tell you. With so many electoral walk-abouts to do, it seems to me a tantamount priority that Mrs Thatcher should rest up as much as possible and eschew tight shoes.

Mrs Root was once bed-ridden for three weeks. No great hardship for the country in her case, but the people can ill-afford Mrs Thatcher's absence from the centre of things for a like period.

Here's a pound. Persuade our Leader to take it easy. I'll leave this to you.

Bring back the rope!

Yours sincerely,

Henry Root

Henry Root.

From
The Rt. Hon. Mrs Margaret Thatcher
Conservative & Unionist Central Office, 32 Smith Square, Westminster SW1P 3HH

18th April 1979

Dear Mr Root,

Thank you very much for your letter of
17th April.

Dr Cosgrave has, I believe, a PhD. This
is as you know an academic qualification
not a medical one. Dr Cosgrave has never
claimed to be a doctor of medicine.

Finally thank you for your very kind
contribution. It is greatly appreciated.

With best wishes,

Yours Sincerely,

Richard Ryder
Private Office

H Root Esq

139 Elm Park Mansions
Park Walk
London, S.W.10.

Dr Dawid de Villiers,
The South African Embassy,   17th April 1979.
South Africa House,
London, W.C.2.

Your Excellency!
        May I say what a rare pleasure it is to have a running scrum-
half at the Court of St James? I don't usually agree with dragging
sport into politics, but I'm happy to make an exception in your case.
        I saw you play a few times in your youth, Sir, and by jingo you
could go a bit! I know what goes on in those scrummages unperceived
by the naked eye in the stands and I never saw you elbow an opponent
in the eye or squeeze a fellow's under-parts. You were a gentleman
scrum-half, Sir.
        Because of the internal difficulties of your great country
(which Mrs Root and I had the great pleasure of visiting a year or
two ago) you'll run into a bit of flack over here from ignorant
elements in our society: professional liberals who, at a safe distance, like to protest at the robust methods by which your hard-
pressed security police uphold the law. I don't have to tell you
not to pay any attention. Peter so-called Hain has no constituency.
What does he know of your country's internal difficulties? It's an
intolerable impertinence, in my opinion, for the citizens of one
country to criticise the customs of another, and I hope very much
that, in the course of your stay with us, you'll be outspoken in your
own criticisms of anyone in this country who holds an opposing view.
        Could you oblige with a photograph? As a philosopher and a
diplomat you may disapprove of personality cults, but I'm trying to
persuade my boy Henry Jr (15) that soccer's a girl's game and I
reckon that a photo of a fine looking man like you in his room might
do the trick.
        Up the Springboks!
        We haven't forgotten Rorke's Drift even if the Zulus have!
        Yours Against Interfering in the Internal Affairs of Another
Country!

Henry Root

Henry Root.

South African Embassy

25 April 1979

LONDON WC2N 5DP

Mr Henry Root
139 Elm Park Mansions
Park Walk
LONDON SW 10

Dear Mr Root

Thank you very much for your friendly letter and warm words of welcome. Your very kind remarks about me are sincerely appreciated.

I am delighted to hear that you have visited South Africa and have gained a favourable impression of our country. We do not ignore the fact that we have pressing problems. However these problems are much more complicated than what most critics are prepared to acknowledge. I am convinced that the peoples of South Africa are in the best position to solve their own problems and will do so, given the opportunity. The majority of the people in South Africa, black and white, are dedicated to resolve the problems in a peaceful and evolutionary way. Great strides have already been taken in that direction.

It gives me pleasure to oblige you in your request for a photo for Henry.

Yours sincerely

Dr D J de Villiers
Ambassador

Best wishes Henry
from David de Villiers!

139 Elm Park Mansions
Park Walk
London, S.W.10.

Nicholas Scott MP,
Chelsea Conservative Party,
1a Chelsea Manor Street,
London, S.W.1.

17th April 1979.

Dear Mr Scott,

Don't get me wrong — I'm a Tory, always have been, always will
be. However, before casting my vote for you in the coming election
I would like to be reassured on one point.

Are you, like our Leader Mrs Thatcher, committed to the re-
introduction of selective hanging? If you are, I'm afraid I will
be unable, as a matter of conscience, to vote for you.

The concept's nonsense, and the one plank in her platform on
which I and Mrs Thatcher (with whom I have been in close touch
throughout the campaign) are unable to agree.

Was the Battle of Britain won by shooting down Jerry selectively? I should say not! We pranged the buggers willy-nilly! Now
that we are engaged in another, and no less desperate, Battle of
Britain we can be certain of one thing: we won't defeat the enemy
in our midst — terrorists, weirdos and extremists under the bed — by
hanging them selectively. We've got to hang the lot!

I look forward to hearing that you agree with me on this vital
issue.

Here's a pound.

Yours for Law and Order!

Henry Root

Henry Root.

Nicholas Scott
Conservative

General Election
3rd May 1979

Chelsea
Campaign Headquarters
1a Chelsea Manor Street,
London, S.W.3.
Tel: 352 0102

Election Agent: R. A. Rogerson

2o April 1979

Dear Mr Root

Thank you very much indeed for your
contribution to the Fighting Fund.

Like you, I do not approve of selective
hanging!

Yours sincerely

Nicholas Scott

Henry Root Esq,
139 Elm Park Mansions,
Park Walk, London S.W.10

Published by R. A. Rogerson, 1a Chelsea Manor Street, London, S.W.3.   Printed by J. G. Bryson, (Printer) Ltd., 156, 164 High Road, N.2

139 Elm Park Mansions
Park Walk
London, S.W.10.

Nicholas Scott MP,
1a Chelsea Manor Street,   26th April 1979.
London, S.W.3.

Dear Mr Scott,
        Thank you for your letter of 20th April, but you will forgive
me if I say your answer to my question on selective hanging was somewhat evasive (typical of a politician!)

        'Like you, I do not approve of selective hanging', you write.
You will agree that this is rather ambiguous to say the least. It
might mean that you are against all hanging (though I can scarcely
bring myself to believe this of a Tory) or it might mean that, like
me, you think everyone should be hanged.

        It's not in my nature to be a bore, and I must apologise for
being so persistent on this point. It's most important to me, however to get an unambiguous reply before voting for you on 3rd May.

        Here's another pound!

        Up our Leader!

        Yours Against Bennery Under the Bed,

        Henry Root

        Henry Root.

P.S. Talking about beds, may I say - without straying into impertinence, I hope - that I trust all is now well between you and Mrs
Scott? It's always sad when the private lives of our public servants
are at sixes and sevens, and it must be said that Tories tend to be
rather weak-willed and easily-led in these matters.

Nicholas Scott
Conservative

General Election
3rd May 1979

Chelsea
Campaign Headquarters
1a Chelsea Manor Street,
London, S.W.3.
Tel: 352 0102

Election Agent: R. A. Rogerson

2o April 1979

Dear Mr Root

Thank you for your further contribution.

I am sorry you found my reaction ambiguous but
I really did think my views on this matter were
well known in the constituency.

I share the views of those of my colleagues in
the Tory Party who are opposed to the principle
of capital punishment.   This is not to say I
am against convicted terrorists spending the
rest of their natural lives in gaol, but I do
not accept that the threat of hanging is a
deterrent to murder and indeed as far as terrorists
are concerned my fear is that it could be tragically
counter-productive.

Thank you for the kind thoughts behind your
personal enquiry.   I do not want to be evasive,
but just at this special moment in time I can
only reassure you that all is well.

Yours sincerely

Nick Scott

Henry Root Esq.

Published by R. A. Rogerson, 1a Chelsea Manor Street, London, S.W.3   Printed by J. G. Bryson, (Printer) Ltd. , 156 164 High Road, N.2

139 Elm Park Mansions
Park Walk
London, S.W.10.

Richard Ryder Esq,
Conservative Central Office,
32 Smith Square,
London, S.W.I.   26th April I979.

Dear Ryder,

    Many thanks for your letter of I8th April.

    It was a great relief to discover that Dr Cosgrave is not,
after all, a chiropodist and indeed that our Leader is in perfect
health.

    May I say how delighted I was to read in yesterday's 'Evening
Standard' that our Leader doesn't 'wish to see the death penalty
used a very great deal'. This dispels the popular idea that she
intends to be personally present at all hangings. This seems to me
to be the right attitude. She should only attend the more important
ones.

    May I also take this opportunity of saying how pleased I was
to read in 'The Sun' today that she has written personally to Mrs
Whitehouse, giving that good lady her personal guarantee that she
will crack down hard on the porno merchants when she comes to power.
I see that young Mr Steel characteristically failed to join in the
dialogue with Mrs Whitehouse on this vital topic. The boy has no
feel for the relevant issues. Mrs Thatcher understands that our
leaders ignore Mrs Whitehouse at their peril. She doesn't have to
be reminded of what happened to those easily-led light-weights, me
noble Lords Lambton and Jellicoe. (You'll notice that I deliberately failed to mention Mr Profumo. It's high time, in my opinion,
that the poor man should be allowed to forget that he slept with a
tart, endangered the security of his country and lied to the House
of Commons.)

    Here's a pound. Use it to crack down on the porno barons.

    Bring back the rope!

    Your Man on the Door-Step!

Henny Root

Henry Root.

P.S. Henry Root's no tell-tale but I think you ought to know that
I've had a most unsatisfactory letter from Nicholas Scott (my local
MP) on the subject of selective hanging. Is it too late to put up
another candidate in this area?

Copy to Nicholas Scott MP.

The Rt. Hon. Mrs Margaret Thatcher

Conservative & Unionist Central Office, 32 Smith Square, Westminster SW1P 3HH

1st May 1979

Dear Mr Root,

Thank you very much for your kind
letter of 26th April. I am most
grateful to you for sending £1
towards our Campaign Fund. It is
much appreciated.

With best wishes.

Yours sincerely,

Richard Ryder
Private Office

Henry Root Esq

Duke Hussey,
The Times,
New Printing House Square,
Gray's Inn Road,
London, W.C.1.

139 Elm Park Mansions
Park Walk
London, S.W.10.

18th April 1979.

Your Grace,

I want you to know that Mrs Root and I were inspired by your performance on 'The News' last night.

"Never go down to the Unions! That's not the way to beat the extremists under the bed.

"We plan to change the philosophy of Fleet Street," you said.

Well, I don't know much about philosophy (I left school at sixteen) but I do know I didn't get to the top in fish by truckling to militants.

I'm a 'Telegraph' man myself, but here's a pound. Not much, but if every 'Telegraph' reader sent you a pound the fight against the trouble-makers would be funded for another month.

Good luck!

Never give in!

Yours sincerely,

Henry Root

Henry Root.

TIMES NEWSPAPERS LIMITED

Registered office: P.O. Box no. 7, New Printing House Square,
Gray's Inn Road, London WC1X 8EZ
Telephone 01-837 1234 Telex 264971 Registered no. 894646 England

April 23rd, 1979

Henry Root, Esq.
139 Elm Park Mansions
Park Walk
London, SW10

Dear Mr. Root,

Thank you so much for your letter of April 18th, and particularly for the £1 note which I am giving to our Widows and Orphans Fund.

We are fighting as hard as we can and we do not intend to give in.

With all good wishes.

Yours sincerely,

M.J. Hussey
Chief Executive and
Managing Director

139 Elm Park Mansions
Park Walk
London, S.W.10.

C.James Anderton Q.P.M., F.B.I.M.
Chester House,
Boyer Street,
Manchester MI6 ORE.   19th April 1979.

Dear Chief Constable,

    I am so sorry not to have replied sooner to your letter
of 27th March. Mrs Root and I are naturally disappointed that
you're unable to address a meeting of 'The Ordinary Folk Against
Porn Society', but we quite understand that you're flat to the
boards chasing porno merchants off your patch. Well done!

    Don't worry about this, because I've had an idea! We'll
come to you!

    Would Tuesday 8th May be convenient? If so we'll muster in
your office at, say, four pm on that day. There'll just be a
handfull of us: myself and Mrs Root, Major Dewdrop, Dr Littlewinkle and his good lady, the Snipes (Fred and Rita) together
with their youngsters, Molly (17) and Bruce (19) and the Smithsons.

    We wouldn't want you to go to any trouble on our behalf,
so please don't lay on much of a show. A cup of tea (Indian
please) and some rock cakes would be just fine. I certainly don't
wan;y to eat into funds that would be better employed putting
pimps in the pokey so I enclose a pound to cover the cost of
any hospitality you arrange.

    Bring back the rope!

    Your pal in the soft south!

Henry Root

    Henry Root.

PS. Please let me know if you can't make it on the arranged date.
I'd hate to run into your office with my party only to find you'd
sugared off early to play golf with the Lord Mayor!

C James Anderton Q.P.M., F.B.I.M.
Chief Constable

Chief Constable's Office
P O Box 22 (S.West PDO)
Chester House
Boyer Street
Manchester M16 0RE
Telephone 061-872 5050

23rd April 1979.

Dear Mr. Root,

I have your letter of 19th April but regret I am not available to meet you as you suggest on Tuesday, 8th May. I am sorry about this.

I doubt if it will be possible for me to meet you and your friends under such arrangements as my busy professional life makes it virtually impossible for me to guarantee such relatively informal contacts.   I hope you will understand.

I am returning the £1.00 note you forwarded with your letter.

Yours sincerely,

Chief Constable.

H.Root, Esq.,
139 Elm Park Mansions,
Park Walk,
London.S.W.10.

139 Elm Park Mansions
Park Walk
London, S.W.10.

Patrick Moore Esq,   19th April 1979.
Selsey,
West Sussex.

Dear Mr Moore,
          I was most interested to read in 'The Sun' yesterday about
the formation of The United Country Party.
          I'm not entirely sure that astrologers like yourself should
get mixed up in the real world of politics, but I like the sound
of your platform. (I hope it's a strong one! Let's face it, you're
no feather-weight!) At least you won't have to rely on the opinion
polls to tell you how you're doing. You'll be able to read it in
the stars! Not that I believe in any of this astrology nonsense.
We're very sceptical, we Capricorns!
          The aims of your party sound sensible. Abolish income tax,
clear the rubbish from the streets and crack down hard on the Welsh.
Just what the doctor ordered. I take it you're in favour of the
immediate re-introduction of hanging?
          I'd be most grateful if you could send me a copy of your
manifesto and also if you could let me know whether you're putting
up up a candidate in this constituency (Chelsea) for whom I can
vote.
          Yours for Law and Order!

          Henry Root

          Henry Root.

VICE-CHAIRMAN & PARLIAMENTARY
CANDIDATE FOR CHICHESTER

Lt.-Col. E. A. L. Iremonger,
Durley, Sidlesham, Sussex.

TREASURER:
G. Gumersall,
93 Drift Road, Selsey.

UNITED COUNTRY PARTY

CHAIRMAN:
Patrick Moore, OBE FRAS

SECRETARIAL ADDRESS:
39 West Street
Selsey, Sussex
Tel: 024361-3668

BANKERS:
Lloyds Chichester.

Dear Mr. Root,

I hasten to stress that I am an astronomer, not an astrologer! -

Details of manifesto enclosed. Hanging is not on our manifesto, as we feel that this is a matter for everyone's own conscience. I am not a 'hanger' myself, but I believe most people are, and we'd prefer a free vote.

We are campaigning hard here.

All good wishes.

Sincerely

Patrick Moore

139 Elm Park Mansions
Park Walk
London, S.W.10.

Mr Nigel Dempsey,   19th April 1979.
The Daily Mail,
Carmelite House,
London, E.C.4.

Dear Dempsey,

     May I say how much I have enjoyed your 'Diary' over the years?
Some folk deride sycophantic gossip about one's social superiors as
a lot of snobbish nonsense, but I am not of their number. Born, like
you, without the advantages, I have acquired, like you, a healthy
respect for my 'betters'. I have seen you described in some pseudo-
intellectual magazine as having the morals of a cocktail waitress.
So what? It happens to be the case that Mrs Root was a cocktail
waitress when I met her and not once has she caused me to rue the
day I plucked her off her bar-stool and made an honest woman of her.

     I write to you now on a matter of some delicacy, but I'm sure
I can rely on your discretion. The excellent firm of Jonathan Cape,
of whom you may have heard, are shortly to publish my first novel,
'Day of Reckoning', and I am naturally eager that it should receive
maximum media exposure.

     I'm not some young idealist with his head in the literary clouds,
but, like you, a down-to-earth businessman, and I haven't climbed to
the top in fish without discovering that you don't get anywhere in
life without - how shall I put this? - 'taking care of' a few in-
fluential people on the way. I expect you have found this out for
yourself.

     I now enclose a fiver on the understanding that you will write
flatteringly about me when the book appears, linking my name with
starlets and suggesting I'm intimate with Barry Sheene and his lady-
friend 'Hotpants' Burbank. (I don't have to teach you your business.)

     This is only the start. There's plenty more where this came
from, so you be good to me and I'll see you're all right!

     If you need some background information on me, please don't
hestitate to let me know. I'm a very busy man but I could squeeze
you in for an interview most mornings before 10am.

     I look forward to reading the first item in your column!

     Yours sincerely,

     Henry Root

     Henry Root.

139 Elm Park Mansions
Park Walk
London, S.W.10.

19th April 1979.

Jonathan Cape Esq,
Jonathan Cape Ltd,
30 Bedford Square,
London, W.C.1.

Dear Cape,

<u>DAY OF RECKONING by HENRY ROOT</u>.

I'm told you're always on the alert for solid yarns with no
unnecessary thrills, so I am now enclosing the synopsis of my
recently completed first novel as above.

Let me say at the outset that the 'property' comes to you
with certain advantages. For the right return on capital outlay,
I'm prepared to help with the financing of the caper (mainly to
ensure maximum media exposure - your people couldn't get a plug
for a bath, I'm told!) and I have taken the precaution of 'fixing'
certain journalists and literary editors. Nigel Dempsey of 'The
Daily Mail', for instance, is 'in my pocket'.

An additional advantage is that I shape up brand new in
public, come across well on camera (or so I was told after being
interviewed on a street-corner by Esther Rantzen on the hilarious
urday night') and I'm fully available with matching luggage to
undertake 'exploitation' tours - though not of Turkey, Greece or
Scandinavia.

Before I accept your offer, I should warn you that from a
business point of view I didn't just fall off a turnip truck.
looking for a heavy advance as a guarantee that you aren't just
messing me about. I've heard of too many young writers for whe
an offer from a publisher turned out to be a stepping-stone to
obscurity.

Let's go!

Yours sincerely,

Henry Root

Henry Root.

Enc: Synopsis of DAY OF RECKONING by HENRY ROOT.

<u>DAY OF RECKONING</u>
By
<u>HENRY ROOT</u>.

<u>Synopsis</u>.

Bronzed, attractive, amazingly fit, 45-year-old Harry Toor, Chairman and Managing Director of Harry Toor Wet Fish Ltd, woke up in the sumptuously appointed bedroom of his luxury mansion in Maidenhead.

He stirred contentedly and, as was usual when he woke, he ran over in his mind his many blessings and possessions: his swimming-pool and tennis courts, his musical cocktail-cabinet and three-piece lounge-room suite in Victoria plum velvet with old-gold lurex edgings (a wedding present from his good mate and next-door neighbour, Michael Parkinson), his Rolls, his yacht in Monte Carlo, his constant supply of willing 'personal secretaries' and, above all, his latest 'companion', the long-legged, full-bosomed 'starlet', Lorraine Pump-tit.

Suddenly he felt strangely ill at ease. Into his mind had come a vision of Barnsley and the back-street slum in which he'd been born and in which his 82-year-old dad and 80-year-old mum still lived. He hadn't visited them in over twnety years. Had it all been worthwhile, his ruthless drive to the top? Did he still know who he was? If he was to visit his old mum and dad now, sample once again his old mum's apple-pie and Yorkshire pudding, play darts with his old dad at the pub on the corner, would he still be able to talk to them, really communicate?

He thought of the little house in which he'd been born, of his old mum and dad, of the lads at the local pork-pie factory who had once been his mates, and of little Janet Gibbens with whom he'd had his first fumbling sexual experience in the back row of the Odeon and he thought:

"Stuff that lot. I'll stay put."

And he went contentedly back to sleep.

<u>THE END</u>.

Henry Root
139 Elm Park Mansions
Park Walk
London, S.W.7.
<u>ALL RIGHTS RESERVED</u>.

JONATHAN CAPE LIMITED
THIRTY BEDFORD SQUARE
LONDON W.C.1

Telephone 01-636 5764
Telex 299080
Answer CBCSER G

Telegrams
CAPAJON, LONDON WC1B 3EL

DB/ME

20th April, 1979

Mr Henry Root,
139 Elm Park Mansions,
Park Walk,
London, S.W.10.

Dear Mr Root,

Thank you for your letter of 19th April and synopsis. We regret
that we do not think it would be worth your while submitting your
typescript DAY OF RECKONING to us, as we do not feel that the
book would be entirely suited to our list.

Please find your synopsis enclosed.

Yours sincerely,

Debra Byron

Debra Byron,
Editorial.

DIRECTORS Tom Maschler Graham C. Greene Lizz...
Registered in England...

Daily Mail

REGISTERED OFFICE
CARMELITE HOUSE,
LONDON, EC4Y OJA
REGISTERED NO. 116035E ENGLAND

TELEPHONE 01-353 6000
TELEGRAPH DGLTMAIL LONDON EC4

GC/JEM

20 April, 1979

Mr. H. Root,
139 Elm Park Mansions,
Park Walk,
London, S.W.10.

Dear Mr. Root,

Thank you for your letter dated 19 April
which Mr. Dempster has passed to me.

It is not Mr. Dempster's habit, or that
of any other member of the Daily Mail
staff, to accept money, or anything else,
on the understanding that stories will
be written. In the circumstances I return
your £5.

Yours sincerely,

G. Cowan

GORDON COWAN
Assistant Managing Editor

DAILY MAIL LTD. (Subsidiary of Associated Newspapers Group Ltd.)

Directors: Hon. Vere Harmsworth (Chairman), P.M. Shields (Deputy Chairman) D. English, P. Grover, J.C. Johnston
J.A. Lewis, S.A. Marler, B.A. Drey, J. Freeman, D.R. Pace, A.A. Robinson, E.J. Wavington-Ingram

139 Elm Park Mansions
Park Walk
London, S.W.10.

Mr Gordon Cowan,
The Daily Mail,
Carmelite House,
London, E.C.4.   22nd April 1979.

Dear Mr Cowan,

        Thank you for your letter of 20th April in reply to my
letter of 19th April to Mr Nigel Dempster.

        Why can't he answer his own letters? I was addressing
myself to the monkey, not the organ-grinder. Is it the function
of an Assistant Managing Editor to act as secretary to the
paper's scandal writer? If so, what does the Managing Editor
do? The Snooker Correspondent's typing?

        Perhaps Mr Dempster will answer this letter. Or does
Mr English deal with your mail? It's all very confusing.

        Pending an explanation, I return the fiver.

        Yours sincerely,

        Henry Root

        Henry Root.

Daily Mail

REGISTERED OFFICE
CARMELITE HOUSE,
LONDON, EC4Y 0JA.
REGISTERED NO. 1160842 ENGLAND

TELEPHONE> 01-353 6000
TELEGRAPH>DAILYMAIL·LONDON·E.C.4.

GC/JEM

2 May, 1979

Mr. H. Root,
139 Elm Park Mansions,
Park Walk,
London, S.W.10.

Dear Mr. Root,

Thank you for your further letter dated April 22.

Whatever you may think about newspaper production, or whatever you may expect, the only acknowledgment you will receive in this matter is from me. Mr. Dempster quite rightly brought it to my attention as the person in charge of editorial administration.

You have now received the courtesy of two letters on the matter and I consider this correspondence closed. I return to you your money and reiterate that we do not accept money from anyone on the understanding that stories will be written about them.

Yours sincerely,

GORDON COWAN
Assistant Managing Editor

DAILY MAIL LTD. (Subsidiary of Associated Newspapers G
Directors: R.M.Shields (Chairman) D.English P.Grover J.C.Johnston
B.A.Olley J.Pearmain A.A.Robinson E.J.Winnington

139 Elm Park Mansions
Park Walk
London, S.W.10.

Mr Brian Clough,
'The Boss!',
Nottingham Forest F.C.,
Nottingham.

23rd March 1979.

Dear Mr Clough,

So you stuffed the Swiss! Magic! Mustard! You and the
lads must be over the moon!

I was a bit disturbed by a pre-match report in my paper
that you were thinking of buying their big striker, Sulser. The
lad looks useful (you must have been as sick as a parrot when he
stuck the ball in the back of the net to make it none one against
you!) but where would this leave the boy Birtles? On top of
which, is it possible for a foreign player to familiarise himself with the English way of doing things? You know what I
mean. I'm talking about being a credit to the game on and off
the field. Short hair, smart appearance, train hard, no cussing
or monkey-business in the changing-room and just one holiday a
year with the wife and kiddies in Majorca.

Now, Henry Root's no snitch, but I think you ought to know
that at half-time against the Grasshoppers, Archie Gemmill ('The
Wee Man') blew his nose onto the pitch. Surely this isn't the
Notts Forest way? I think you should remind your players that
when they're on TV they are guests in our lounge-rooms and the
last thing we want to see is them blowing their noses onto the
lounge-room floor.

Anyway, here's a pound towards Sulser's fee. In spite of
my reservations as expressed above, I recognise that you're the
boss and that what you say goes.

You'll never walk alone!

Yours ever,

Henry Root

Henry Root.

139 Elm Park Mansions
Park Walk
London, S.W.10.

Mr Brian Clough,
'The Boss',
Nottingham Forest F.C.,
Nottingham.

23rd April 1979.

Dear Mr Clough,

Did you get my letter of 23rd March, enclosing a pound for the boy Sulser? Since you don't strike me as being the sort of man who'd pocket a pound without so much as a 'ta very much, lad', I assume my letter must have gone astray. In the circumstances, here's another pound. Let me know if this one doesn't arrive either.

Now - about the return with Cologne. I've got a daring suggestion to make. Drop the Big Man, Shilton! Let's face it, he failed to dominate 'the box' in the first leg and I ask myself whether he's got the bottle for the big occasion. Remember what happened in the World Cup against Poland? Perhaps in preferring Clemence, Mr Greenwood is turning out to be less stupid than he looks.

As for the two big centre-backs, well, one of them's got to go. Why don't you buy Toddy? I don't have to tell you of all people that he's still the most cultured No 6 in the world and I see he's now playing in the Everton Reserves, having had no less than sixteen of his majestic lapses in four minutes against West Bromwich last week. You could probably pick him up for a song or swop him for the wild-man Burnsy, who is not your sort of player. Some of us haven't forgotten how, against Arsenal last season, he saved a certain goal by knocking the opposing No 9 as cold as a stoat with an Army-surplus sandbag he'd taken with him onto the park. Effective, but not the Notts Forest way.

I'm glad to be able to report that at half-time in the first-leg against Cologne, Archie Gemmill ('The Wee Man') didn't blow his nose onto the pitch or do anything else to bring the game into disrepute. Possibly this was because he wasn't still on the field, having gone crook after a few minutes. I hope he's recovered now. He's a bonny wee fighter and you need him in the side.

Good luck in the return leg!

You're the Boss!

You'll never walk alone!

Your pal in the stands!

Henry Root

Henry Root.

Nottingham Forest Football Club

City Ground
Nottingham NG2 5FJ
Telephone 868236
Information Desk 860232
Pools Office 864808

Telegrams
Forestball Nottingham

Manager:
Brian Clough

Secretary/Treasurer:
Ken Smales

Founded 1865

Football League Division 1
Champions 1977-78
Football League Division 1
Runners Up 1966-67

Football League Cup Winners
1977-78

F A Cup Winners 1898 1959

Anglo Scottish Competition
Winners 1976-77

President G N Watson J P
Chairman S M Dryden J P
Vice-Chairman G E Macpherson J P

Committee
R M Alcock F C A
B J Appleby Q C
E G T Thorpe
E Reacher
F T C Peel F C A
D C Pavis
D L Loch

Ref. BC/JMT

24th April, 1979.

Mr. H. Root,
139 Elm Park Mansions,
Park Walk,
London S.W.10.

Dear Mr. Root,

Thank you for your letters dated 23rd March and 23rd April, and I must apologise for not replying to you sooner, but having spent so much time with the players recently, due to playing four to five games per week, and I have had hardly any time to sit in the office and answer my correspondence. I have had to plough through a pile of over a one hundred letters to find your original correspondence, but I can assure you that you would have had a reply in due course.

I am returning the second pound note you sent me, but will put the original one into our "Sulser Fund", and hope that you will not mind us using it for another transfer fee should say, Kevin Keegan, come onto the market first.

Once again, sorry for the delay, but I hope you understand my position.

Yours sincerely,

B. Clough,
Manager.

139 Elm Park Mansions
Park Walk
London, S.W.10.

Mrs Joan Pugh,
London Weekend Television Ltd,
London, S.E.1.

23rd April 1979.

Dear Mrs Pugh,

    I am applying for the job of Programme Researcher in your new
'Minorities Unit', as advertised in this week's 'Spectator'.

    Don't get me wrong. I've made my pile, I'm semi-retired and
I certainly don't need the work. But I'm glad to see your company's
leading the long over-due crackdown on the minorities in our society –
homosexuals, immigrants, drug addicts and young people – and I'd like
to support you. Quite frankly, after such unaffirmative shows as
'The London Programme' (in which, if Godfrey Hodgson isn't making
hearsay allegations against the Metropolitan CID, a sharp-nosed young
lady called Yvonne Roberts is poking up back alleys after prostitutes)
I'm agreeably surprised that you're at last taking a responsible line.
Worried about your licence being renewed? Nothing wrong with that.

    Here are the facts of my life in a nut-shell:

    Born 4th January 1935. Left school at 16 with one 'O' level
in geography (so I know my way around the world), but continued my
education at the University of Real Life, than which, you will agree,
there is none better.

    From the age of 16 to 18 worked as a porter in Billingsgate
Fish Market. Gained invaluable experience of the English working
class's dislike of ethnic minorities and so-called intellectuals.
From 18 to 20 did my National Service in submarines under the legendary Captain 'Crap' Myers VC. Commissioned.

    On being demobbed, started my own wet fish business. Worked
like a black (but paid myself rather better) and was able to sell
the business for a tidy sum in 1976. Now find myself with time on
my hands. Looking for new challenges with a societal bias.

    Personal details: 5ft 8¾ins, 15 stone, English on both sides
of the family as far back as can be traced (1904). Expert shot.
Front upper denture due to boxing mishap sustained during National
Service. (17 fights, 2 convictions.) Married Muriel Root (née Potts)
in 1958. Two youngsters – Doreen (19) and Henry Jr (15.)

    May I say how much I'm looking forward to joining your team and
to flushing out the ethnic woodworms from the fixtures and fittings
of our society.

    Yours Against Minorities!

Henry Root

    Henry Root.

P.S. I don't want to influence your decision one way or another,
but I think I ought to tell you that Mr Michael Grade is a personal
friend of mine, as the enclosed letter will show.

P.P.S. I'm a bit concerned about your address. Isn't S.E.1. rather
out of the picture media-wise? Can you assure me that, located as
you are on the wrong side of the river, you don't find yourselves
somewhat isolated from where it's happening? I don't want to be
stuck up some dead-end back-water.

LWT
London Weekend Television

South Bank Television Centre, Kent House, Upper Ground, London SE1 9LT. (Registered Office)
Telex: 918123. Cables: Weekendtel London SE1. PBX Telephone: 01-261.3434.

Direct Line: 01-261

29th March, 1979

Henry Root Esq.,
139 Elm Park Mansions,
Park Walk,
LONDON S.W.10.

Dear Mr. Root,

Thank you for your letter,

Yours sincerely,

MICHAEL GRADE
DIRECTOR OF PROGRAMMES

LWT
London Weekend Television

South Bank Television Centre, Kent House, Upper Ground, London SE1 9LT. (Registered Office)
Telex: 918123. Cables: Weekendtel London SE1. PBX Telephone: 01-261.3434.

Direct Line: 01-261 -3140

10th April, 1979

Henry Root, Esq.,
139, Elm Park Mansions,
Park Walk,
London SW10

Dear Mr. Root,

Thank you for your letter of the 9th May. I am sorry
that you have not received a reply to your application for the
London Minorities Unit vacancy, but I am afraid this may take
some time as we have had over 600 applications. You will however be notified if you are to be called for interview or not.

Thank you for your interest.

Yours sincerely,

Mrs. Joan Pugh,
Staff Officer

139 Elm Park Mansions
Park Walk
London, S.W.10.

The Rt Hon William Whitelaw,
Conservative Central Office,
32 Smith Square,
London, S.W.1.   24th April 1979.

Dear Mr Whitelaw,

Following the disgraceful and unprovoked attempt by left-wing
extremists to break up the perfectly lawful National Front meeting
in Southall last night, I was most relieved to hear you say on 'News
at Ten' that you would make no attempt as Home Secretary (which, God
willing, you soon will be) to ban further National Front rallies,
marches or meetings.

Don't misunderstand me - I'm no supporter of the Front. The pity
is that successive Governments, both Tory and Labour, have, by weak-
kneed policies on immigration, played into their hands. It remains
true, however, that a citizen has a basic human right to express his
views - however obnoxious these views may be. That's what we call
freedom of speech and it was reassuring, Sir, to hear you assert this
freedom on the News last night with all the considerable eloqence at
your command.

One thing bothers me, however. You will agree, I hope, that while
every citizen should have the right to express his opinions openly -
however unpleasant and prejudiced these opinion may be - this right
should not be granted to pornographers.

It is one thing to daub racist slogans in public places, quite
another for sweetshops and newsagents to openly display photographs
of naked ladies where kiddies can see them. You will agree, I think,
that our young folk are far more likely to be depraved and corrupted
by the latter than by the former.

Can I have your assurance, Sir, that as Home Secretary under Mrs
Thatcher, you will do nothing to impede the passage through Parliament
of Mr Hugh Rossi's sensible Obscene Displays Act, but that if, say,
The National Party of Pornographers and Pederasts tried to hold a
meeting in Southall you would stamp down on them with all your considerable weight?

I have two youngsters of my own, Sir, and I can assure you that
I would rather they exposed themselves to Mr Enoch Powell than that
they should be confronted in their local sweetshop by the naked bosoms
of some so-called 'topless model'.

Here's a pound. Use it to enforce law and order!

Yours for Freedom of Speech except for Pornographers!

Henry Root

Henry Root.

Copy to Mr Richard West.

PENRITH and THE BORDER CONSTITUENCY

PARLIAMENTARY ELECTION - 1979

CONSERVATIVE CANDIDATE
WILLIE WHITELAW

Election Agent:
N. B. DENT

CENTRAL COMMITTEE ROOMS,
31 CHISWICK STREET, CARLISLE
Telephone: Carlisle 21192

27th April, 1979

Dear Mr. Root,

    Thank you very much for your kind donation to our Conservative Party.

    I will always defend free speech in our country although I do equally vehemently oppose extremists who use violence utterly alien to our democratic tradition.

    I can confirm that our Conservative Party will take action against pornography. Mr. Rossi's Bill revived legislation which our Government prepared in 1973 but which the present Government ignored on taking power.

          Yours sincerely,

Annabel Dent

          Dictated by Mr. Whitelaw
          and signed in his absence
          by his secretary.

Henry Root, Esq.,
139 Elm Park Mansions,
Park Walk,
London, S.W.10.

VOTE WHITELAW

**POLLING DAY
THURSDAY,
MAY 3rd**

Published by N. B. Dent, Election Agent, 31 Chiswick Street, Carlisle, and Printed by Reed's Ltd., King Street, Penrith.

139 Elm Park Mansions
Park Walk
London, S.W.10.

Mr Leslie Crowther,
c/o Thames Television Ltd,
306 Euston Road,
London, N.W.1.   26th April 1979.

Dear Leslie,

Could you settle a dispute between me and Mrs Root? (You're her favourite comedian - I can't think why! No, I'm only joking!) Anyway, she holds that you're in your sixties, but I say that that's impossible unless you've had your face lifted. But if you had had your face lifted you wouldn't be able to smile all the time like you do now. Your ears would drop off! I say you're only in your late fifties. Could you settle this argument for us, once and for all?

Congratulations on your recent show on Thames! It was most amusing - good clean family entertainment with no allusions to matters appertaining to the water-works. (That's rare enough these days, alas.)

Here are a couple of wise-cracks you could use on your next show. Just give me the credit. Say 'Additional wise-cracks by Henry Root'. That would be okay.

1. Bob Monkhose. "You know, Dickie, it's not easy making millions of people laugh".

Dickie Henderson: "Sensible of you never to have tried, Bob!"

2. Question. "What's an innuendo?"

Irish Literary Critic: "An Italian suppository!"

Could you possibly oblige with a photo for Mrs Root? She'd be really thrilled! I expect you get literally millions of letters from ordinary folk like me, so I enclose the postage for your convenience.

You're okay!

Yours,

Henry Root

Henry Root.

```
                        Temple Court,
                        Corston,
                        Nr. Bath,
                        Avon.




Dear Henry,
        Many thanks for your delicious
letter which arrived in time for breakfast.
        Here is the photograph for
Mrs. Root - I could not get one of Bob
Monkhouse - which I hope she will like.

        Yours sincerely,     Good Luck !!
                                   Leslie Crowther
                        Leslie Crowth
```

Good Luck !!   Leslie
Leslie Crowther

139 Elm Park Mansions
Park Walk
London, S.W.10.

26th April 1979.

General Zia-ut-Haq,
The Strong Man!,
The President's Office,
Islamabad,
Pakistan.

Mr President!

In recent weeks you will have read unflattering reference
to yourself in our so-called liberal press. Pay no attention!
Most of us realise that a backward people such as yours needs,
and appreciates, the smack of firm government.

We are not a backward people, of course, which makes our
sad National Decline in recent years all the harder for patriots
to stomach.

Many take it as the final straw that in Kent - the garden
of England, I might remind you, Sir, - the county cricket team
is currently captained by a dusky character who rejoices in some
such unlikely name as Asif Iqbal!

Happily for us, Margaret Thatcher - a strong man like yourself - is about to come to power. As she stomps the country, in-
voking the glorious example of such great Englishman from our
island story as St Francis Drake and Sir Walter Pidgeon, the streets
ring with the sound of do-gooders breaking wind and taking to the
boats. Some will find a welcome, no doubt, in the licensed brothels
and drug-parlours of Holland and Denmark, but most will be blown
onto the rocks of obscurity by the hot wind of her rhetoric.

Her first priority - and one which will greatly appeal to
you, Mr President - is the immediate restoration of capital punishment, not least for those who have committed murder. There's
a long way to go before Britain once again rules the world, of
course, but this is a step in the right direction, I think you'll
agree.

Could you oblige with a photo, Mr President? It would have
pride of place, next to the late lamented Generalissimo Franco, in
my gallery of great International Conservatives.

You're all right!

Yours respectfully,

Henry Root

Henry Root.

بِسْمِ اللهِ الرَّحْمٰنِ الرَّحِيْمِ

THE ISLAMIC REPUBLIC OF PAKISTAN

General M. Zia-ul-Haq

ISLAMABAD
57/2/CMLA
06 May 79

Henry Root, Esq
139 Elm Park Mansions
Park Walk
London, S.W. 10
U.K.

Dear Mr Root,

Thank you for your letter of 26 April 79.

I appreciate your thoughtfulness in writing to me to convey certain very pertinent views.

Enclosed is my photograph which you have requested. I have also signed it.

Wishing you all the best,

Yours sincerely,

General
(M. Zia-ul-Haq)

Root, with my
and very best wishes
M. Zia

139 Elm Park Mansions
Park Walk
London, S.W.10.

Ms Audrey Whiting,
Royal Correspondent!
The Sunday Mirror,
Holborn Circus,
London, E.C.1.

30th April 1979.

Dear Ms Whiting,

I was deeply shocked to read your article in yesterday's
'Sunday Mirror' about the acute shortage of 'Royals' and the
consequent strain on Her Majesty the Queen.

I have a suggestion to make. We now have Life Peers. Would
it not be sensible to apply this concept to the creation of Life
Royals?

I have in mind folk of the utmost probity, folk who, like Her
Majesty, are above the rough and tumble of mere politics, folk who
have swum resolutely against the tide of declining morality over
the past years and have managed, lke Her Majesty, to affirm the
traditional values and family virtues in all they've done.

I'm talking about people such as Group Captain Sir Douglas
'Hang 'em all' Bader, Miss Mary Kenny, Mr John Junor, Dr J.P.R.
Williams, Mr Bobby Charlton, Sir Richard Attenborough, Sir 'John'
Mills, Dame Ninette de Neagle, Miss Nanette Newman, Mr Laurie McMen-
emy ('The Big Man!'), Mary O'Hara the dancing nun from Glasgow (to
keep the Scots in their place) and Ms Val Doonican (ditto the Welsh.)

You will notice that not all these people are from what might
be called 'the top drawer'. But the same could be said, let's face
it, of some of our present Royals. The criteria for being a Life
Royal should have nothing to do with 'class' as such. Life Royals,
like actual Royals, should be ordinary, but exceptional, folk up whom
lesser folk will naturally look but with whom they can relate.

What do you think?

Yours sincerely,

Henry Root

Henry Root.

Copies to: Her Majesty the Queen.
            Miss Mary Kenny.
            Mr John Junor.

139 Elm Park Mansions
Park Walk
London, S.W.10.

Her Majesty the Queen,
Buckingham Palace,
London, S.W.1.   30th April 1979.

Your Majesty,

    I enclose a copy of a letter I have sent today to Ms Audrey
Whiting, 'The Sunday Mirror's' Royal Authority.

    I was most shocked to read Ms Whiting's article about the
reluctance of certain members of your family to attend Royal Occasions
of the sort that Lord Delfont keeps arranging for you and I think
my concept of Life Royals might be the answer. (What a shame, incidentally, that I couldn't include Lord Delfont among my suggested
candidates for enroyalment. He would have been ideal, but by creating him a Life Peer, Sir Harold Wilson foolishly rendered him
unviable.)

    I was so sorry to read about the trouble you're having with
Princess Anne. My Doreen (19) is off the rails too, so I know what
it's like.

    Could you oblige with a photo, Ma'am? I'd be very honoured.

    Your humble subject,

Henry Root

Henry Root.
Copy to Miss Mary Kenny.

FROM THE
EDITOR
OF THE
SUNDAY EXPRESS

FLEET STREET, LONDON
01-353 8000

1st May 1979

Dear Mr. Root,

Thank you very much for having sent me a copy of your letter to the
Sunday Mirror.

I am greatly flattered by your nomination of me as a "Life Royal".
But I very much doubt if the Royal Family would find me an
acceptable substitute!

With all good wishes,

Yours sincerely,

JOHN JUNOR

Henry Root Esq.,
139, Elm Park Mansions,
Park Walk,
London. S.W.10.

BUCKINGHAM PALACE

10th May, 1979.

Dear Mr. Root,

      I am commanded by The Queen to
write and thank you for your letter and
enclosure, the contents of which have
been noted.

      In answer to your request for a
photograph of Her Majesty, I have to
explain to you that owing to The Queen's
rules in these matters, it is not possible
to do as you ask.

      When I tell you of the many similar
requests that Her Majesty receives, I feel
sure you will understand the reason for
these rules and that The Queen would not
wish to break them for one and not for others.

Yours sincerely,

Susan Hussey.

Lady-in-Waiting

Henry Root Esq.,
139 Elm Park Mansions,
Park Walk,
London, S.W.1.

139 Elm Park Mansions
Park Walk
London, S.W.10.

The Prime Minister! (Mrs Margaret Thatcher!)
10 Downing Street,
London, S.W.1.

4th May 1979.

Dear Prime Minister!

Congratulations! We did it! What a day! History has been made!

Enough of that. As you said when you arrived at No 10 this afternoon: "There's work to be done."

That's right. It's straight down to business. (Don't worry! There'll be plenty of time later for women's work like measuring for new curtains!) We've got to form a Cabinet of hard-nosed men to prosecute our number 1 priority: the crackdown on the unions, the work-shy, law-breakers and homosexuals. I hope there won't be too many 'Oxbridge' men in our Cabinet. Dragged from the lecture-room into real life, they have trouble, in my experience, in discovering what day of the week it is. I'd like to make three suggestions:

1. For Home Secretary - Mrs Whitehouse. The self-appointed intellectuals sneer at her, but she's a mother like yourself. I read recently in 'The Sun' of how she visited you in your room at the House and how you showed each other pornographic pictures and knelt of the floor and prayed together. That was moving.

2. For Minister of Defence - Laurie McMenemy. As you may know he's the manager of Southampton FC at the moment, but he's got the shoulders to shine on a wider stage than the green turf of Wembley. Southampton have played in Europe, so he's had invaluable experience of 'kicking the foreigners into the stands'. I assume he's a Tory, but I'm writing to him on your behalf to check. I certainly never saw a Socialist with a back as straight as his.

3. For 'Our Man in Europe' - Paul Johnson. All right! All right! So they say he's a carrot-haired loony! So they call him Colonel 'Bonkers' Johnson! So what? Have they forgotten General Wolfe, the victor at Quebec? He was as mad as a hatter but he sent the Frogs packing! Johnson said to my father once:

"Root! You and I are old enough to remember a time when you could walk from one end of the Champs Elysées to the other without seeing a Frenchman! Those were the days!"

Johnson won't let you down, but watch out for the softies in the party. I don't much care for the look of Norman St John Stevas.

My father taught me two things I've never forgotten.

"Mind this, son," he used to say. "Never spit in a man's face unless his moustache is on fire. And never trust a man who wears mauve underpants at tea-time."

I don't think we should have any bachelors in our Cabinet unless it's entirely necessary.

Here's a pound!

Bring back the rope! Let's go!

Your man on the door-step!

Henry Root

Henry Root.

Copies to: Mr Laurie McMenemy, Mr Paul Johnson and Mrs Whitehouse.

10 DOWNING STREET

10th May 1979

Dear Mr Root,

The Prime Minister has asked me to
thank you very much for your kind
letter of 4th May. Your message
of congratulations is greatly
appreciated and thank you very much
for sending us another £1 for our
party funds.

With best wishes.

Yours sincerely,

Richard Ryder
Political Office

Mr Root Esq

SOUTHAMPTON FOOTBALL CLUB LIMITED Founded 1885

Registered office:
The Dell, Milton Road,
Southampton SO9 4XX

telephones:
(0703) 23408 & 28108

commercial office:
(0703) 36616

Manager:
Lawrie McMenem[y]

Commercial Mana[ger]
Malcolm Price

Secretary:
Brian Truscott

LM/VG.

Dear Mr. Root,

16th May, 1979.

Thank you for your considerations and I am very flattered that you
put my name forward to Mrs. Thatcher. Should she decide to call on me
perhaps you could let me know as soon as possible before I make too many
plans for next season!

Seriously, I think she must have chosen her Cabinet by now and, like
yourself, I do hope she does a good job.

Best wishes.

Yours sincerely,

L. McMenemy,
Manager.   (Signed in his absence.)

Directors: A.A. Woodford (Chairman), John Corbett, B.G.W. Bowyer TD, JP,
Lt. Col. Sir George Meyrick Bart. MC, F.G.L. Askham FCA, E.T.Bates.

VAT Reg. No:
Reg No: 53

139 Elm Park Mansions
Park Walk
London, S.W.10.

The First Sea Lord,
The Admiralty,
Whitehall,
London, S.W.1.

17th April 1979.

My Lord,

I was alarmed to read a recent article in 'The Spectator' by Mrs Thatcher's chiropodist, Dr Patrick Cosgrave, concerning the imminent outbreak of hostilities with the Soviets.

Has a definite date been fixed? Mrs Root is pressing me to take her on a sun-shine holiday for two to the Canary Isles, but as an ex-serving officer I naturally don't want to be out of the country when the balloon goes up.

I may say that in the performance of my National Service it was my pleasure to be under the legendary Captain 'Crap' Myers VC in the Med. He it was, as you'll remember, who during the last show took a bolshie rating onto the casing of his submarine and shot him as dead as a skunk - or so the story goes.

I'm on red alert here and can leave for my ship at the drop of a bollard, but I shall need to know where to go and how to interpret my coded orders. No point in ex-serving officers all over the country receiving a telegram from the Admiralty reading: "Pigshit! Scuttle!" and not being able to decipher it.

I am awaiting your signal, my Lord.

Let's not have a cock-up like last time!

Yours for the defence of this once great country!

Henry Root

Henry Root. (Ex-Sub Lt, RNVR.)

PS. I know what Navy efficiency is like so I am enclosing a stamp to expedite the promulgation of my orders.

NO REPLY!

139 Elm Park Mansions
Park Walk
London, S.W.10.

The Rt Hon Francis Pym,
The Ministry of Defence,
Whitehall,
London, S.W.1.

8th May 1979.

Dear Mr Pym,

May I say how much more easily in our beds we ordinary folk
will sleep now that we once again have a Minister of Defence ready
to stand up to the Soviets?

Tourist in Whitehall: "Excuse me, can you tell me which side
the War Office is on?"

Englishman: "Ours, I hope."

A joke, possibly, but not, you will agree, a very funny one.

On 17th April, having read an article in 'The Spectator' by
Mrs Thatcher's chiropodist, Dr Patrick Cosgrave, about the imminent
outbreak of hostilities with the Warsaw Pact countries, I wrote to
the First Sea Lord alerting him to my availability and requesting
information as to what would be the signal telling me to join my
ship (I am an ex-submarine officer.)

To my amazement, I received no reply! Under a Socialist
Government it was not so surprising, I suppose, that we would once
again have been up the creek, due to those in charge of our affairs
having been caught with their trousers down.

You, Sir, will change all this, I know. I would be most
grateful if you would look into this matter for me and let me know
why ordinary folk like me, prepared to fight for our country, should
be treated with such high-handed contempt by the authorities.

I look forward to hearing from you, Sir.

Stand up for our country!

Support the Iron Lady!

Yours for a good scrap,

Henry Root

Henry Root.

NAVAL PERSONNEL DIVISION 2
MINISTRY OF DEFENCE
Old Admiralty Building Spring Gardens London SW1A 2BE

Telephone (Direct Dialling) 01-218
(Switchboard)   01-218 9000 } ext 3040

H Root Esq
139 Elm Park Mansions
Park Walk
LONDON SW10

Your reference

Our reference D/NP2/12/8/47

Date   16 May 1979

Dear Mr Root

The Secretary of State for Defence has asked me to
thank you for your encouraging letter of 8 May and I
am to inform you that your willingness to serve in
the Royal Navy in the event of hostilities has been
noted.

I can assure you that no slight was intended by the
delay in answering your earlier letter and you should
shortly receive a reply from the Office of the
First Sea Lord.

Yours faithfully

G.W. Owens

G W OWENS

From: Captain W.A. Higgins, Royal Navy

Secretary to First Sea Lord
MINISTRY OF DEFENCE
Main Building, Whitehall, London SW1A 2HB
Telephone (Direct Dialling) 01-218
(Switchboard) 01-218 9000

No. 3300/13/2

16th May 1979.

Dear Mr Root,

First Sea Lord was most grateful for your letter of
17th April offering your services should hostilities break
out and he has asked me to pass on his thanks. However,
in view of your age I am sorry to say that there is no
prospect of us being able to employ you in the Reserves
despite your earlier service.

I hope you will be relieved to learn that we have no
reason to believe that war is imminent but the only sure
way to deter any possible Soviet adventurism in the future
is by keeping our defences well up. The fact that our
Government intends to do this is surely emphasised by the
prominence given to Defence in yesterday's Queen's Speech.

Yours sincerely

Bill Higgins

Henry Root, Esq.

139 Elm Park Mansions
Park Walk
London, S.W.10.

8th May 1979.

Lord Hailsham,
The House of Lords,
London, S.W.1.

My Lord,

May I say what a great pleasure it is to have once again a man with a broad bottom on the woolsack?

May I also say what a relief it is to ordinary folk such as myself to have a Lord Chancellor with some determination to uphold Law and Order?

As the enclosed letter will show, I wrote to your Socialist predecessor on 28th March on a matter of great public concern. It was naive of me, perhaps, to expect a reply. While expressing his vote, generalised concern for the common man when canvassing his vote, Socialists, in my experience, treat him individually with the utmost contempt, ignoring, when they come to power, his hopes, his fears, his worries and his desires.

I know that you, my Lord, are a public servant of a very different kidney, and I look forward to hearing that you, unlike your uncaring predecessor, will be taking strong action in this disgraceful episode concerning Judge Joseph Zigmund (sic) and this country's finest policeman, Mr James Anderton.

Bring back the rope!

Yours faithfully,

Henry Root

Henry Root.

Enc: Letter dated 28/3/79 to the Lord Chancellor.

COPY.

139 Elm Park Mansions
Park Walk
London, S.W.1.

The Lord Chancellor,
The House of Lords,
London, S.W.1.

28th March 1979.

My Lord,

     As an ordinary member of the public, I must protest in
the strongest possible terms at the unwarranted rebuke Mr James
Anderton (the Chief Constable of Manchester and this country's
finest policeman) and his devoted body of men recently received
from so-called Judge Joseph Zigmund.

     Allow me, my Lord, to remind you of the relevant details.
After much diligent police work (which involved fifty of Manchester's
best detectives lurking for an irksome nine months in a public
house, when they might have been more amusingly employed picking
prostitutes off the streets, raiding family newsagents in search
of offensive material and visiting so-called massage parlours) a
Mrs Lillian Semmonds (sic) was brought before the court, accused
of the vile offence of controlling a prostitute.

     Fining her a derisory £50, the Judge proceeded to tell the
police that they had been wasting everyone's time and then observed
that the prostitute and Mrs Semmonds had anyway been enjoying a
lesbian relationship! As though that mitigated the offence!

     As you will agree, my Lord, this evil woman should have
received a five year prison sentence for controlling a prostitute
and another five years (to run consecutively) for being a lesbian.

     Who is this Judge Joseph Zigmund? Why doesn't he practise
law in his own country? Is it a consequence of our joining the
Common Market that foreigners are now allowed to preside over our
courts?

     With the greatest respect, my Lord, I await your explanation
and to hearing what action you are taking to punish Judge Joseph
Zigmund and to defend the good name of Mr James Anderton: a man
who has been compared (by himself) to Christ and who, single-handed,
is engaged on the lonely task of combatting the forces of darkness.

     Yours faithfully,

Henry Root

Henry Root.

LORD CHANCELLOR'S DEPARTMENT
Neville House Page Street London SW1P 4LS

Telephone Direct line 01-211
Switchboard 01-211 3000

Mr H Root,
139, Elm Park Mansions,
Park Walk,
LONDON SW10.

Your reference

Our reference

Date 9th May 1979

Dear Mr. Root

I am writing on behalf of the Lord Chancellor to thank you for your letter of 28th March and apologise for the delay in replying.

I hope you will understand when I say from the outset that because our system of justice is based upon the independence of the courts from Government, it would be seen as a serious breach of this principle of judicial independence if the Lord Chancellor or any official of his department were to express views on the propriety of a sentence for any particular offence.

Parliament has given to all courts a complete discretion in the matter of sentencing subject in general to the maximum sentences which may be imposed for particular offences. The appropriate sentence for any individual case must be dependent on the circumstances of that case and the court, which has before it the full facts of the offence and usually the assistance of reports about the defendant's personal background and character, is in the best position to decide the correct way of dealing with him.

I do not know whether or not your attention was drawn to this case from newspaper reports, but if so, you will appreciate such reports must, of necessity, be brief and cannot possibly reflect all the conflicting factors that judges must consider when passing sentence.

It is not possible for me to be more helpful.

Yours sincerely

M A STEWART

Lord Hailsham,
The House of Lords,
London, S.W.1.

139 Elm Park Mansions
Park Walk
London, S.W.10.

10th May 1979.

Dear Lord Hailsham,

Well done! I wrote to your predecessor on 28th March with a stiff complaint and what happened?

Nothing!

I then put the whole matter in your hands and what happened?

I got a reply by return of post!

That's the Tory way! Keep it up!

Support Mrs Thatcher!

Yours sincerely,

Henry Root

H Root.

Curtis Brown Ltd,
1 Craven Hill,
London, W.2.

139 Elm Park Mansions
Park Walk
London, S.W.10.

8th May 1979.

Dear Sir or Madam,

Please find enclosed a copy of my original stage play 'The
English Way of Doing Things'.

It is a light-hearted romp in two acts about a Police Commissioner who sets forth in good shape to arrest the inmates of
a bawdy-house but is flummoxed by the fact that they out-rank him
socially. In a hilarious denouement he finds himself taking the
bookings!

I would like to offer the part of the Police Commissioner to
Sir Robert Mark.

As you will see, it's a small but telling part towards the
end of the play, and I would venture to suggest exactly the sort
of key but technically undemanding role that Sir Robert should be
essaying at this stage of his acting career.

I think he could handle it, but we would of course require
him to read for us.

I look forward to hearing from you.

Yours faithfully,

Henry Root

Henry Root.

CURTIS BROWN
LIMITED
1 Craven Hill London W2 3EP
Telephone 01-262 1011

11th May 1979

Henry Root, Esq.,
139 Elm Park Mansions,
Park Walk,
London, S.W.10.

Dear Mr. Root,

Thank you very much for sending us THE ENGLISH
WAY OF DOING THINGS. I am sorry to say that
Sir Robert Mark is away in Australia for the
next few months and does not in any case feel
that his talents lie in the direction of acting.

I am therefore returning your script and I am
sorry to give you such a negative answer.

Yours sincerely,

Kate Marsh

Kate Marsh

A MEMBER OF THE CURTIS BROWN GROUP LTD LONDON SYDNEY NEW YORK

Directors Graham Watson (Chairman) Peter Grose (Managing) Diana Baring Andrew Best Felicity Bryan
Richard Odgers Michael Shaw Mollie Waters George Webster

Telex 264536 Cables Browncurt, London W2 Registered Office address as above Registered in London 1030815

139 Elm Park Mansions
Park Walk
London, S.W.10.

Head of Script Unit,
BBC Television Centre,
London, W.12.   9th May 1979.

Dear Sir,

Last night, Mrs Root and I were watching the excellent
American TV (television) show 'McMillan & Wife', when I was
struck by a sharp idea!

How about an English version of the show, called 'McNee
& Wife', based of the crime-fighting exploits of our own Commissioner? Over the past few weeks I've been in close touch with
Sir David McNee about his somewhat stodgy, not 'one 'o the People'
image and I know he's keen to come across as less of a big Glasgow
pudding to the general public. For this reason, I'm sure he'd
cooperate if you came up with some good scripts based on his
working day, showing him (like Rock Hudson) solving crimes and
bringing wrong-doers to book with the able assistance of his
lady wife and the family cook.

I happen to know he's very busy at the moment, so he might
not have time to play the central role (though I could put it to
him on your behalf.) It doesn't really matter, because I've had
a second sharp idea! Now that he's an actor, who better to play
the main character than Sir Robert Mark?

What do you say? I have a lot of clout with Sir Robert's
agents, Curtis Brown, and I'll get straight on to them as soon
as you give me the go-ahead.

As for the '& wife' character in the series, I doubt whether
Lady Mark (not being a thespian like her husband) could handle it.
Casting the part authentically should present no problems, however.
Mrs Root is familiar with Lady Mark from afternoon bingo sessions
in Esher and she tells me that either Hylda Baker or Thora Hird
could portray her to the life. Whichever you preferred. Let's
not butt heads over a minor character.

I look forward to receiving your go-ahead!

Yours sincerely,

Henry Root

Henry Root.

B B C TV

BRITISH BROADCASTING CORPORATION
TELEVISION CENTRE WOOD LANE LONDON W12 7RJ
TELEPHONE 01·743 8000   TELEX 265781
TELEGRAMS AND CABLES TELECASTS LONDON TELEX

Reference 35/JS/GE   28th June, 1979

Dear Mr. Root,

I have received your letter of the 1st June and seen a copy of the
letter to the Director General. As we receive 8,000 scripts a year
which we deal with in strict rotation there is inevitably some delay
in replying to authors. However, we have looked at your idea and
I have to tell you that it is not remotely possible for television
in this country for legal and copyright reasons not to mention the
fact that it is our normal practice to only employ actors who are
Equity members. Regarding copyright this is a very shady area and
there is no strict copyright in ideas. For a brief outline of
copyright law I refer you to the Writers' and Artists' Yearbook which
should be available from your local public library.

Yours sincerely,

Jdn Scotts

JOHN SCOTNEY
Head of Television Script Unit

139 Elm Park Mansions
Park Walk
London, S.W.10.

The Managing Director,   3rd May 1979.
Keyser Ullman Ltd,
25 Milk Street,
London, E.C.2.

Dear Sir,
          I wish to acquire the publishing house of Jonathan Cape Ltd,
of 30 Bedford Square, London, W.C.1.
          You have been recommended to me as people who can handle a
delicate situation, so I'd be happy for you to act for me in the
matter.
          Don't charge in like a bull at a gate. Use a little stealth.
I don't want Cape to see me coming, so in the first instance just
'ask around' about the strength of the present set-up. Who the
present shareholders are, whether we can 'get anything on them' etc
etc. I don't have to teach you your business.
          We'll discuss your fees in the matter when you get in touch
with me with your initial report.
          I look forward to hearing from you.
          Yours faithfully,

          Henry Root

          Henry Root.

NO REPLY!

<u>VERY URGENT</u>.

139 Elm Park Mansions
Park Walk
London, S.W.10.

The Managing Director,
Keyser Ullman Ltd,
25 Milk Street,
London, E.C.2.

8th May 1979.

Dear Sir,

Please ignore for the moment my letter of 3rd May with reference to my takeover of Jonathan Cape Ltd.

I have only just read the Department of Trade's so-called 'Selmes Report' and in the circumstances you will quite understand that I cannot allow you to proceed on my behalf until I have had you cleared.

I will be in touch with you with further instructions once I have checked out your present standing with the Department of Trade.

<u>Do nothing until you hear from me again</u>.

Yours faithfully,

Henry Root

Henry Root.

139 Elm Park Mansions
Park Walk
London, S.W.10.

The Managing Director,
Hambros Bank Ltd,
41 Bishopsgate,
London, E.C.2.

9th May 1979.

Dear Sir,

For personal reasons which needn't concern you I am anxious
to acquire the book publishing house of Jonathan Cape Ltd.

You were not, in fact, my original choice to handle this
matter on my behalf. I first contacted the firm of Keyser
Ullman Ltd, but having read the so-called 'Selmes Report' I
decided to take my business elsewhere.

Not wishing to slip twice on the same banana skin, I had
my people run you through the computer. I have the print-out
on my desk now and I am glad to be able to tell you that you've
come up brand new. Well done! Indeed my people could find
nothing on you to suggest you're anything other than an honest
and diligent enterprise with no bad eggs under the table or
skeletons of an embarrassing nature in the cupboard.

In the circumstances I'd be happy for you to negotiate
the purchase of Jonathan Cape Ltd on my behalf. Perhaps you
could find out (without in the first instance divulging the
name of your client) the names of the present shareholders,
whether they could be 'induced' to sell, how many shares I
would have to buy to gain control and what the total cost to
myself would be.

I look forward to receiving your ihitial report and to
hearing what your own charges will be <u>if</u> we're successful.

Yours faithfully,

Henry Root

Henry Root.

Hambros Bank Limited

Your ref.

Our ref.   CFD/ARB/MEB

41 Bishopsgate London EC2P 2AA
Telephone 01-588 2851 Telex 883851
Telegrams Hambro London EC2

11th May 1979

Henry Root, Esq.,
139 Elm Park Mansions,
Park Walk,
London, S.W.10.

Dear Sir,

Your letter of 9th May addressed to the Managing Director has been passed to me. Jonathan Cape is a wholly owned subsidiary of Chatto, Bodley Head & Jonathan Cape Ltd. and I would have thought it unlikely that it would be for sale on its own.

However, if you want to discuss this matter further, please do not hesitate to contact me.

Yours faithfully,

A.R. Beevor,
Director.

139 Elm Park Mansions
Park Walk
London, S.W.10.

The Department of Trade,
1 Victoria Street,
London, S.W.1.

25th May 1979.

Sir,

I seek your advice on a matter of considerable urgency.

A week or two ago - before the publication of the so-called
'Selmes Report' - I instructed the merchant banking house of
Keyser Ullman Ltd to purchase Jonathan Cape Ltd, publishers of
30 Bedford Square, London, W.C.1., on my behalf.

I was naturally most concerned when I read the Selmes Report
and now wonder whether I should leave the matter in the hands of
Keyser Ullman.

Could you let me know (confidentially, of course) how Keyser
Ullman shape up at the moment?

I cannot believe that Mr Edward du Cann - the man, let it
not be forgotten, who put Mrs Thatcher where she is today - could
have been associated with an enterprise that reflected incompetence.

I look forward to hearing from you.

Yours faithfully,

Henry Root.

Henry Root.

DP

DEPARTMENT OF TRADE
COMPANIES DIVISION
2 - 14 Bunhill Row London EC1Y 8LL

Telephone 01.606 4071 ext 12

Henry Root Esq
139 Elm Park Mansions
Park Walk
London
SW10

Your reference

Our reference COS 452
19

Date 6 June 1979

Dear Mr Root

RE: FERGUSON & GENERAL INVESTMENTS LTD
(formerly known as Dowgate & General Investments Ltd)
C S T INVESTMENTS LTD

Thank you for your letter of 25th May. I regret
however, that the Department is unable to advise you
as to whether or not, in the light of the Inspectors'
Report, to proceed with the purchase, through
Keyser UllmanLtd, of the Publishers, Jonathan
Cape Ltd.

Yours sincerely

M B WOOLF

139 Elm Park Mansions
Park Walk
London, S.W.10.

The Managing Director,   12th June 1979.
Keyser Ullman Ltd,
25 Milk Street,
London, E.C.2.

Dear Sir,
        Please ignore <u>completely</u> my previous letters to you on the
subject of my purchase of Jonathan Cape Ltd.
        My man at the Department of Trade has now written to me as
follows:
        'I regret that the Department is unable to advise you as
to whether or not, in the light of the Inspector's Report, to
proceed with the purchase, through Keyser Ullman Ltd, of the
publishers, Jonathan Cape Ltd'.
        In the circumstances I have decided to instruct Hambros Ltd
to act in this matter for me.
        If you have already contacted (against my instructions) any
of the principles involved in the matter, I must ask you to write
to them immediately explaining that your company <u>is in no way</u>
associated with Henry Root Wet Fish Ltd.
        Yours faithfully,

        Henry Root

        Henry Root.

NO REPLY!

139 Elm Park Mansions
Park Walk
London, S.W.10.

Peter Barnes Esq,
The DPP's Office,   11th May 1979.
4 Queen Anne's Gate,
London, S.W.1.

Dear Mr Barnes,

Mrs Root and I were both flabbergasted by your 'performance' on 'TV Eye' last night.

I find it extraordinary that at a time when our Leader, Mrs Thatcher, has appealed to the public to support the police you, a public person, should see fit to go on television to blackguard them.

No doubt your assessment, ringingly broadcast to the country at large, that 95% of the Metropolitan CID are as bent as a kangaroo's hind-leg is largely correct. Do you really believe, however, that it is conducive to law and order for the man in the street to be aware of this? Could anything be better calculated to undermine the thin blue line which stands between us and the abolition of pay-beds than for the public at large to know that the Met employs more criminals than it catches?

I look forward to receiving an explanation, Sir, for your extraordinary outburst.

Support Mrs Thatcher!

Yours sincerely,

Henry Root

Henry Root.

Director of Public Prosecutions
4-12 Queen Annes Gate London SW1H 9AZ

Telephones Direct line   01-213 5110 or 7363
Switchboard 01-213 3000

Henry Root Esq.
139 Elm Park Mansions
Park Walk
LONDON S.W.10

Your reference

Our reference   PAD(M)

Date   14th May 1979

Dear Mr. Root,

I answer to your letter of 11th May, I can assure you that in the T.V. Eye programme I neither said nor implied that 95% of the Metropolitan CID are corrupt.

Indeed my personal view is that the percentage of corrupt policemen is very small although, as I did point out in the interview, it is very hard to get sufficient evidence to ensure the conviction of those few.

The overwhelming majority of the police do a magnificent job and they fully deserve the support and confidence of the public.

Yours sincerely,

P.R. BARNES

139 Elm Park Mansions
Park Walk
London, S.W.10.

The Rt Hon William Whitelaw,
The Home Office,   18th May 1979.
Whitehall,
London, S.W.1.

Dear Mr Whitelaw,

Well done! You gave me your assurance in your letter of 2nd April that when you came to power you 'intended to build up the strength and quality of the police to give them a better opportunity to investigate and prevent crime'. Already you have raised their pay! Congratulations! Soon the 'thin blue line' will become the 'thick blue line'! How splendid to have a Government which fulfils the promises in its manifesto!

However. In your letter to me of 27th April you wrote:

'I can confirm that our Conservative Party will take action against pornography'.

Excellent. But what bothers me is this. I read recently that 60% of all drugs on the black-market had been put there by the police. No sooner are drugs seized, it seems, than they are recycled onto the street by the arresting officers!

Can you assure me that the same thing won't happen with pornography? It would be a scandal, in my opinion, if all the material confiscated from family bookshops turned up a few weeks later, and, as is the case with drugs apparently, at a grossly inflated price, due to the Porn Squad's profit margin having to be tacked on the top.

I know our Leader, Mrs Thatcher, is in favour of private enterprise, but this is the free market gone mad! I don't want to see the price of 'Rendezvous' going through the roof just because some ambitious Detective Inspector (spurred on, no doubt, by Mrs Thatcher's exhortations that he should stand on his own two feet) is buying a new split-level maisonette with lounge-diner in Godolming.

One would have somewhat greater faith in the average policeman's awareness of what constitutes an acceptable profit had not Mr Peter Barnes of the DPP's office gone on television last week to announce in 'TV Eye' that in his opinion most of the Metropolitan CID were as bent as corkscrews.

Yours for the Market Economy Within Reasonable Limits!

Henry Root

Henry Root.

NO REPLY!

Kenneth Rose Esq,
The Sunday Telegraph,
Fleet Street,
London, E.C.4.

139 Elm Park Mansions
Park Walk
London, S.W.10.

14th May 1979.

Dear Mr Rose,

Your gossip column in 'The Sunday Telegraph' is often lively.
Well done! But yesterday you had an item perplexing to the self-
made man such as myself who has taken well to the paper after a
poor start.

Writing of Mr Gordon Richardson, the Governor of the Bank of
England (nice job!), you call him a man of 'civilised tastes'.
What are these? For my sort you must spell things out. With
Mrs Thatcher pouring the sherry wine it will be even more important,
if one wants to hold on in the lounge-rooms of power, to know what
civilised tastes are.

Don't misunderstand me, Kenneth. I don't walk around with a
straw up my nose and my trousers held at the knee with harvesting
twine. I know, for instance, that one shouldn't ask one's hostess
for directions to the 'toilet', listen to Shirley Bassey records
or tell German jokes in the presence of the Royal Family. But Mr
Richardson must know more about 'civilised tastes' than this, otherwise I'd be Governor of the Bank of England. Right?

I'd appreciate some guidelines in this area and to this end
I enclose three colour snaps of myself and Mrs Root taken at the
Derby last year.

I want you to come straight out and tell us whether we shape
up. Don't pull your punches. If you think Mrs Root looks like an
old belter, you say so. Bear in mind, however, that following a
bit of luck on the 4.30 she's being escorted off the course by a
constable prior to being booked on a D & D infringement. Even Mr
Richardson wouldn't be at his best in such a corner, I think you'll
agree.

And how about me? I might say that my suit and topper are not
on hire by the hour from Covent Garden or bought with coupons. No
sir. They put me back a couple of hundred quid.

Perhaps I should say that I'm 45, that I've made a fortune in
wet fish and, since I've sold my business and retired, that I've
got time on my hands in which to devote myself to the study of
'civilised tastes'.

Let's hear from you!

Cheers!

Henry Root

Henry Root.

to fin:

SUNDAY TELEGRAPH

135 FLEET STREET LONDON EC4P 4BL TELEPHONE: 01-363 4242 TELEGRAMS: TELESUN LONDON EC4
TELEX: 22874 TELENEWS LONDON

May 15, 1979

Dear Mr. Root,

Thank you for your letter of
May 14, which I interrupt a
holiday to answer.

By Gordon Richardson's "civilised
tastes" (in the context of his possible
appointment as head of an Oxford
college) I meant that he is
well-read with an impressive knowledge
of pictures and music.

I write a weekly column and
do not run correspondence courses on

SUNDAY TELEGRAPH LIMITED REGISTRATION NO. 667848 ENGLAND
REGISTERED OFFICE 135 FLEET STREET LONDON EC4P 4BL

etiquette: So I should regard it as very impertinent on my part to suggest how others should behave in matters of speech or recreation.

All I would say of the photographs you send me (and which I now return) is that you seem to be having more fun than most people at the Derby. Did you back the winner?

Glad to hear you made a fortune out of film. That, I suppose, is why I can no longer afford it!

All good wishes,

Yours sincerely,

Kenneth Rae

139 Elm Park Mansions
Park Walk
London, S.W.10.

H.R.H. The Prince of Wales,
c/o Buckingham Palace, (please forward)
London, S.W.1.   18th May 1979.

Your Royal Highness,

        Inspired by the example of your uncle, Lord Mountbatten, I
have decided to throw my flat open to the public on Saturday 9th
June.

        I reckon to pull in the Japs and the more gullible of our
American friends. The idea is to show them how an _ordinary_ English
couple lives.

        I'll take the mugs on a conducted tour of the premises while
Mrs Root and my two youngsters, Doreen (19) and Henry Jr (15), continue doing what any average family does at weekends: that is to
say stretching the family budget by bottling plums, lolling about
painting one's finger-nails and carrying out the weekly bullworker
maintenance. Mrs Root will be bottling plums, Doreen will be oiling
her bullworker and Henry Jr will be painting his finger-nails, but
that's young people these days.

        Would you consider performing the opening ceremony? We'd be
very honoured and it would be nice for you to meet my Doreen. If
you found yourself a little short, I'd be prepared, like your uncle
Lord Mountbatten, to sock you the pound entrance fee till you
straightened up.

        I look forward to hearing from you, Sir.

        Support Mrs Thatcher!

        Yours respectfully,

        Henry Root

        Henry Root. A naval man like yourself!

PS.   Sorry to send this care of Her Majesty, but you don't seem
to be in the phone book.

BUCKINGHAM PALACE

From: The Assistant Private Secretary to H.R.H. The Prince of Wales

4th June, 1979

Dear Mr Root,

The Prince of Wales has asked me to thank you very much for your letter to him of 18th May in which you asked if he would be able to visit your flat on Saturday 9th June.

I am afraid His Royal Highness will be unable to accept your kind invitation since he has already made his plans for that day.

Yours Sincerely

Oliver Everett

Oliver Everett

Henry Root, Esq.

139 Elm Park Mansions
Park Walk
London, S.W.10.

H.E. The Greek Ambassador,
The Greek Embassy,   30th April 1979.
1a Holland Park,
London, W.11.

Your Excellency,

I write to you on a matter which could have serious international repercussions.

Yesterday afternoon Mrs Root was hosing down the family Rolls
under my supervision when her knees gave forth, causing her to sit
in the bucket and rick her back. A massage appeared to be the answer,
so we summoned a young lady whose advertisement in the window of our
local newsagent proclaimed 'Greek Masseuse. Full Theatrical Wardrobe'.
(Mrs Root naturally didn't want some fancy man offering to oblige
her separately.)

All was proceeding according to the book, when Arianna — for
that was the young lady's name — suddenly sat athwart Mrs Root and
suggested sapphic alternatives with the door closed.

Sir, is this the Greek way of doing things? Is this some
indigenous custom of your once great country, instigated by such
celebrated homosexualists as Plato the Great and General Alexander
and kept alive by such as the big warbling pudding who crops up from
time to time on 'Top of the Pops'?

Mrs Root screeched like a gibbon and Arianna high-tailed it
out of the flat with her bag of tricks, but Mrs Root was so shaken
by the incident that I had to get my own dinner. In the circumstances
we have thought it best to cancel a sunshine holiday for two we had
planned to take this summer in your part of the world, where no doubt
swimming without clothes and the eating of raw fish is now encouraged.

I would suggest, Mr Ambassador, that you take immediate action
to dissuade those of Miss Arianna's stripe from bringing the rest of
you into disrepute.

Such incidents as the one I have described could never have
happened under the Colonels.

Yours respectfully,

Henry Root

Henry Root.

Copy to The Foreign Office.

                                        139 Elm Park Mansions
                                        Park Walk
                                        London, S.W.10.

The Greek Ambassador,
1a Holland Park,
London, W.11.   1st June 1979.

Your Excellency,
        I am astonished that you haven't had the common civility to
reply to my letter of 30th April re Mrs Root's experience at the
hands of one of your masseuses.
        What's going on over there in Holland Park? Get a grip on
yourself, my good man!
        I look forward to hearing from you by return.
        Yours sincerely,

        Henry Root

        Henry Root.
Copy to Sir Ian Gilmour, The Foreign Office.

CONSULATE GENERAL OF GREECE

1A HOLLAND PARK, LONDON W11 3TP   TEL.: 01-727 8040

7th June, 1979

Henry Root, Esq.,
139 Elm Park Mansions,
Park Walk,
LONDON S.W.10.

Dear Sir,

We acknowledge receipt of your letters dated 30th April and 1st June addressed to His Excellency the Ambassador and which have been forwarded to me.

I am sorry for the trouble which has been caused to your wife but, as you will understand, it is not a matter of the competence of this Consulate General and I suggest that if you wish to pursue the matter you should contact the competent British authorities.

Yours faithfully,
For Consul General

P. Vlassopoulos
Consul

Foreign and Commonwealth Office
London SW1A 2AH

Telephone 01- 233-5097

Henry Root Esq
139 Elm Park Mansions
Park Walk
LONDON SW10

Your reference

Our reference

Date 6 June 1979

Dear Mr Root

I have been asked to thank you for your
letter of 1 June to Sir Ian Gilmour, the
contents of which have been noted. The
incident you describe is indeed regrettable.
I hope that Mrs Root's back is better.

Yours Sincerely

A L S Coltman
Southern European Department

139 Elm Park Mansions
Park Walk
London, S.W.10.

Mr A.L.S. Coltman,
Southern European Department,
The Foreign and Commonwealth Office,   21st June 1979.
London, S.W.1.

Dear Mr Coltman,

Thank you for your letter of 6th June re the incident of Mrs Root and the Greek 'masseuse'.

She's on the mend now, you'll be relieved to hear, though she still gets the jitters from time to time, being unable to watch without qualms Miss Esther Rantzen on TV or confront a portion of moussaka.

Please thank Sir Ian Gilmour for taking an interest in this matter. Don't bother Lord Carrington with it. I'm sure he's got enough to worry about what with one thing and another here and there.

Perhaps I could seek your advice on another matter while I have your attention. Having cancelled our annual holiday for two in Greece consequent upon Mrs Root's 'experience', we are now wondering whether the sunshine island of Ibiza might make a viable alternative. Once was when the holder of a British passport could move through Europe and other parts knowing that his person and the persons of his family were adequately protected by the signature of Her Majesty's Foreign Secretary on page 1. Not anymore, it seems. I have heard rumours that even in Spain matters are not, since the sad death of General Franco, all that they might be re law and order. As so often happens, democracy, it seems, has brought in its wake swarms of local Pedros who roam the streets putting their hands up ladies' skirts and infiltrating to their own ends the wallet-pockets of package tourists.

Can you, Sir, as a Southern European expert, tell me whether these practices have now reached the Balearics or whether in fact Mrs Root and I could safely visit Ibiza this summer without incident?

Yours sincerely,

Henry Root

Henry Root.

Foreign and Commonwealth Office
London SW1A 2AH

Telephone 01-

Henry Root Esq
139 Elm Park Mansions
Park Walk
London SW10

Your reference

Our reference

Date

27 June 1979

Dear Mr Root

Thank you for your letter of 21 June. I am glad that Mrs Root is better.

I know no reason why you should not visit Ibiza. But the activities to which you refer are indeed apt to occur in most popular tourist centres. A travel agent should be able to advise on this aspect.

Yours Sincerely

A L S Coltman
Southern European Department

139 Elm Park Mansions
Park Walk
London, S.W.10.

C. James Anderton Q.P.M., F.B.I.M.,
Chief Constable's Office,
Chester House,
Boyer Street,
Manchester MI6 ORE.

21st May 1979.

Dear Chief Constable,

May I congratulate you on your fine showing on the TV programme 'Jaywalking' yesterday evening?

You came over as forceful and sincere - in marked contrast,
I may say, to our own Sir David McNee, who recently made a very
poor fist of being interviewed on 'Thames at 6'. He shaped up
well physically, but under Andrew Gardner's relentless probing
his brain fell out and he admitted, among other things, that half
his force was corrupt! Not very good for the morale of those
under him! You'd never fall into such an obvious trap!

One slight criticism. Questioning you about your sensible
decision to give full police protection (at a cost of hundreds of
thousands of pounds to the rate-payers) to a recent National
Front rally on your patch (as you so rightly understand, freedom
of speech - however obnoxious - <u>must</u> be protected by the law,
though this freedom must <u>never</u> be extended to pornographers), Miss
Jay said:

"Was that a moral decision or a police decision?"

My eldest, Doreen, who is reading philosophy and sociology
at Essex University, said that either this was a category mistake
(whatever that might be!) or Miss Jay was implying that a police
decision can never be a moral decision.

If my Doreen is correct (and it wouldn't be the first time,
I might add), may I ask you why you didn't thrust Miss Jay's
question back down her throat by saying something along the lines
of:

"Are you suggesting, madam, that there must always be a clear
distinction between a moral decision and a police decision? I
recognise no such distinction."

Apart from this one slight lapse - a really splendid performance! Well done!

Keep it up!

Christians demand the return of the rope!

Your pal in the soft south!

Henry Root

Henry Root.

C James Anderton Q.P.M., F.B.I.M.
Chief Constable

Chief Constable's Office
P O Box 22 (S.West PDO)
Chester House
Boyer Street
Manchester M16 0RE
Telephone 061-872 5050

22nd May 1979.

Dear Mr. Root,

It was kind of you to write to me on 21st May and I appreciate your good wishes.

Your daughter Doreen is absolutely right in her opinion of my handling of the question to which you specifically refer. The trouble is that, in a lengthy television interview during which questions come thick and fast, it is not possible always to sort out one's thoughts quickly enough to meet the situation correctly. In any event, the whole thing was pre-recorded and later chopped about in such a way that one cannot guarantee that the questions and answers are put together properly. You will know television interviewers often film their own questions again later to complete the programme.

If I had dealt with the question better to meet the point raised by your daughter, I am quite sure it would not have featured in the programme at all.

Thank you for your interest.

Yours sincerely,

Chief Constable.

Henry Root, Esq.,
139 Elm Park Mansions,
Park Walk,
London. S.W.10.

139 Elm Park Mansions
Park Walk
London, S.W.10.

The Producer,
'Brass Tacks',
BBC,
Manchester.

23rd May 1979.

Dear Sir,
        I wish to protest most strongly at the scandalous treatment
this country's finest policeman, Mr James Anderton, received on
your programme last night.
        To sit a fine Christian gentleman down in close proximity to
an unsavoury crowd of prostitutes was bad enough. Even worse was
to allow him to be humilaited intellectually by the afore-mentioned
rabble (when you must have known perfectly well that it is not given
to mere policemen, as it is to street-walkers, to think coherently
on their feet.) Worst of all was your irresponsible decision not
to cut out the ringingly audible aside made by one of the ladies
of the night, who suddenly turned to the painted strumpet sitting
on her left and said, in a whisper which must have echoed round the
country:
        "This sanctimonious, dirty-minded half-wit really gets on
my tits! I hate to think how <u>he</u> gets his rocks off!"
        Your programme, apart from being an aid and comfort to every
prostitute in the land, Sir, must have put the cause of Law and Order
back by fifty years.
        I await your explanation.
        Yours disgusted,

        Henry Root

        Henry Root.
P.S. I would be grateful if you could supply me with the phone
number of the young lady with red hair who sat in the centre and
did most of the talking. I would like to contact her with reference
to my own researches.

BRITISH BROADCASTING CORPORATION

NEW BROADCASTING HOUSE PO BOX 27 OXFORD ROAD MANCHESTER M60 1SJ

TELEPHONE AND TELEGRAMS 061-236 8444

20th June, 1979.

Mr. Henry Root,
139, Elm Park Mansions,
Park Walk,
<u>London, S.W.10.</u>

Dear Mr. Root,

In the absence of our Editor, Roger Laughton, your letter has
been passed to me by the Programme Controller's office for reply.

As you know, at the end of BRASS TACKS we advertise a service to
viewers who wish to express a point of view on the subject under
discussion. That's in a programme called RETURN CALL transmitted
on the Monday following the programme. In fact, an excerpt from
your letter was used in that programme on 28th May 1979.

> "Your programme, apart from being an aid and comfort to
> every prostitute in the land, Sir, must have put the
> cause of Law and Order back fifty years."

As you will realise the response to such a subject was overwhelming
and we received several hundred letters, which makes it quite
impossible to furnish individual replies to all of them. May I
say that of all the people who have written with a point of view
on the subjects we have covered, this is the first time that anyone
has objected to not getting a personal reply.

To take up some of the other points in your first letter, a copy
of which we retain on our files, I have reviewed the tape of the
original transmission and can at no point hear anyone saying:

> "This sanctimonious, dirty-minded half-wit really gets
> on my tits! I hate to think how <u>he</u> gets his rocks off!"

Finally, I am afraid it is not our policy to release the telephone
numbers of programme guests. However, if you wish, I am quite
happy to forward a letter from you to the young lady in question
and then leave it to her discretion as to whether or not she
chooses to reply.

Yours sincerely,

Eric Robson,
Presenter,
BRASS TACKS.

139 Eln Park Mansions
Park Walk
London, S.W.10.

Mr Eldon Griffiths MP,
The House of Commons,
London, S.W.1.

26th May 1979.

Dear Eldon,

I was delighted to read in the paper this week that you are
already planning to raise the 'restoration of hanging' issue in
the House. Well done! Once again ordinary folk have a Government
which cares a little for their safety.

I have a suggestion to make, on which I'd appreciate your
comments. One of the arguments for capital punishment rests on
the deterrent value of the rope. Couldn't it be argued that hanging is too swift a method of execution to deter the really hard-
line criminal?

I expect you were as impressed as I was to read of the recent
execution in Florida of a character called John Spenkelink in the
electric chair. It seems a full six minutes passed before Spenkelink was dead, during which time he hopped about like a prawn on
a hot-plate.

That will have taught him to think twice in future before
shooting innocent people.

Wouldn't the prospect of being slowly fried to a crisp be
more alarming to the terrorists and sex fiends who are making it
impossible for decent folk to walk our streets than the mere
prospect of dangling at the end of a rope?

Let me have your views on this.

Support Mrs Thatcher!

Yours for the introduction of the chair!

Henry Root

Henry Root.

Eldon Griffiths M.P.

acknowledges with thanks the receipt of your communication
of the 26th May

the contents of which have been noted.

8/77 12m 335617 LP1-2029

H.C. 85

139 Elm Park Mansions
Park Walk
London, S.W.10.

Mr George Hardy,
Derby County Football Club,
The Baseball Ground,   28th May 1979.
Derby.

Dear George,
        I'm a busy man, but you're in a deep hole with the Rams and
I'm prepared to dig you out. I'm hereby nominating myself for the
job of manager, as advertised.
        Right. Down to cases. You'll want to know what experience
I've had of running a football club.
        None at all!
        So what? The name of the game is motivation and psychology,
and that I know about. Why do you suppose Mr Clough consistently
delivers the goods? Because he terrorises the lads into turning
it on for him, that's why. I'll be the same. I'll have the lads
so psyched up they'll run round the park like demented threshing-
machines, reducing even Liverpool's Red Army to a bunch of dancing
woofters.
        In one respect only will I carry on with the policies of my
predecessor, the Doc. I'll get rid of all the good players. (He
only left two behind - Daly and the boy Hill - so this won't take
long.) Psychology again, you see. The players who stay behind
will feel less bad about their uselessness out there on the park.
        I gather you've got a few bad eggs under the board-room table.
They'll have to go. Leave this to me.
        It so happens that I'll be in Derby on business on Tuesday
12th June. If I don't hear from you to the contrary, I'll assume
it will be okay for me to drop in and see you at the Baseball
Ground at about 12.30. We can finalise the details - salary, perks,
kick-backs etc - then.
        Let me know if you can't make it. I'd be as sick as a parrot
to run into your office only to discover that you were visiting
your 'masseuse'.
        Up the Rams!
        It's all about winning!
        Yours,

        Henry Root

        Henry Root.

DERBY COUNTY FOOTBALL CLUB LIMITED

All Communications to be addressed to the Secretary   Registered in England No. 49139

Our ref: GH/SAB

12th July 1979

Dear Sir

We thank you for your letter applying for the position of Manager with
our Club.

We regret to inform you that your application was unsuccessful, the Club
having appointed Mr. Colin Addison to the position.

May we thank you for your interest and we wish you every success in the
future

Yours faithfully

George Hardy
Chairman

The Baseball Ground, Derby DE3 8NB   Telephone: Derby **40105/6/7**   Grams: FOOTBALL DERBY

Chairman GEORGE HARDY   Manager ~~DANNY BOCHES~~   **General Secretary STUART WEBB**

139 Elm Park Mansions
Park Walk
London, S.W.10.

Nicholas Scott MP,
The House of Commons,
London, S.W.1.

28th May 1979.

Dear Mr Scott,

During the recent election campaign you were good enough to answer my questions most promptly.

In the event, I'm afraid I was unable to vote for you (as you will remember, we were unable to resolve our differences over the selective hanging issue) but you are, for better or worse, my MP, so I wonder if I might trouble you again.

Following the adverse publicity given to the behaviour of the Scottish football fans on Saturday last, the false and mis-leading comparisons between the dangers of alcohol and so-called cannabis are once again being made. The 'legalise cannabis' lobby in the media has been quick to draw our attention to the violence, blood-shed and damage to property caused by the high-spirited Tartan Army, and equally quick to point out that far from inducing this kind of anti-social behaviour cannabis, in fact, has a strange-ly peaceable and law-abiding effect on those who take it.

So what? A drop of the hard stuff never hurt anyone. Most parents, as I'm sure you will agree, would infinitely prefer that their youngsters were exposed to a bit of boisterous horse-play by a few thousand bottle-throwing football fans than that they should 'drop out' of reality by taking cannabis.

Can I have your assurance that you will never vote for any bill designed to legalise cannabis or one to restrict the easy distribution of alcohol?

Support Mrs Thatcher!
Yours for a wee drop!

Henry Root.

Nicholas Scott, MBE, MP

House of Commons
London SW1

7 June 1979

Dear Mr Root

Thank you for your letter.

'Never' is an extravagant word in the political lexicon, but I do fully share your views about the dangers of legalising cannabis and I have little fear that I shall become hooked on the evidence of counter-vailing opinion.

As for alcohol, I must admit it would be against my natural inclinations and better judgement to seek to control its consumption.

Yours sincerely

Nicholas Scott

Henry Root Esq.

139 Elm Park Mansions
Park Walk
London, S.W.10.

Mr 'Larry' Lamb,   25th May 1979.
The Sun,
30 Bouverie Street,
London, E.C.4.

Dear Mr Lamb,

I wish to protest most strongly about a story which appears on the front page of 'The Sun' today.

Under a picture of a foreign 'actress' (no doubt French) called Suzanne Danielle, we are informed that she lives with a Mr Patrick Mower in a Buckinghamshire cottage.

I don't want to know that! Nor, I may say, does Mrs Root.

Is it due to some sub-clause in the Treaty of Rome that we now have to be brought up to date over our breakfast corn-flakes with the immoral arrangements of foreign 'actresses' living in this country? Such information should be tucked away on page 3, if anywhere.

Why can't you publish on your front page a picture of the gracious and talented English actress, Miss Nanette Newman, with the information that she is living with her husband, the equally talented Mr Bryan Forbes, in a villa in Virginia Water?

I look forward to receiving your explanation, Sir, for this thinly veiled attack on family values.

Support Mrs Thatcher!

Yours sincerely,

Henry Root

Henry Root.

Copy to Sir David Nicholson (56, married, 3 grown-up children – candidate.)

Sir David Nicholson,
10 Fordie House,
Sloane Street,
London, S.W.1.

139 Elm Park Mansions
Park Walk
London, S.W.10.

25th May 1979.

Dear Sir David,

I enclose a copy of a letter I have today written to
Mr 'Larry' Lamb of Sun Newspapers Ltd.

Before I cast my vote for you in the coming European
election, could you let me know where you stand on this sort
of issue?

In my view the Common Market should be about morality
as well as butter mountains. What do you think?

I see from your leaflet that you speak fluent French
and have a knowledge of Germans. Do you know something we
don't know?

Support Mrs Thatcher!

Yours sincerely,

Henry Root

Henry Root. Anti-Marketeer.

NEWS GROUP NEWSPAPERS LTD
A Subsidiary of News International Ltd

Registered Office:

30 Bouverie Street, Fleet Street, London, EC4Y 8DE.

Registered No. 679215 England
Telex Sunnews 267827
Telephone 01-353 3030
EDITOR'S OFFICE

May 30th, 1979.

AL/MD

Henry Root, Esq.,
139, Elm Park Mansions,
Park Walk,
London, SW10.

Dear Mr Root

Thank you for your letter.

I understand - without necessarily accepting - your point of view.

We are in the business of supplying information. Doctor Who is a very popular programme. Mr. Mower is a very popular actor.

To record the fact of his domestic arrangement with Ms. Danielle surely does not imply approval of the arrangement

My apologies to Mrs. Root!

With best wishes,

Yours sincerely,

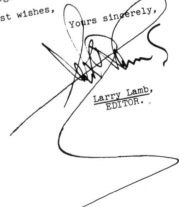

Larry Lamb,
EDITOR.

DAVID

LONDON CENTRAL
EURO-CONSTITUENCY

NICOLSON

CONSERVATIVE CANDIDATE

CENTRAL COMMITTEE ROOM: 90, EBURY ST. SW1W 9QD ★ TEL: 730 8181 ★ ELECTION AGENT: B. VILLETTE

Henry Root. Esq.,
139, Elm Park Mansions,
Park Walk,
<u>LONDON S.W.10.</u>

30th May, 1979.

Dear Mr Root,

Many thanks for your letter of May 25th, and I can
only say that I too deplore the kind of article to which you refer
and which appears so often in the popular press.

I believe if we had a proper national objective once
again and concentrated on other things, we could certainly improve
standards of morality.

Yours sincerely,

David Nicolson

Published by: B. Villette, 90 Ebury Street, S.W.1. & Printed by: Errington & Martin, 25 Elsdale St., E.9.

139 Elm Park Mansions
Park Walk
London, S.W.10.

30th May 1979.

The Chairman,
The Parole Board,
50 Queen Anne's Gate,
London, S.W.1.

Dear Sir,

May I, a mere member of the general public, congratulate you on your enlightened decision to release ex-Commander Kenneth Drury, late of the Flying Squad?

In my opinion a policeman should never be sent to prison, no matter what he's done. It's outrageous that he should be obliged to mingle with common criminals, many of whom he will have been obliged to 'fit up' in the execution of his duty.

Perhaps I could take this opportunity of suggesting parole for the so-called Luton Post Office killers. Not because they happen to be innocent. In the interests of law and order that's neither here nor there. No, I suggest clemency merely on the grounds that their sentence seemed a little harsh. Ten years is about right for something you didn't do; twenty is definitely too long.

I look forward to hearing your views on this suggestion.

Yours faithfully,

Henry Root

Henry Root.

Copy to Mr Timothy Raison MP.

PAROLE BOARD

Queen Anne's Gate
LONDON, SW1H 9AT

LM

Direct Line 01-213
Switchboard 01-213 3000

Your Ref ....

Any communication on the subject of this letter
should be addressed to:
THE SECRETARY
and the following reference quoted:

....

17 July 1979

Mr H Root
139 Elm Park Mansions
Park Walk
LONDON
SW10

Dear Mr Root

Thank you for your letter of 30 May to which the Chairman of the Parole Board has asked me to reply on his behalf. The delay in replying is regretted.

I should perhaps explain that the Parole Board is an independent non-judicial advisory body only and can only consider and recommend on cases which have been referred to it by the Home Secretary. This applies equally to prisoners with determinate sentences or with life sentences, and **until** the Home Secretary sees fit to refer the cases you mention to it, the Parole Board has no authority to comment on the matter of their parole suitability.

I should also add that the question of a prisoner's guilt or innocence is not a matter for the Parole Board. The Board can only proceed on the premise that parole candidates are guilty of the crimes they have been convicted of by the Courts and sentenced accordingly.

I have copied this correspondence to the Home Office for their information.

Yours sincerely

Marcella Hargreaves

JD

 HOME OFFICE
Queen Anne's Gate London SW1H 9AT

Direct line 01-213
Switchboard 01-213 3000

H Root Esq
139 Elm Park Mansions
Park Walk
LONDON
SW10

Your reference

Our reference
PDP/M 0910/9/14
Date

2 7 July 1979

Dear Sir

You wrote to Mr Raison on 1 June asking for his comments on a copy of a letter which you had sent to the Chairman of the Parole Board.

On the first point (that police officers convicted of offences should not be sent to prison) the sentence to be imposed in a particular case is, within the limits provided by the law and subject to the right of appeal, for the Court to decide in the light of all the information before it about the offence and the offender. It would be wholly inappropriate for the Home Secretary, or any Government Minister for that matter, to attempt to interfere with the Court's discretion in an individual case.

On the second point (that those convicted of the murder of the Luton sub-postmaster should now be released on parole) prisoners serving life sentences are not eligible for parole as such but are released on a life licence under the terms of which they may be recalled to prison at any time during the remainder of their lives should their conduct make this necessary. But the Home Secretary cannot order the release of a life sentence prisoner unless he is recommended to do so by the Parole Board and after he has consulted the Lord Chief Justice and, if he is available, the trial judge. Each case is dealt with individully on its own merits and, in considering the case of any life sentence prisoner, the Parole Board and the Home Secretary must proceed on the basis that the prisoner was rightly convicted. The cases of those convicted of the murder of the Luton sub-postmaster will be considered in precisely the same way as those of all other prisoners serving life sentences for murder.

Yours faithfully

V. K Storey

MRS V K STOREY

                                        Root House
                                        139 Elm Park Mansions
                                        Park Walk
                                        London, S.W.10.

Lord Grade,
ACC Ltd,
ATV House,
London, W.1.   1st June 1979.

Dear Lord Grade,
        I'm presently getting together a consortium of plausible
businessmen to take over the publishing house of Jonathan Cape.

        I don't know whether you're familiar with this company.
It once enjoyed a solid reputation in the world of letters, but
recently, due to lack of editorial know-how and ability to pick
winning manuscripts with lucrative subsiduary rights situations
attached, it has gone back badly.

        It is my opinion, however, that with the right go-go man-
agement (me) directing its affairs, in place of the grey-beards
and dizzy young girls now in control, it could once again have
a relevant contribution to make to the literary scene.

        Would you be interested in joining the consortium? My
bankers, Hambros, are pressing me for a meeting, but first I
want to arrange some financial back-up. Under-capitalised, I'd
be running through Hambros' door in nothing but my bowler hat
and that would create a doubtful impression.

        You appeal to me as a man who can make up his mind quickly
(well done!) so if the concept strikes you as valid perhaps you'd
like to have lunch (on me!) at the Mirabelle at 1 o'clock on
Friday 15th June.

        May I say how much I'm looking forward to your Euro-Gala
from the Theatre Royal, Drury Lane this Sunday? Miss Petunia
Clark is a splendid artiste and melodies to catch the ear always
appeal to the family.

        You're a true European!

        I look forward to hearing from you.

        Yours for family entertainment!

        Henry Root

        Henry Root.

Associated Communications Corporation Limited

ATV House
17 Great Cumberland Place
London W1A 1AG
telephone 01-262 8040
cables and telegrams
Ayteevee London W1
telex 23762

From the office of the Deputy Chairman
and Deputy Chief Executive

6th June, 1979

JFG/MANL

H. Root, Esq.,
139 Elm Park Mansions,
Park Walk,
London S.W.10

Dear Mr. Root,

Lord Grade has passed to me your letter of the 1st June concerning your proposition to buy the book publishing house of Jonathan Cape Limited. We actually looked at this particular company some twelve months ago and decided not to attempt to purchase it.

We hope that you will be successful in obtaining someone else to join your consortium.

Yours sincerely,

Jack Gill.

Registered Office: ATV House 17 Great Cumberland Place London W1A 1AG
Registered in England No. 544144

139 Elm Park Mansions
Park Walk
London, S.W.10.

Miss Debra Byron,
Editorial,
Jonathan Cape Ltd,   2nd June 1979.
30 Bedford Square,
London, W.C.1.

Dear Miss Byron,
        Thank you for your letter of 20th April with regard to my
original novel, 'Day of Reckoning'. I must apologise for not
getting back to you before now.
        You'll be delighted to know that your prompt and courteous
rejection of the book as it then stood in no way drove me from
my typewriter! Rather the reverse! This, I suspect, was your
intention. As you quickly perceived, you weren't dealing with
silly young girl with her head filled with maudlin literary
dreams of an Irish slant, but with a plain-speaking man with whom
you needn't pull your editorial punches.
        I know one can't expect instant success. After all, isn't
it the case that Freddy Forsyth's 'The Day of the Jackass' was
turned down with ill-concealed contempt by no less than 37 of
the top houses including your own (well done!)
        So did I give up? No sir! I had a long hard look at the
piece (particularly the ending - so often the weakest part of
a first book) and came to the conclusion that there might be
something valid in what you said.
        So I went to work! Here, after six hard weeks are the
fruits of your editorial know-how and my perseverence. What I
have done, as you will quickly see, is tighten up the prose and
cut ruthlessly (without, I hope, destroying the book's artistic
integrity) so we are left with nothing but the hard muscle of
the narrative line. Now the reader is led unerringly by the
nose to the book's psychological centre - our hero's actual
moment of reckoning, the moment when he discovers who he really
is.
        Other deft touches have been to alter the main character's
name to Harry Toro (this renders the work less distractingly
autobiographical) and to change the name of a subsiduary character
from Lorraine Pumptit (weak) to Desiree Thunderbottom (much
stronger).
        Okay, the ball's back in your court! Let's go!
        Yours sincerely,

        Henry Root

        Henry Root.

DAY OF RECKONING
By
HENRY ROOT

2nd Draft.

Amazingly attractive, 45-year-old Harry Toro, chairman of Harry Toro Wet Fish Ltd woke up in the bedroom of his luxury mansion in Maidenhead.

He began to count his blessings. His Rolls, his swimming-pool, the expense account trips to Paris and New York with his latest 'companion', the long-legged, full-bosomed 'starlet', Desiree Thunder bottom.

Suddenly he felt guilty. He thought of the back-streets of Barnsley in which he'd been born and in which his aged parents still lived. Were he to get up now, take the Rolls from the garage and drive himself, literally and metaphorically, back to his origins would he still have anything to say to his old mum and dad, to his mates at the local factory and to little Janet Gibbens with whom he'd had his first 'experience' at the local Odeon?

"Who cares?" he thought, and he went happily back to sleep.

THE END.

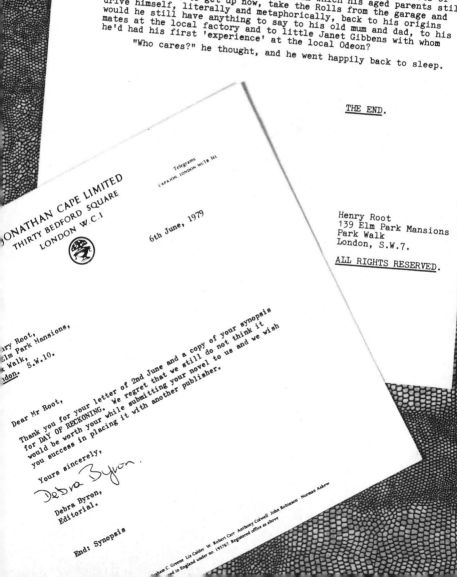

Telegrams
CAPAJON, LONDON WC1B 3EL

JONATHAN CAPE LIMITED
THIRTY BEDFORD SQUARE
LONDON W.C.1

6th June, 1979

Henry Root
139 Elm Park Mansions
Park Walk
London, S.W.7.

...ry Root,
...Elm Park Mansions,
... Walk, S.W.10.
...don,

Dear Mr Root,

Thank you for your letter of 2nd June and a copy of your synopsis for DAY OF RECKONING. We regret that we still do not think it would be worth your while submitting your novel to us and we wish you success in placing it with another publisher.

Yours sincerely,

Debra Byron

Debra Byron,
Editorial.

End: Synopsis

...ham C. Greene Liz Calder W. Robert Carr Anthony Colwell John Robinson Norman Askew
...d in England under no. 195767. Registered office as above

139 Elm Park Mansions
Park Walk
London, S.W.10.

Petal Model Agency Ltd,
28 Walpole Street,
London, S.W.3.

6th June 1979.
(D-Day plus 35 years!)

Dear Sir or Madame,

In case you are unfamiliar with my work, let me say at once that I am a photographer not without experience and flair, known for the standard of my finish here and there. Also fully equipped with Hasselblad and strobe.

You have been given to me as the people to supply the best type of girl for outdoor photography without clothes.

Here's the concept. Now that we have joined the Common Market it is particularly deplorable, in my opinion, that magazines of the sort that male readers participate in privately with the door shut still consider exotic locations abroad as the proper setting for figure shooting on the sands.

What's wrong with this country? Why does it always have to be Denise, Stephanie, Fifi and Kerry-Jane soaking up the sun on the beaches of Ibiza and then joining the photographer, Heinz, in the champagne a go-go bar of the Hotel Player Real?

Why not Denise, Stephanie, Fifi and Kerry-Jane in the car-park of the Red Bull Hotel Staines and, later, enjoying a shandy with the photographer, Henry de Root, in the Executives Bar of the same hotel?

I invisage a lay-out for 'Penthouse' entitled 'Away Day in Staines' and to this end I would like to book four of your best types while the weather holds.

Please let me know what would be the price of each girl for participating in erotic tableaux in Staines throughout the day and early evening (nothing distasteful).

I look forward to hearing from you.

Yours sincerely,

Henry de Root

Henry de Root. Photographer.

Petal Model Agency,
28 Walpole Street,
London, S.W.3.

139 Elm Park Mansions
Park Walk
London, S.W.10.

16th June 1979.

Dear Sir or Madame,

Why haven't I heard from you in reply to my letter of
6th June with regard to the proposed lay-out in 'Penthouse'?

Never mind! I can come to you! I'll hop into your office
at 3.30 pm on Tuesday 26th June to run my eye up and down a
line-up of your best types.

Do you happen to represent the delightful lass currently
participating in the 'Lilt' commercial on TV (television)? If
you do, get her there on the 26th. She'd be fine for what I
have in mind. Also those two blonde girls - don't know their
names, I'm afraid - who apart from modelling without benefit of
clothes also form a popular singing duo. I think one of them
may be called Nina. Or if it's not her, then it's the other
one. Have them there on Tuesday week if you represent them.
Plus any others you deem appropriate to my concept.

I look forward to becoming acquainted with you and the
girls on the 26th. Kindly let me know well in advance if for
any reason this date is not suitable for you. I'd hate to run
through your door and find no one there but a couple of dozey
typists painting their finger-nails and considering their personal involvements.

Let's make money here!

Yours sincerely,

Henry de Root.

Henry de Root.

PETAL

PETAL MODEL AGENCY LTD. 28 WALPOLE STREET, CHELSEA, LONDON, SW3 4QS

U.K. Bookings: Press, Television, Film, 01-730 7284 International Bookings 01-730 7285 Telex: Petal 21879
Accounts: Invoices 01-730 1902 Bought ledgers 0295 4491

Mr. Henry de Root,
139 Elm Park Mansions,
Park Walk, London, S.W.10.

18th June, 1979.

Dear Mr. de Root,

Thank you for your letter of the 16th June.

Unfortunately we do not have any models suitable for your
proposed lay-out for 'Penthouse'.

The model in the 'Lilt' advertisement is Stefanie Marrian, who
is with Askew's model agency. Also the two blond models you mentioned
are currently making a record but can be found at Bobton's.

I'm sorry we can't help you, but perhaps you could ring Geoff
Wootton Agency 736 0191.

Yours sincerely,

Dawn Wylie-Harris

Dawn Wylie-Harris

The Director of Public Prosecutions,
The DPP's Office,
4 Queen Anne's Gate,
London, S.W.1.

139 Elm Park Mansions
Park Walk
London, S.W.10.

Sir,

19th June 1979.

I have before me the so-called girlie magazine Penthouse, Vol 14 No 4, and refer specifically to 'Emma Jane's Diary' which purpor to be a regular column written by a self-alleged call-girl entitled Miss Emma Jane Crampton.

I make no comment on the fact that a call-girl is allowed to advertise her services by writing a column in a widely read magazine. That the authorities allow such a state of affairs to continue hardly surprises one these days.

However, I do object most strongly to her opening remarks, which read as follows:

'Disgusted to find in my 'Observer' today a long and sycophantic interview with the increasingly absurd Mrs Thatcher, in the course of which she keeps referring to something she calls 'ordinary folk'. It so happens that I shall shortly be interviewing Mrs Thatcher myself on behalf of 'Penthouse' and I can say here and now that if she dares to call me 'an ordinary folk' I shall lean forward and, with one deft movement, pull her knickers down.'

Can one say this? Surely any unauthorised reference to Mrs Thatcher's knickers illegal and a threat to pull them down by a private citizen unacquainted with Mrs Thatcher tantamount to civil disorder? So-called Miss Crampton continues:

'In my experience most suburban ladies find it a most disconcerting tactic and I urge 'ordinary folk' throughout the land to adopt this highly effective form of political comment should they have the misfortune to meet Mrs Thatcher in the course of one of her vote-losing walk-abouts'.

There we have it! A direct instruction to ordinary folk everywhere (and what's wrong with being an ordinary folk I ask?) to pull our Leader's knickers down! And what could be more offensive than Miss Crampton's suggestion that only suburban ladies would find such treatment discouraging? She continues:

'I assure you that the manoeuvre is easier than you might suppose - the element of surprise usually proving decisive. I did it to Mrs Whitehouse outside the Old Bailey after the Gay News trial and, as you will have seen for yourselves, she hasn't been the same since'.

I look forward to receiving your assurance, Sir, that you have already started proceedings against Miss Emma Jane Crampton and the magazine for which she writes. Failing this, I must tell you that I shall have no hesitation in instigating a private prosecution. I am not without means and am acquainted with Sir James Goldsmith.

Yours faithfully,

Henry Root.

Copy to Mrs Mary Whitehouse.

NATIONAL VIEWERS' AND LISTENERS' ASSOCIATION

Hon. Treasurer
Mr R. C. Standring
'Still Waters'
Pine Walk, East Horsley
LEATHERHEAD, Surrey
Tel. East Horsley 2573

President:

Vice-President: Miss C. J. FitzGerald

Hon. Gen. Sec.
Mrs Mary Whitehouse
Ardleigh, COLCHESTER
Essex, CO7 7RH
Tel. Colchester 230 123

26th June 1979

Mr. Henry Root,
139 Elm Park Mansions,
Park Walk,
London SW10.

Dear Mr. Root,

Thank you very much for your letter of 19th June and for the copy of the letter you have sent to the Director of Public Prosecutions.

Miss Crampton's story is pure fabrication as far as I am concerned - I am grateful for your concern over this but I am of the opinion that any legal action on our part over this would simply give publicity to this very stupid woman.

Yours sincerely,

Mary Whitehouse

The Director of Public Prosecutions
acknowledges receipt of Mr. HENRY ROOT 's
communication of 19th JUNE 1979

4/12 QUEEN ANNES GATE,
LONDON SW1H 9AZ
2 6 JUN 1979

(2437) 3-318902/000824 1/74 2m MC8 82

139 Elm Park Mansions
Park Walk
London, S.W.10.

The Director of Public Prosecutions,
The DPP's Office,
4 Queen Anne's Gate,
London, S.W.1.

7th August 1979.

Dear Sir,

I wrote to you on 19th June 1979 in the matter of so-called
Miss Emma Jane Crampton's suggestion in the 'girlie' magazine
'Penthouse' that ordinary folk should, if presented with the
opportunity, pull Mrs Thatcher's knickers down (surely there's
a 'D' Notice on these?)

I said that unless I had your immediate assurance that you
were about to institute proceedings against Miss Crampton and
the magazine for which she writes, I would commence a private
prosecution myself.

On 27th June I received a curt printed acknowledgement (on
a postcard!), but since then I have heard nothing.

I must ask you again, Sir, whether you intend to prosecute
'Penthouse' and Miss Crampton, and if not, why not.

Yours faithfully,

Henry Root

Henry Root.

Director of Public Prosecutions
4-12 Queen Anne's Gate London SW1H 9AZ

Telephone   Direct line 01-213 **6142**
Switchboard 01-213 3000

Mr. Harry Root   Your reference
139 Elm Park Mansions
Park Walk   Our reference
London   MDW/IP/MISC/3/79
SW10   Date
                                         8 August 1979

Dear Sir

Thank you for your letter dated 7 August, 1979.

I do not intend to prosecute 'Penthouse' or
Miss Crampton, because in my view such a course
is not justified.

Yours faithfully

D. G. WILLIAMS

Assistant Director of Public Prosecutions

139 Elm Park Mansions
Park Walk
London, S.W.10.

Sir James Goldsmith,
Cavenham Foods,
Millington Road,
Hayes.

18th June 1979.

Dear Sir James,

I've been watching you for some time and you're all right!
If you decide to go into politics you can count on at least one
vote. Mine!

The way you stand up against the pinko conspirators in the
media is an inspiration to decent folk everywhere!

If we stick together we can beat them. How much money do
they have? Not enough!

Here's a pound. Although you always win your court cases
against the weasels of 'Private Eye' it's my experience that
cowardly bullies don't settle their bills as quickly as they prom-
ulgate an innuendo. The pound's to help you bridge the gap.

I believe you're presently showing a high profile in the
publishing game. Well done! I'm about to go into publishing
myself with the purchase of the house of Cape. Do you know them?
All right once, not too sweet now. Perhaps we might get together
on this one. I'm looking for ██ investors so if you're interested
why don't we grab a bite to eat some time?

What do you say we meet for lunch at your favourite watering-
hole, the Clermont Club, on Friday 29th June? I'd make it sooner,
but I'm flat to the boards at the moment with one thing and another.

I'm not a member of the Clermont myself, but no doubt you
can fix that. You get me in and I'll pay for lunch. How's that?
Fair enough?

I look forward to meeting you on the 29th.

Freedom of speech except for blackmailers! Let's go!

Yours sincerely,

Henry Root

Henry Root.

139 Elm Park Mansions
Park Walk
London, S.W.10.

14th June 1979.

Mr A.R. Beevor,
Hambros Bank Ltd,
41 Bishopsgate,
London, E.C.2.

Dear Beevor,

Please forgive me for not having been back to you sooner
with reference to my take-over of Jonathan Cape Ltd.

The fact is I've been flat to the boards here trying to
raise the wind to get the caper off the ground.

Don't hesitate to let me know if you have any sharp ideas
yourself in this direction! I could use them!

Stay cool. I'll be back to you soon.

Yours sincerely,

Henry Root

Henry Root.

TELEPHONE: 01-480 5876.

65-68, LEADENHALL STREET
LONDON,
EC3A 2BA.

20th June 1979

Henry Root, Esq.,
139 Elm Park Mansions,
Park Walk,
London SW10

Dear Mr. Root,

Thank you very much for your letter which
I appreciated enormously. I am grateful for the
£1 which I will send to the appropriate charity
for retired journalists. I do so because I know
that the bulk of them are decent.

I wish you much good luck in your new venture.
At the moment I am fully involved in my own publishing
venture and I am afraid NOW magazine will take up all
the time and financial resources currently available!

Perhaps a little later in the year we can be in
touch again.

Yours sincerely,

James Goldsmith

139 Elm Park Mansions
Park Walk
London, S.W.10

Mr Paul Johnson,   30th May 1979.
The Evening Standard,
Fleet Street,
London, E.C.4.

Dear Johnson,

I would like you to know how much I appreciate your articles in various newspapers and periodicals. More than any other journalist, you did more, it seems to me, to ensure that in the recent election only a very small majority voted against Mrs Thatcher.

I write to you now, in fact, concerning your article in yesterday's 'Evening Standard', entitled 'Will Norman stop the Tate dropping bricks?'

'Of all Margaret Thatcher's appointments,' you wrote, 'the one which I have heard most widely applauded - at any rate among the London intelligensia for the arts'. is her decision to give Norman St John Stevas responsibility for the arts'.

I don't doubt you're right, but can you tell me who precisely constitutes 'the London intelligensia' and where they live? It seems to me that they must be an exceptionally close-knit group, all living in the same vicinity and meeting every evening, otherwise even someone as well-connected as you could not, in the relatively short time since the election, have canvassed their opinion of Norman's appointment.

As a plain man who's kicked up it's never been my privilege to meet 'London's intelligensia' and I'd like to put this right before it's too late. Can you advise me how to set about it?

A little later in the same article you say 'Norman is an experienced boulevardier'. What's this exactly? I don't speak much French, but a literal translation would seem to suggest that Norman's an experienced street-walker. Can this really be the case? Does Mrs Thatcher know?

I'd be most grateful if you could clear up these two problems for me. I wouldn't normally trouble such a busy and important person with trivialities of this nature, but it's always struck me that, though an aristocrat yourself, you care about the problems of those you refer to as 'the people'.

Yours sincerely,

Henry Root

Henry Root.

Copy to The Rt Hon Norman St John Stevas.

From PAUL JOHNSON, Copthall, Iver, Buckinghamshire. Iver 653350

Saturday 7th July '79

Please accept my apologies for not having answered your letter before: I have been in Washington, then in the Middle East, and have many unanswered letters. I have no secretary at present — and large numbers of people write to me, often posing questions I cannot answer. A boulevardier is a man-about-town who knows his way around; but how you are to meet the intelligensia is a query which cannot be satisfied if it is necessary to frame it. P.J.

139 Elm Park Mansions
Park Walk
London, S.W.10.

The Officer-in-Charge,
The Criminal Record Office,
New Scotland Yard,
London, S.W.1.

30th May 1979.

Sir,

I would be grateful if you would run the following people through the computor at Hendon and let me know whether they all come up brand new. I don't think my reasons for wanting this information need concern you. Suffice it to say that they are people with whom I may be coming into contact, socially or in a business context, in the near future.

Mr Ray Cooney. Impresario and immigrant (possibly illegal). c/o The Whitehall Theatre, London.

Mr Edward du Cann. MP and one-time chairman of Keyser Ullmann Ltd of Milk Street, E.C.1. (not an address to inspire confidence). Rumoured to be descended from Miss Nell Gwynne.

Mr Russell Harty Plos. Chat show host. London Weekend Television Ltd, London, S.E.1.

Mr Norman St John Stevas. Minister for 'the Arts'. Alleged to be a boulevardier (or streetwalker.)

Mr Jonathan Cape (deceased). Publisher. Late of 30 Bedford Square, London, W.C.1.

Mr Richard West. Cricket commentator, Rugby correspondent of 'The Times', one time 'host' of 'Come Dancing' and presently Morals Correspondent of 'The Spectator', 56 Doughty Street, London, W.C.1.

Thanking you.

Yours faithfully,

Henry Root

Henry Root.

NO REPLY!

The Officer in Charge,
Criminal Records Office,
New Scotland Yard,
London, S.W..1.

139 Elm Park Mansions
Park Walk
London, S.W.10.

16th June 1979.

Dear Sir,

Did you get my letter of 30th May asking you to feed certain people through your computor at Hendon?

I imagine you can't have done, otherwise I would have heard from you by now.

If it always took as long as this to check out someone's deep background and personal standards you'd never catch anyone, least of all other policemen!

They'd be up and away while you were waiting for the print-out!

Let me know if you didn't get my letter and I'll send you a copy.

Yours faithfully,

Henry Root

Henry Root.

NO REPLY!

139 Elm Park Mansions
Park Walk
London, S.W.10.

The Officer-in-Charge,
Criminal Records Office,
New Scotland Yard,
London, S.W.1.

3rd July 1979.

Dear Sir,

I've been sitting here wondering why you haven't replied to my letters of 30th May and 16th June, requesting you to feed certain 'faces' through your computor.

Now I know! I should have bunged you!

Reporting the case of The Police and The Playboy Club v Ladbrooks Ltd in the matter of the Gaming Act, today's 'Daily Express' tells us that for a private citizen to obtain confidential information from the computor a 'drop' of 50p per name is levied by the policeman in charge.

Sorry! I should have been cognisant of this.

Although there were six names on my list originally, my own 'people' have been able to discover all anyone would want to know about Mr Richard West and Mr Russell Harty Plos. I now only need the deep background on Mr Ray Cooney, Mr Edward Du Cann, Mr Norman St John Stevas and Mr Jonathan Cape.

I enclose £2 being 50p for each name.

Sorry about my ignorance of the 'system'.

Yours faithfully,

Henry Root

Henry Root.

The Commanding Officer,
'B' Division (the best!),
Chelsea Police Station,
2 Lucan Place,
London, S.W.3.

139 Elm Park Mansions
Park Walk
London, S.W.10.

Dear Commander,

21st July 1979.

Over the past few weeks I have been corresponding with the Criminal Records Office at Scotland Yard re getting the deep background on certain people with whom I was about to come in contact.

Receiving no reply to my letters, I eventually sent them a couple of pounds to 'aid the due processes', as it were.

On the morning of Friday 13th July, two of your best men (an Inspector and a Sergeant) ran trough my door with two pounds in an envelope and pointed out that 'dropping' the CRO wasn't good form.

Fair enough. However, they also pointed out that I had wasted their valuable time. Being a great supporter of Law and Order (particularly in Chelsea) I feel rather bad about this. In the circumstances I would like to make a contribution to a police charity which is on the up-and-up and I consequently now return the two pounds. I recently sent a fiver to Sir David McNee and he popped it into the Police Dependants' Trust. That would be fine by me.

The post being what it is these days (don't worry - Sir Keith Joseph will get that right), I'd like to hear that the money has arrived safely, but please don't bother to send any of your young men round to thank me personally.

Yours sincerely,

Henry Root

Henry Root.

139 Elm Park Mansions
Park Walk
London, S.W.10.

Sir Joseph Cantley,
Carpmael Buildings,
Temple,
London, E.C.4.   6th July 1979.

M'Lud,

    Now that the dust's settled after the so-called 'Trial of
the Century', I judge it to be the time to congratulate you on
the fine showing you put up throughout. You tipped the jury
the right way and some of your jokes were first-class! Well done!

    Some folk thought Thorpe was for the high jump at last, but
you never looked to me like the sort of man who'd send an Old
Etonian to the pokey on the say-so of an Italian air-line pilot,
a discredited businessman with dyed hair from L.A. (Los Angeles)
a dusky-hued character from the Channel Islands and a 'male model'
with the unlikely name of Josiffe.

    What a courageous example Mrs Thorpe set by the way she 'stood
by' her husband throughout his ordeal! (Perhaps you could have
made more of this in your closing speech for the defence). Most
wives would have popped the family valuables and had it away on
their toes to South America. And where, might I ask, were the
wives of Bessell, Josiffe and 'Gino' Newton? Conspicuous by their
absence!

    Here's a pound. I would have sent it to you during the trial,
but I was advised that you might rule this contempt of court and
pack me off with my tooth-brush for a night or two in Brixton! It
might also have been construed as an attempt to pervert the course
of justice, and I knew I could safely leave that to you.

    Yours respectfully,

Henry Root

Henry Root.

The Commissioner,
The City of London Police,
26 Old Jewry,
London, E.C.2.

139 Elm Park Mansions
Park Walk
London, S.W.10.

24th July 1979.

Dear Commissioner,

Some two weeks ago I had occasion to send a pound to Mr Justice Cantley. This was a token of my esteem following the way he conducted himself during the so-called Thorpe trial.

Imagine my surprise, last Friday morning, when two of your officers returned this money in person on the grounds that His Lordship didn't need it at the moment. They were most courteous, of course, but did murmur something about it being a waste of time and money having to hop round to my place personally. Being a great supporter of the force (and a friend of Mr James Anderton, the Chief Constable of Manchester) I was somewhat shocked to think that I of all people had been responsible for using up the time of two fine young officers who would have been better employed clearing our streets of punks, muggers and demonstrating mimes on their way to pester Mrs Thatcher re VAT.

In the circumstances, I am now returning the pound (it may not be the same one, I'm afraid - money slips through the fingers so quickly these days, don't you find?) and I would be most pleased if you'd put it towards some worthy police charity.

I'd like to know that this small contribution to the fight against orchestrated extremism has arrived safely (the post being what it is these days - no marks to Sir William Barlowe!), but please don't bother to send any of your men round to thank me personally. Frankly the sudden presence in my lounge-room of two young constables on duty can have a negative bearing on a business deal. I'm sure you'll understand.

Yours sincerely,

Henry Root.
Henry Root.

Telephone 01-606 8866

Ext.

Telegrams: ADJUTOR. LONDON. TELEX

Official Letters to be addressed:-
THE COMMISSIONER OF POLICE
FOR THE CITY OF LONDON.

Please quote Ref.   F.14/80

Your Ref.

CITY OF LONDON POLICE,
26, OLD JEWRY,
LONDON, EC2R 8DJ.

6th August, 1979

Dear Mr Root,

I am directed by the Commissioner of Police for the City of London to thank you for your letter of 24th July, 1979 and acknowledge safe receipt of your kind donation of £1.00, which has been allocated to the City of London Police Benevolent Fund as you requested.

Yours sincerely,

A/Chief Superintendent

H Root Esq
139 Elm Park Mansions
Park Walk
London SW10

139 Elm Park Mansions
Park Walk
London, S.W.10.

Mr Kenneth Kendall,
BBC News,   12th July 1979.
Lime Grove,
London, W.12.

Dear Kenneth,
        I hope you won't mind my calling you Kenneth. Your face
has been appearing for so long in my lounge-room that I feel
you're a friend of the family. Still, I expect that's what
they all say.
        Sorry to read in the paper today that your teeth fell out
while you were reading the news last night. Most awkward for
you.
        Here's a pound. Get yourself a tube of Dentu-Fix, but be
careful where you keep it. Mrs Snipe, who lives opposite, confused hers with the Polyfilla tube and all her windows fell out.
        How about a photo for Mrs Root? You're her favourite
newscaster. Do you merely read the news or do you make it up
as well? I've often wondered.
        All the best,
        Yours sincerely,

        Henry Root

        Henry Root.

BBC tv

BRITISH BROADCASTING CORPORATION

TELEVISION CENTRE WOOD LANE LONDON W12 7RJ

TELEPHONE 01-743 8000   TELEX: 265781

TELEGRAMS AND CABLES: TELECASTS LONDON TELEX

July 23rd 1979

Dear Henry,

Thank you for the sympathetic note and the £1! All charges for fixing the fallen crown will be born by my dentist - and if Dentu-fix is needed he can jolly well supply it - so here's your £1 back!

No, we don't write the news - we read it.

I enclose a photo for Mrs Root.

All good wishes

Kenneth Kendall

To Mrs Root
With my best wishes
Kenneth Kendall

139 Elm Park Mansions
Park Walk
London, S.W.10.

Lord Ted Dexter,
The Sunday Mirror,
Holborn Circus,
London, E.C.1.

18th July 1979.

My Lord!

Your articles in 'The Sunday Mirror' are often good, as are your live commentaries on TV. Well done! It seemed to me that after lunch in the last Test you had difficulty getting your tongue round the names of our Indian friends. Here's a tip. Don't bother with their names. Just say: "Oh dear! The ball went straight through the little sooty's legs!" That sort of thing.

I write to you now to ask your opinion of our present skipper, Brearley. He is more to blame than anyone, it seems to me, for the introduction of compulsory crash helmets when batting. I appreciate that he's an intellectual and as such will not wish to have his brains rattled too often by a piece of hard leather travelling at speed, but how many of those under him are intellectuals? None at all, I'd guess, least of all the lad Botham and the big man, Hendrick. 'Rags' too strikes me as being alert in the field rather than a deep thinker. So what's their excuse? I myself have been hit on the head many times and this didn't stop me getting to the top in fish.

I was concerned too by certain passages in Brearley's book now being serialised in 'The Observer'. On the recent tour of Australia horse-play took place, it seems, with the skipper's approval, with the lad Botham putting himself about the English dressing-room and introducing ice-cubes into Boycott's socks. Did this sort of thing go on in your day? Surely not!

I'm not happy either about all the pansy kissing and hand-holding which now takes place in the middle, particularly at the fall of a wicket. The photo above Brearley's article in yesterday's 'Observer' of Botham clasping the boy Gower to his bosom might well have been misconstrued by those of a mind to do so.

What's your opinion of these developments?

Could you oblige with a photo? I'd like to stick it up in my boy Henry Jr's room as an example of what can be done with an upright stance and a straight bat. You were a true Corinthian and some of your drives through mid-off would, on contact, have loosened a rhino's balls. Of how many can one say that these days?

Yours ever,

Henry Root

Henry Root.

5 Warwick Dene.
Ealing Common.
London. W5 3JG
01-567 3206.

Monday.

Dear Mr Root,

I don't keep prices about the place these days - sorry

How your lad goes the right way with his cricket.

Keep him <u>sideways</u> both batting and bowling.

I never see people make many runs with helmets!

Sincerely

Ted Dexter

139 Elm Park Mansions
Park Walk
London, S.W.10.

Mr Peter Saunders,
The Mousetrap Man!,
The Vaudeville Theatre,
London, W.C.2.

23rd July 1979.

Dear Mr Saunders,

May I be the first to congratulate you on your engagement to the TV personality, Lady Katie Boyle? She's still a handsome woman and her advice at the back of 'The TV Times' is sometimes sound.

That's enough of that - down to business! As far as I know you've never put on a dirty show (well done!) so I am now enclosing for your evaluation my original stage play THE ENGLISH WAY OF DOING THINGS by HENRY ROOT. You'll find it an amusing romp in two acts with only enough unnecessary explicitness to suck in our Japanese friends over here to photograph Her Majesty and buy their underwear in Oxford Street.

I'd be prepared to take your theatre for a season on sensible terms. I read in 'The Sunday Express' the other day that you keep in your office a fridge full of champagne for visiting actors and other more serious folk, so unless I hear from you to the contrary I'll drop in on you at about 11.30 on Tuesday 7th August to discuss the deal. This will give you more than a week to assess the play's potential and jot down casting ideas (though I'll have the final say, of course, in this department.)

Have you come across the work of an actress called Glenda Jackson? She'd be fine for the part of the old boiler who comes to grief early in Act 1, but don't waste your time considering 'Sir' Robert Mark for the role of the stupid Police Commissioner because he's already turned it down on the grounds that he doesn't after all want to be an actor (after his TV deodorant commercial who's surprised?)

I'd want first crack at the ingenue, of course, but you could be second cab off the rank. I'd not say a word to your good lady as long as you didn't drop me in it with Mrs Root!

Who gets the ice-cream sales? Do we share? I'll take care of the critics. A fiver's on its way to Irving Warble of 'The Times' and since Mrs Root is about to join Arriana Stassinopulos's 'Levi-tation and Deep Personal Awareness' group I'll be able to 'get to' Bernard Levin.

Let's make money here!

Yours for family theatre,

Henry Root

Henry Root.

Enc: THE ENGLISH WAY OF DOING THINGS by HENRY ROOT.

PETER SAUNDERS LTD

DIRECTORS: PETER SAUNDERS (Chairman & Managing) L. H. MITCHELL F.C.A. VERITY HUDSON
REGISTERED ENGLAND 002331

VAUDEVILLE THEATRE OFFICES
10, Maiden Lane, London, WC2E 7NA

Tele: 01-240 3177 (all lines)
Telegrams & Cables: Saunplays London WC2

30th July 1979

GEN/SH/86

Henry Root Esq
139 Elm Park Mansions
Park Walk
LONDON   SW10

Dear Mr Root

　　Thank you for your letter of the 25th July and for your congratulations.

　　Please don't come in on the 7th August as firstly, as I have a meeting which will last most of the day and secondly, I have quite a stock of plays to read and it is better to see if I like it first.

Yours sincerely

PETER SAUNDERS

PETER SAUNDERS LTD

DIRECTORS: PETER SAUNDERS (Chairman & Managing) L. H. MITCHELL F.C.A. VERITY HUDSON
REGISTERED ENGLAND 002331

VAUDEVILLE THEATRE OFFICES
10, Maiden Lane, London, WC2E 7NA

Tele: 01-240 3177 (all lines)
Telegrams & Cables: Saunplays London WC2

5th September 1979

GEN/SH/PLA

Henry Root Esq
139 Elm Park Mansions
Park Walk
LONDON   SW10

Dear Mr Root

"The English Way Of Doing Things" by Henry Root

　　Thank you for sending me this play but I don't think it is one that I would care to take on especially as I have another attraction to follow the current one at the Vaudeville.

　　Of course, I do indeed know Glenda Jackson but she has committed herself to another play in February of next year.

　　I am so sorry not to be more helpful but I don't think a meeting would really serve any purpose.

Yours sincerely

PETER SAUNDERS

Enc

139 Elm Park Mansions
Park Walk
London, S.W.10.

Ms Debra Byron,
Jonathan Cape Ltd,
30 Bedford Square,
London, W.C.1.

29th August 1979.

Dear Ms Byron,

You'll be wondering why you haven't heard from me since your sensible letter of 6th June.

Don't worry! I've been hard at work on a money-making concept that could do us both a bit of good.

Have you by any chance heard of a book entitled 'Man Watching' by a keeper at the London Zoo called Desmond Morris? I imagine you may have done because your outfit published it. It's a psychological pot-boiler, lacking that certain something to take it to the top of the hot-hundred list, but at least it had the merit of giving me this solid idea.

How about WOMAN WATCHING by HENRY ROOT? What do you think? And it would have the added advantage of being comprehensively illustrated by myself. You may not be aware that as well as being a writer I am also a fully equipped photographer of style ever at the ready with my system set, so I am taking this opportunity of enclosing my portfolio of girls snapped from an unexpected angle.

Here's the scheme. Financed by you I'll lurk unusually in places not normally available to men. No doubt you will yourself have visited 'The Sanctuary' in Covent Garden, a 'girls only' sauna and swimming club where dancers and others of that ilk strip off and recline on benches. With a letter of introduction from you, I'll hop incognito through the door in a pair of ballet pumps and, with a cry of "Straighten up ladies! I've been sent by Cape!", I'll take unusual photos before ejection.

How does it strike you? Let's be positive on this one!

What I need is a letter of authority from you enabling me to enter premises not generally available for figure shooting in the afternoon. I suggest something along the following lines:

TO WHOM IT MAY CONCERN:

This is to confirm that Mr Henry Root is engaged for us on a viable undertaking entitled WOMAN WATCHING. We would be most grateful if you could give him your full cooperation and, after he has finished, forward the account to us for settlement.

Signed: Debra Byron.
        p.p. Jonathan Cape Ltd.

With your help I should be able to have the first draft on your desk by the end of October.

Let's go!

Yours sincerely,

Henry Root

Henry Root.

P.S. In case you're of a mind to utilise my photos to illustrate other books in your pipe-line, I should warn you that they are fully protected by the Copyright Act 1959, and I enclose a stamped addressed envelope for their safe return.

Telephone 01 636 5764
Telex 299080
Answer CBCSER G

JONATHAN CAPE LIMITED
THIRTY BEDFORD SQUARE
LONDON W.C.1

Telegrams
CAPAJON, LONDON WC1B 3EL

DB/ME

Mr Henry Root,   31st August, 1979
139 Elm Park Mansions,
Park Walk,
London. S.W.10.

Dear Mr Root,

Thank you for your letter of 29th August together with photographs.
We regret that we do not think it would be worth your while sending
us a finished copy of WOMAN WATCHING. We wish you sucess in placing
it elsewhere.

Please find your photographs enclosed.

Yours sincerely,

Debra Byron.
Debra Byron,
Editorial.

DIRECTORS Tom Maschler Graham C. Greene Liz Calder W. Robert Carr Anthony Colwell John Robinson Norman Askew
Registered in England under no. 195767 Registered office as above

139 Elm Park Mansions
Park Walk
London, S.W.10.

The Headmaster,
Langley Grammar School,
Langley,
Berks.   27th July 1979.

Dear Headmaster,

My friend Paul Johnson - who, as you may or may not know,
is one of Mrs Thatcher's closest advisers - recently wrote in
'The Evening Standard' that your school isn't a seminary for
subversives, has no great reputation for Marxist studies, drugs
or violence and that its staff do not spend their spare time
engaged in race-demos and assaults on the police.

Well done!

In the circumstances I'm prepared to entrust to your care
my boy Henry Jr, now 15. Frankly, he's not shaping up. He wears
girls' blouses and plays the guitar to excess. We all know where
that leads. A recent study shows that one hundred per cent of
youngsters on hard drugs had at some time in their lives listened
to so-called pop music.

When can he start? On the assumption that you believe in
private enterprise, I enclose a fiver. This is for you personally,
you understand, and is merely the tip of the ice-berg. There's
more to come if you manage to slip him to the top of the queue.

I'll pay generously for what I want, so if there's anything
you need - a new pav for the playing fields, perhaps, or a colour
TV for the Senior Common Room - just let me know.

Shall I come and see you? Just give me the word and I can
be your way in 24 hours.

I look forward to doing business with you.

How are you off for fish?

Support Mrs Thatcher!

Yours sincerely,

Henry Root

Henry Root.

P.S. I take it capital punishment still takes place in your school.
Let me know about this. Youngsters must learn what's what.

Royal County of Berkshire
Department of Education

Langley Grammar School

Reddington Drive, Langley, Slough, SL3 7QS
Telephones:
Headmaster—Slough 43222 Staff—Slough 43223

Headmaster:

A. G. Robinson, M.Sc., Ph.D., C.Chem., F.R.I.C.

16 August 1978

Henry Root Esq
139 Elm Park Mansions
Park Walk
London SW 10

Dear Mr Root

Thank you for your letter of the 27 July enquiring about a possible
place here for Henry Junior.

The only possible suggestion which I cna make is that we test Henry
here at the school with a view to him entering our 5th year.   The
criterion for entry is usually the 12+ selection test conducted by
the Berkshire County Council.   The staff would be prepared to test
him at this stage in the various subjects.   If he was successful a
place would be offered.   You would then have to write to the Director
of Education at Kennet House, King's Road, Reading, with a view to
having this confirmed.   The difficulty would be the fact that you
reside in Greater London and this means taking the matter up with
them as well.

We assemble back for the Autumn Term on Tuesday, September 4th and if
you wished us to proceed with the testing this will be arranged.
Perhaps you would kindly let me know if you wish this to take place.

I am on holiday 17 - 31 August so if you contacted me on the phone
here at the school, Slough 43222, on Tuesday 4 September I will then
be in a position to suggest a date for testing.

Many thanks for your kind comments about the school.   I am forwarding
your £5 to the treasurer of the Langley Grammar School Fighting Fund
and he will send you a receipt in due course.

Looking forward to seeing you.

Yours sincerely

pp A. G. Robinson

Headmaster

Dictated by Dr Robinson but signed in his absence.

AN.

139 Elm Park Mansions
Park Walk
London, S.W.10.

The Senior Tutor,
Magdalene College,
Cambridge.

29th July 1979.

Dear Senior Tutor,

Yours is a college at which brains are neither here nor there, I'm told. Indeed, my enquiries lead me to understand that duffers are more than welcome so long as their fathers measure up financially.

This being the case, I'm prepared to send my boy to you in three years time. He's 15 now and shows every sign of needing all the advantages money can buy. You'll have seen many like that.

I'll leave the subject to you. Not sociology.

Places are tight, I dare say, (many being snapped up at birth by Etonians and such) but I'm prepared to pay 'over the top' to achieve equality of opportunity. That's the Tory way. We voted for Mrs Thatcher so that those of us who had indulged in prudent house-keeping down the years could give their youngsters a flying start.

I enclose a small cash advance (this is for you personally, you understand) against a heavy financial contribution to the college if you can 'fix' a place for my boy.

What do you need? Do you have a decent library? If not, just say the word. I'd be happy to endow you with sufficient funds to build one. I'd want some sort of credit, of course. Something along the lines of 'This Library has been generously gifted to the College by Henry Root Wet Fish Ltd'. If you wanted to put this in Latin, that would be okay with me. Or what about a new pavillion for your playing-field? What, come to that, about a new playing-field? Exercise, in my experience, takes boys' minds off matters on which they'd be better not to dwell till later.

I look forward to hearing from you.

Yours against student participation,

Henry Root

Henry Root.

T. E. B. HOWARTH, M.C., M.A.,
SENIOR TUTOR AND TUTOR FOR ADMISSIONS

MAGDALENE COLLEGE
· CAMBRIDGE CB3 0AG
TELEPHONE 61543

31 July 1979

Henry Root Esq.,
139 Elm Park Mansions,
Park Walk,
London S.W.10.

Dear Mr. Root,

   Thank you for your letter. I am afraid I do not know who you are, but you are
evidently either an ingenious hoaxer or labouring under a massive misapprehension.
I therefore return your £5 note herewith.

      Yours sincerely,

139 Elm Park Mansions
Park Walk
London, S.W.10.

Major-General Wyldbore-Smith, C.B., D.S.O., O.B.E.,
Conservative Board of Finance,
32 Smith Square,   7th August 1979.
Westminster,
London, S.W.1.

Dear Major-General Wyldbore-Smith,

I'm a blunt man, accustomed to plain-speaking, so I'll come straight to the point.

What's the going price for getting an honour?

I'm not talking about an M.B.E., an O.B.E. or a C.B.E. They seem to be for ballet dancers, disc-jockeys, crooners and those who are quick over the high hurdles. (No offence meant. I see that you yourself have the O.B.E. Nothing wrong with that. Well done!) No, I'm talking about a life peerage, or, at the very least, a knighthood like my friend Sir James Goldsmith.

In the course of the past year I have contributed steadily and generously to Tory Party funds. Your understrapper Brigadier L.H. Lee C.B.E. will confirm this. (I am writing to you rather than him, incidentally, because you seem to outrank him and because you have the more sensible name.) I realise, however, that I will have to think in terms of a rather more substantial lump sum in order to secure a place near the top of Mrs Thatcher's New Year hand-outs.

Can you give me an idea of the approximate amount?

I read recently that a 'drop' of as little as £25,000 to one of our leading politicians was enough to obtain a seat in the Lords for the donor.

Has inflation bumped up the price?

Let me know. I'm waiting here with my cheque-book ready!

Support Mrs Thatcher!

Yours sincerely,

Henry Root

Henry Root.

P.S. It goes without saying that there could be 'something in this' for you personally.

CONSERVATIVE BOARD OF FINANCE

Chairman
R ALISTAIR McALPINE

Director
MAJOR-GENERAL F.B. WYLDBORE-SMITH,
C.B., D.S.O., O.B.E

Deputy Director
BRIGADIER I. H. LEE, C.B.E

32 SMITH SQUARE,
WESTMINSTER, SW1P 3HH
TELEPHONE: 01 222 9000

14th August 1979

Henry Root Esq.,
139 Elm Park Mansions
Park Walk
<u>London SW10</u>

Dear Mr. Root,

Thank you for your letter of the 7th August. I think I must make it absolutely clear that there is no question of buying Honours from the Conservative Party.

However, I am most grateful to you for the support which you have given to the Party over the past few months.

Yours sincerely,

F.B.Wyldbore-Smith

THE FURTHER LETTERS OF

HENRY ROOT

139 Elm Park Mansions
Park Walk
London, S.W.10.

Mrs Thatcher,
10 Downing Street,
London, S.W.1.   24th July 1979.

Dear Prime Minister,

        <u>Double</u> the VAT on theatre tickets, that's my advice!

        Strolling down Whitehall this afternoon on business that
needn't concern you, I ran head-first into a rabble of chanting
rowdies, many of whom were in full make-up even though it was
not yet tea-time. Taking it to be a student demo out of hand,
I cried "slash student grants!" and passed among them with my
stick. It was then that one old party, whom I took to be a
teacher, announced that they were in fact actors marching to
No 10 in protest against the price of theatre seats.

        On hearing this, I naturally redoubled my efforts, realisin
that you wouldn't want the decision-making processes to be inter-
rupted by a march of painted mimes. I tried to head them back to
their various play-houses and rehearsal-rooms, but many got
through, I fear, and for this I blame myself.

        Don't misunderstand me, Prime Minister. This is a free
country for those who can afford it and I would always defend the
right of jugglers and ballet dancers to pursue their activities
in authorised places. What I <u>do</u> object to, however, is that
their efforts to amuse should be subsidised out of the pockets
of tax-payers.

        It so happens that my own play THE ENGLISH WAY OF DOING
THINGS by HENRY ROOT will shortly be opening at the Vaudeville
Theatre in the Strand. Should it fail to attract an audience,
I won't run bleating to Norman St John Stevas, the boulevardier,
demanding that he support it out of public funds.

        There are many theatres in the West End occupying prime
sites for the purveyance of hamburgers and soda. Such as cannot
pay their way should be pulled down and reconstituted on a sound
commercial footing.

        Cut back subsidies to the arts!

        Your man on the door-step,

        Henry Root

        Henry Root.

Chancellor of the Duchy of Lancaster

PRIVY COUNCIL OFFICE
WHITEHALL. LONDON SW1A 2AT

9th August 1979

Henry Root Esq
139 Elm Park Mansions
Park Walk
LONDON SW10

Dear Mr Root,

Your letter of 24th July which you sent to
the Prime Minister about the Equity demonstration has been passed to the Chancellor
of the Duchy of Lancaster who is responsible
for the Arts.

The Chancellor is at present abroad on an
official visit but I am sure that he would
be most interested to read your views and
I will bring your letter to his attention
on his return.

Yours sincerely

Miss M E Giles
<u>Private Secretary</u>

139 Elm Park Mansions
Park Walk
London, S.W.10.

The Picture Editor,
The Daily Express,   1st May 1979.
Fleet Street,
London, E.C.4.

Dear Sir,
        Enclosed you will find a selection of prints typical of my
work. They are entitled:

        Ducks on Pond.

        Old Greek Saddler and Wife.

        Nude with Banana.

        My Cat Ben.

        Footpath with Sign Post.

        A Beach Somewhere.

        I am slowly building up a photo library (approx 400 new pics
per year) of the urban and rural environment. I use a Hasselblad
616X for maximum sharpness and expense.

        I am prepared to accept commissioned work exclusively on a
free-lance basis.

        I enclose a stamped addressed envelope in case you are unable
to utilise any of these prints at the moment.

        Yours faithfully,

        Henry de Root

        Henry de Root. Photographer.

DAILY EXPRESS

Express
Newspapers
Limited

121 Fleet Street
London EC4P 4JT
Telephone
01-353 8000
Telex No 21841
Cable Address
Express London

9th May, 1979

Henry de Root,
139 Elm Park Mansions,
Park Walk,
London, S.W.10

Dear Mr. de Root,

Thank you very much for sending the photographs,
but I am afraid they are not suitable for
publication in the Daily Express.

Enclosed are the photographs.

Yours sincerely,

Andrew Harvey
picture Editor

enc.

Registered in London No 141748.
Registered office: 121 Fleet St London EC4P 4JT

139 Elm Park Mansions
Park Walk
London, S.W.10.

The Resident Team,
'Junior That's Life',
The BBC,
London, W.12.   11th August 1979.

Dear Team,

I gather that you want to make monkeys of singing grannies on 'Junior That's Life'.

What a great idea!

I'd like to nominate Mrs Root's mother, Enid Potts, aged 79. She's no Shirley Bassey, but she is bad. Her repertoire consists mainly of excerpts from 'The Dancing Years', but she occasionally essays some of the up-to-date stuff too. Some years ago she won third prize for her Petunia Clark impression on a senior citizens' away day.

What if the old tart kicks the bucket on camera? It would be good TV, but what about recompense? Will you have her insured?

I suppose that as with senior 'That's Life' you are presently looking for healthily vulgar contributions from the general public. I append hereunder a new ode which I hope you will consider apposite in the circumstances.

'There was an old granny from Chislehurst
Who before she could pee had to whistle first.
One sad day in June
She quite lost the tune
And what do you know? - her bladder!'

Not bad, eh? Will Cyril be with you to read out these contributions from the viewing public? I think it might be more amusing to have a knowing little basket aged eight in Cyril's chair. Still, not for me to advise. You know what you're doing. When would you like me to wheel Mrs Root's mother in for an audition?

Cheers!

Henry Root

Henry Root.

M

889077 PO FD G
299992 PO TS G

H71 1133 LONDON TELEX 28

HENRY ROOT 139 ELMPARK MANSIONS PARK WALK
LONDONSW10

PLEASE RING BBC THATS LIFE RE SINGING GRANNY REVERSING CHARGES
743 1272 EXTENSION 6374/5
REGARDS CHRIS SERLE

139 SW10 C1 743 1272 6374/5
992 PO TS G
077 PO FD G

139 Elm Park Mansions
Park Walk
London, S.W.10.

The Earl of Longford,
Sidgwick and Jackson Ltd,
1 Tavistock Chambers,
London, W.C.1.

11th August 1979.

Dear Lord Longford,

I read recently that Miss Mary Kenny is doing you a book on God. That's one to look forward to! Well done! Will it be in the shops in time for Christmas! That's always a good idea. Catch the mugs with money in their pockets and long shopping-lists. Promoted with verve I can see this one being as big a stocking-filler as Ronnie Barker's 'Book of Bedtime Boobs'.

Miss Kenny's concept has given me this solid idea. Why not a series of similar books? That is to say, studies by ordinary unqualified folk like Miss Kenny of great thinkers and their influence. Such a series, unlike the stuff written by University boffins would be readily intelligible to the man in the street.

I was talking over the idea with my daughter Doreen (20), who is reading philosophy and sociology at Essex University and who therefore thinks she knows more about these things than I do, and in no time at all she had come up with the enclosed outline for such a series.

I hope you like it. If you do, I suggest you appoint my Doreen as General Editor. She'll be leaving Essex in a year and I'm sure she'd be happy to work with you.

I enclose a stamped addressed envelope for the safe return of my Doreen's outline, should you not wish to utilise the concept at this time. I should warn you, perhaps, that the idea is fully protected by The Copyright Act (1957), so I don't advise you to 'borrow' it to your advantage without due credit to myself! I know what you publishers are like!

Let's make money on this one!

Yours sincerely,

Henry Root.

Henry Root.

Enc: Draft outline for SEMINAL THINKERS IN A NUTSHELL - a new series edited by DOREEN ROOT.

SEMINAL THINKERS IN A NUTSHELL.
General Editor - DOREEN ROOT.

Draft Series.

God - Mary Kenny.
Plato - Jimmy Hill.
Christ - Miss Vicki Hodge.
Hegel - Richard Afton.
Marx - Arthur Askey.
Tolstoy - Richard Ingrams.
Nietzsche - Diana Dors.
Darwin - Christopher Booker.
Popper - Malcolm Allison (Big Mal!)
Sir Winston Churchill - Dr Patrick Cosgrave (Mrs Thatcher's chirop-
                                                                odist).
Lenin - Carol Channing.
Mohammed Ali - Taki (the little Jap).
Aristotle - Shirley Conran (the cook).
Newton - James Herriot (the vet).
Freud - Anna Raeburn.
Chomsky - Richard West.
Kant - Jean Rook.
Descartes - Patricia Boxall.
Einstein - Michael Parkinson.
Thatcher - George Gale.

N.B. © DOREEN ROOT
139 Elm Park Mansions
Park Walk
London, S.W.10.

SIDGWICK & JACKSON
Limited
PUBLISHERS

Telegrams: Watergate, London
Telephones: 01-242 6081/2/3

Place of Registration: London, England
Registered Number of Company: 100126

Registered Office:

1 Tavistock Chambers

Bloomsbury Way, London W.C.1A 2SG

20th September 1979

Dear Mr. Root

Thank you for your letter of September 15th. I have now had an opportunity of studying your earlier letter and the very interesting proposals put forward by your daughter. Please allow me respectfully to congratulate you on some excellent ideas.

Alas! we ourselves would not be able to make use of them, but I do hope that you would find a more enterprising publisher.

May I apologise if I have been a long time in replying to you, due to myself and my secretary being on holiday for the last month.

Yours sincerely with renewed apologies

[signature]

Henry Root, Esq
139 Elm Park Mansions
Park Walk
S.W.10

139 Elm Park Mansions
Park Walk
London, S.W.10.

Mr Michael Wolff,
Wolff Olins Ltd,
22 Dukes Road,
London, W.C.1.   14th August 1979.

Dear Mr Wolff,

I recently saw your firm featured in 'About Business' on
Thames TV and I was quite impressed. By <u>you</u>, that is. Your
partner, Olins, made a frightful nonsense, if you remember, of
creating a new 'image' for a kraut Count whose pencil company
had gone back badly. His brief was to come up with a new design
scheme which emphasised all the products the company made <u>other</u>
than pencils. Olins and his men went into a creative trance
which lasted for some weeks and then flew, with evidence of
their labours, back to Germany. The board were called to a
meeting at which Olins ran his new visual image up the flag-pole.
And what was it? A pencil! It wasn't until you were called
in that a 'concept' was thrashed out which met with the Cunt's
approval. Well done!

Do you create 'images' for the man in the street, or do
you deal only in company 'images'?

I ask because I'm currently going flat out for a seat in
the Lords under Mrs Thatcher and when I become Lord Root I want
to measure up. As it happens, I'm not too concerned about myself,
but Mrs Root causes misgivings. I enclose some photos of ourselves
taken at a recent outing and as you can see she's not too sweet.
Can you do anything with her? If not, I may have to dump her.
I imagine I wouldn't be the first life peer compelled to take
this step. Where, after all, is <u>Lord</u> Falkender on state occasions
which involve Black Rod and others? Conspicuous by his absence!

I must emphasise that I want this account to be handled by
you personally, and not by Olins. I can't afford to be messed
about the way the kraut Count was.

Let me have your prices on a top-to-toe 'image' job.

Yours sincerely,

Henry Root

Henry Root.

WOLFF OLINS

Henry Root
9 Elm Park Mansions
ark Walk
London SW10

30 August 1979

Dear Mr Root

I am just back from a swimming holiday in France
and have just seen your most intriguing letter.

The problem you pose, is a familiar one. We often
have requests of this kind. It is difficult to say
whether anything substantial can be done or not
merely by looking at the photographs, and I
recommend that before Wolff Olins makes any formal
proposal to you, we carry out the following
procedure which will give me a better idea of what
is possible in your particular case.

At a mutually convenient time, I suggest that both
Mrs Root and you walk from Victoria Station through
Green Park to the Ritz Hotel where you have afternoon tea. In addition to this, and on another
occasion, I suggest that you have dinner with
Mrs Root in the Connaught Hotel. I will make arrangements for someone from Wolff Olins to be there to
observe, either myself or one of our senior consul-
tants but certainly not Wally Olins. From this we
would get an idea of how you behave together, both
in a relaxed situation and formally in public. This
would give us a much better basis on which to see
how we could contribute and what sort of fees you
should expect to pay. We would not charge you any
fees for this preliminary investigation, but we
would expect you to cover our expenses.

2

Thank you so much for your enquiry. I am gla
you enjoyed the TV programme.

Yours sincerely

Michael Wolff

PS
It would be sensible not to inform
Mrs Root at this stage.

Mr Michael Wolff,
Wolff Olins Ltd,
22 Dukes Road,
London, W.C.1.

139 Elm Park Mansions
Park Walk
London, S.W.10.

6th September 1979.

Dear Mr Wolff,

Thank you for your letter of 30th August.

You seem to have grasped the concept well and your suggestion that you should monitor me and Mrs Root in an observation situation meets with my approval.

Due to Mrs Root's leg, however, it would not be advisable to undertake the slow walk from Victoria to the Ritz Hotel. I suggest we commence the manoeuvre at the Ritz and accordingly Mrs Root and I will take tea in the foyer there between 4 and 5 pm on Monday 24th September. Should there be dancing to a trio you will find our performance adequate if lacking in elaboration.

Mrs Root would be suspicious were I to escort her in public twice in the same calender month, so I suggest that 'Operation Connaught Hotel' should take place on the evening of Friday 5th October. If you would care to let me know that this date is con-venient for you, I will make the necessary booking.

I take it you will bill me in thses two matters when you deliver your initial report and comments.

No doubt you will wish to hang on to the photographs of myself and Mrs Root for identification purposes, but I must ask you to keep them in a safe place. It would be difficult to explain their permanent loss to Mrs Root who keeps an album.

I look forward to doing business with you image-wise.

Yours sincerely,

Henry Root

Henry Root.

Mr Henry Root
139 Elm Park Mansions
Park Walk
London SW10

13 September 1979

Dear Mr Root

Thank you for your letter. Friday 5th October is
fine but I'm afraid Monday 24th September is not
suitable. I could manage the 26th, 27th or 28th,
and I would be grateful if you could let me know
which of these is convenient for both of you as
soon as possible.

Please be assured that your photographs are absolutely safe.

Yours sincerely

Michael Wolff

---

139 Elm Park Mansions
Park Walk
London, S.W.10.

Mr Michael Wolff,
Wolff Olins Ltd,
22 Dukes Road,
London, W.C.1.   19th September 1979.

Dear Mr Wolff,

        Thank you for your letter of 13th September, which (due, no
doubt, to the extraordinary performance of Sir William Barlow) has
only just arrived on my desk.

        You seem to be on the ball. Well done. I like that in a
man.

        Of the dates you suggest for 'Operation Tea at the Ritz',
the 28th of this month would be the most suitable. If I hear
nothing further from you, Mrs Root and I will be observable from
a position in the foyer between 4 and 5 pm on that day.

        Perhaps it would be best if you were to submit both reports
after stage 2 - 'Operation Dinner at the Connaught' on Friday 5th
October. Do you wish me to effect a booking for you on the 5th,
or can you arrange that yourself? And for how many will it be?
I would expect your operative to have an observational assistant,
but I wouldn't like to suppose he'd take advantage of the situation
to give his 'personal secretary' a night on the tiles. I shall be
vetting his expenses most carefully.

        Yours sincerely,

        Henry Root

        Henry Root.

WOLFF OLINS

Mr Henry Root
139 Elm Park Mansions
Park Walk
London SW10

2 October 1979

Dear Mr Root

Since you were not able to be at the Ritz
or able to let me know that you weren't
going to be there, I suppose that you probably either wish to postpone or not to
proceed with the project, so unless I hear
from you before Friday, we will not be at
the Connaught.

Yours sincerely

Michael Wolff

---

139 Elm Park Mansions
Park Walk
London, S.W.10.

Mr Michael Wolff,
Wolff Olins Ltd,
22 Dukes Road,
London, W.C.1.

3rd October 1979.

Dear Mr Wolff,

What on earth's going on? Mrs Root and I were in position
at the appointed time and partook of tea and sandwiches for the
specified period.

I assumed that the couple in hats lurking two tables away
were yourself and a female operative. Small wonder that my various
signals unsettled them to the point of departure early.

If you failed for some reason to attend I will have to pass
my expenses in the matter over to you. Unless, that is, you redeem
yourself somewhat by performing better in the course of Stage 2 -
'Operation Dinner at the Connaught Hotel' this Friday. Mrs Root
and I will certainly be there participating a la carte and I trust
you will be present too.

For goodness sake let's not have another cock-up!

Yours sincerely,

Henry Root.

139 Elm Park Mansions
Park Walk
London, S.W.10.

Mr Geoffrey Wheatcroft,
The Spectator,
56 Doughty Street,
London, W.C.1.

23rd August 1979.

Dear Mr Wheatcroft,

I gather you are the Literary Editor of 'The Spectator'. The style has greatly improved of late and I take it you are responsible for this. Well done! All the contributors now commence each paragraph with some such urbane remark as 'Trollope would have been amused by....', 'Wasn't it Flaubert who said....', 'After an agreeable lunch with....' etc etc. This is excellent and most civilised.

I have recently commissioned myself to put together an anthology of great modern British prose, to show that proud and stately phrasemaking didn't die with Dornford Yates, and I wonder whether I might have your permission to quote the following passages which have appeared in your journal.

1. Dr Patrick Cosgrave writing about the late Airey Neave:

   'On the last occasion I saw Airey, he said: "I know one thing. When they come for me it will be from behind. They aren't soldier enough to look me in the face".

2. Mr Richard West in 'The Spectator' of 16th June 1979.

   'I was sad to read of the death in Zimbabwe of Major André Dennison, who only recently won the country's top award for courage.. He was a witty and most agreeable drinking companion. I notice he received his last, fatal bullet resisting a ZANLA attack on the ~~the~~ bar of the Zimbabwe Ruins Hotel. He would have liked to have gone that way.'

3. Mr Taki in 'The Spectator' of 4th August 1979.

   'The last two years of his life he suffered terribly. Both of his legs were amputated. Needless to say he never complained. He died without tears. Although I am a Christian there are times when I begin to doubt. Why should Tony Galento have suffered?'

4. Mr George Gale in 'The Spectator' of 18th August 1979.

   'If the captain of a ship left the deck knowing a storm was imminent he would lose his command. If a foreign correspondent left his base, knowing big stories were about to break, he would lose his posting. Mr Atkins is a former naval officer. He knows about discipline and he knows about duty. As Northern Ireland Secretary he possesses proconsular and vice-regal powers: under direct rule he is Northern Ireland's ruler. He must have known that August was ominous'.

I look forward to receiving the necessary permissions to quote these fine and ringing passages.

Yours sincerely,

Henry Root

Henry Root.

Spectator

56 Doughty Street London WC1N 2LL Telephone 01-405 1706 Telegrams Spectator London Telex 27124

Henry Root Esq.,
139 Elm Park Mansions,
London SW10

20 September 1979

Dear Mr Root,

I am sorry that you had no reply to your letter of 23 August. Unfortunately Geoffrey Wheatcroft is on holiday at the moment and will not therefore be able to answer your enquiry about reprinting the Hope-Wallace obituary until his return at the beginning of next month. Though the party conferences will be taking much of his time just then I will try to ensure that you get an answer as soon as possible.

I am so sorry about the delay.

Yours sincerely,

Clare Asquith

Clare Asquith

Proprietor: Henry Keswick

Mr Richard Ryder,
10 Downing Street,
London, S.W.1.

139 Elm Park Mansions
Park Walk
London, S.W.10.

30th August 1979.

Dear Ryder,

The Prime Minister's courageous Ulster initiative last
week was an inspiration to ordinary folk throughout the land!
Please tell her this from me.

Never has she seemed less like a woman and more like a
Tory! The shots of her on TV and her cry of "Let me speak to
my people!" as she broke away from her security guards and
reached out both hands to the cheering common folk made one
proud to be English for the first time since we dumped the
Hun at Wembley in '66.

Is it possible to obtain a photograph of her in battle-
dress and combat helmet snapped at the precise moment, as shown
on TV, when the wind from her personal helicopter blew up her
skirt to reveal World War 2 Women's Airforce knickers worn below
the knee? How her enemies must have trembled!

I enclose a pound to cover the expense.

Incidentally, I have recently been in contact with old
Major Wyldbore-Smith at Conservative HQ about the possibility
of an honour for myself in the Prime Minister's new year list.
I pointed out that I was prepared to make a substantial contribution to party funds, but he has indicated that titles can't be
purchased from the Tories!

Could you tell the old duffer to smarten up? You'll
appreciate how I'd hate to join the Liberals!

Yours sincerely,

Henry Root

Henry Root.

Let's have further initiatives here and there!

10 DOWNING STREET

7th September 1979

Dear Mr Root,

I am writing to thank you very much indeed for your letter of 30th August.

In answer to your request for a photograph of the Prime Minister, taken while she was in Ulster, I am afraid that we do not have the photograph and I would suggest that you write direct to the newspaper concerned. I am returning the pound which you enclosed.

With best wishes,

Yours sincerely,

Richard Ryder
Political Office

Henry Root Esq

139 Elm Park Mansions
Park Walk
London, S.W.10.

The Editor,
Burke's Peerage,
56 Walton Street,   4th September 1979.
London, S.W.3.

Dear Sir,
      I would appreciate your advice on a certain matter.
      Having supported the Tories steadily for some time now I
expect to be raised to the peerage in the near future.
      I naturally wish to have my new cutlery, matching shot-guns,
luggage and stationary (duly embossed and crested) ready in good
time for answering communications from others in respect of
weekends in the country shooting this and that, so I am giving
some thought to what my title should be.
      I would prefer, of course, to be Lord Root, but I have a
suspicion that there was once a car dealer of this name, and for
all I know there still might be. I certainly wouldn't want to
be confused with him, particularly since I recall his wife rather
letting him down in public by wearing leopard-skin drawers and
standing on her head. Or was that Lady Docker? Anyway, what
happens in this sort of double-up situation? Could he be persuaded to change his name? Perhaps to Lord Warren Street? I
am not without means.
      Are you experts too on forebears and heraldic matters? I
have in mind my coat of arms and am considering (since I have
spent my life in fish) two prawns rampant and a cock crab en
suivant.
      I'd appreciate your advice at your earliest convenience.
      Yours faithfully,

      Henry Root

      Henry Root.

Burke's Peerage Limited

PUBLISHERS

56 Walton Street London SW3 1RB Telephone 01-584 8134 and 1106
Registered No. 210290 England Registered Office: 42 Curzon Street London W1

Henry Root Esq
139 Elm Park Mansions   Wednesday
Park Walk   5 September
LONDON   1979
SW10

Dear Mr Root

Thank you for your letter of 4th September in which
you inquire about whether the can be two Lord Roots.

To the best of our knowledge there is no Lord Root.
There is however, a Lord Rootes which could be the
Peer you were thinking of.

I hope this information has been of some value to you.

Yours sincerely

P.P. Katharine Heneage

<u>Felicity Mortimer</u>

Chairman & Managing Director Jeremy Norman. Directors John Brooke-Little MVO (Richmond Herald of Arms).
John Cook. The Earl of Lichfield. Dr. Remington Norman. Hugo Vickers. Felicity Mortimer.

139 Elm Park Mansions
Park Walk
London, S.W.10.

Mr Bernard Levin,
The Sunday Times,
200 Grays Inn Road,
London, W.C.1.

1st September 1979.

Dear Mr Levin,

You will be interested to hear that Mr Peter Saunders (The Mousetrap Man!) will shortly be presenting on the West End stage my original comedy in two acts, THE ENGLISH WAY OF DOING THINGS by HENRY ROOT. It concerns a Police Commissioner who sets forth in fair shape to apprehend the inmates of a bawdy-house, but who is so over-whelmed to discover that they outrank him socially that, in a side-splitting climax, he finds himself taking the bookings!

On the assumption that 'The Sunday Times' will be back on the streets in time for the first night, I now enclose a fiver for yourself to ensure that you review it favourably.

While I have your attention perhaps I could trouble you for the address of your 'young lady', Miss Arianna Stassinopulos. I'm eager that Mrs Root should join her Levitation and Deep Personal Awareness Group as soon as possible. I'm told that city gents who've joined now wear foam rubber under their bowler hats so that when in a trance they levitate too sharply to the ceiling they don't drive their heads on impact clean into their chests. No, I'm only chaffing, Bernard! As it happens, I don't have much time for any of this mystical nonsense from the east, with elderly Indians in their underwear manifesting themselves up ropes, but I dare say your young lady knows what she's doing and I'm keen to get Mrs Root out of the house from time to time. If that costs me a hundred and fifty notes, well it's cheap at the price.

I look forward to hearing from you.

Yours sincerely,

Henry Root.

Henry Root.

THE TIMES

Times Newspapers Limited. P.O. Box no. 7, New Printing House Square,
Gray's Inn Road, London WC1X 8EZ (registered office)
Telephone 01-837 1234 Telex 264971 Registered no. 894646 England

6th September 1979

Mr. Bernard Levin regrets he
cannot do as you ask.

139 Elm Park Mansions
Park Walk
London, S.W.10.

R. Alistair McAlpine Esq,
Conservative Board of Finance,
32 Smith Square,
London, S.W.1.   4th September 1979.

Dear McAlpine,

Seeing myself as apt material for a peerage, I wrote to
your Board on 7th August asking how much I would have to slip the
Tories' way to secure a seat in the Lords.

To my surprise, this reasonable question was fielded by
Major-General Wyldbore-Smith and fired back at me stump-high.

"It's not possible to buy a peerage from the Tory Party,"
he said.

Delightful! Well, he's a military man, of course (and nothing
wrong with that) and I expect he's still got his nose so deep into
Queen's Regulations that he hasn't got time to be as <u>au courant</u> as
you and I with the ways of the world.

I realise now that I should have 'dealt with' you in the
first place. Horses for courses.

I contributed generously to the Tory Party during the recent
election campaign, but I'm realistic enough to understand that I'll
have to do rather better than this to get a peerage.

What would do the trick? £50,000? £100,000?

Perhaps we could meet to discuss the matter? Are you a member
of the Carlton? I'm not, but if we met there, you could enrol me at
the same time. Two birds with one stone. Just give me a date and
time. Perhaps you could make the booking.

Needless to say there would be 'something in this' for you
personally, and I now enclose a pound (for yourself) to show that
I am a serious person.

I look forward to hearing from you.

Support Mrs Thatcher!

Yours sincerely,

Henry Root

Henry Root.

Conservative and Unionist Central Office
Treasurers' Department.

HONORARY TREASURER
CONSERVATIVE & UNIONIST PARTY
R. ALISTAIR McALPINE
DEPUTY TREASURER
ROBIN HOLLAND-MARTIN

32 Smith Square
Westminster, SW1P 3HH

6th September, 1979

<u>PERSONAL</u>

Dear Mr Root

I am writing to acknowledge receipt of your letter of the 4th September enclosing a £1 note.

I am sure you are well aware, and have also been so informed by General Wyldbore-Smith that there is absolutely no question of purchasing a peerage from the Conservative Party. I cannot emphasise this too strongly.

No useful purpose can be served by continuing this correspondence, and I return your £1 note herewith.

Yours sincerely,

R. ALISTAIR MCALPINE

Henry Root, Esq.,
139 Elm Park Mansions,
Park Walk,
London S.W.10

```
                              139 Elm Park Mansions
                              Park Walk
                              London, S.W.10.

Mr R. Alistair McAlpine,
Conservative Central Office,
32 Smith Square,
London, S.W.1.              8th September 1979.


Dear McAlpine,
     I am in receipt of your astonishing communication of 6th
September.
     This is to inform you that I have now joined the Liberal
Party.
          Support John Pardoe!
          Yours sincerely,

          Henry Root

          Henry Root.
Copy to the Prime Minister.
```

139 Elm Park Mansions
Park Walk
London, S.W.10.

The Treasurer,
The Liberal Party,
1 Whitehall Place,
London, S.W.1.

11th September 1979.

Sir,

Here's a pound! Let's go!
Support John Pardoe!
Yours faithfully,

Henry Root

Henry Root.

139 Elm Park Mansions
Park Walk
London, S.W.10.

The Treasurer,
The Liberal Party,
1 Whitehall Place,
London, S.W.1.

2nd October 1979.

Sir,

On 11th September I sent you £1, with the promise implied
that there were larger sums in the offing and that I might be on
the point of joining the party.

I haven't heard a word from you!

This is <u>not</u> a very promising start!

I would hate to think that I was about to receive the same
treatment from you as that handed out to my friend Mr 'Union Jack'
Haywood.

Support John Pardoe!

Yours faithfully,

Henry Root

Henry Root.

Telephone: 01-839 4082

LIBERAL PARTY ORGANISATION
HEADQUARTERS

1, Whitehall Place,
London SW1A 2HE.

Henry Root Esq,,
139, Elm Park Mansions,
London, S.W.10.

3rd October 1979

Dear Mr. Root,

Thank you for your kind donation which is
very much appreciated and I apologise for the
delay in sending this acknowledgement.

If you do decide to join the Party please
contact

Miss Edna McGregor (Hon Sec. Chelsea LA)
Flat K8, Sloane Ave. Mansions, SW3.
tel: 584 7754

I am sure they would welcome your support!

In the meantime I enclose a Bankers Order-
should you wish to donate to the Party on a
regular basis

Yours sincerely

Dee Doocey.
Finance Officer

139 Elm Park Mansions
Park Walk
London, S.W.10.

The Rt Hon David Steel,
The House of Commons,
Westminster,
London, S.W.1.

6th October 1979.

Dear Mr Steel,
    No doubt you have on your desk various letters between myself
and your Finance Officer, Mr Dee Doocey, re my joining the Liberals
and contributing towards the pending fund.
    Being new to liberalism I'm afraid I stepped off the pavement
with the wrong foot, as it were, by not checking first as to the
current leadership situation and by closing my letters with 'Support
John Pardoe!' At least I knew it wasn't Jeremy Thorpe! (What was
all the fuss about? I thought Norman St John Scott, so-called 'Gino'
Newton and Peter Bessel got a fair trial. What did you think?).
    Congratulations on your conference showing down in Broadstairs!
I wasn't able to get down there myself to support your motions since
I was flat to the boards last week organising a 'Support the Springbok
Rugby Players' march.
    Might I say that contrary to rumours circulating in the corri-
dors of power I am <u>not</u> the mysterious Mr X referred to recently by Mr
Sam Silkin and pardoned by same as per the old-boy network? I am not
of the old-boy network, nor am I a sodomite. Does this matter? Let
me know.
    Support the SPG! Let's go!
    Yours sincerely,

    Henry Root

    Henry Root. Liberal!

THE RT. HON. DAVID STEEL, M.P.

HOUSE OF COMMONS
LONDON SWIA OAA

October 8th 1979.

Dear Mr. Root,

In Mr. Steel's absence abroad I am writing to thank you for
your letter of October 6th and for your generous donation
to Party Funds which we have now sent on to Liberal Party
Headquarters.

Mr. Steel will see this for information on his return to
London and I am sure that he will be most interested to
have your views and most grateful to you for your generosity.

Thank you for taking the trouble to write.

Yours sincerely,

Nali Dishaw

Private Office.

Henry Root, Esq.,
139 Elm Park Mansions,
Park Walk,
London S.W.10.

139 Elm Park Mansions
Park Walk
London, S.W.10.

Mrs Shirley Conran,
c/o Sidgwick & Jackson Ltd,
1 Tavistock Chambers,
London, W.C.1.

5th September 1979.

Dear Mrs Conran,

I want you to know that until I read your book 'Superwoman' recently (better late than never!) I had always supposed that a married man had to forego the comforts of a well-run home. Like most men, indeed, I had always assumed that the only way of getting a decent meal on time was to cook it oneself or hire a chef. You have done much, it seems to me, to remove this silly prejudice against female house-keepers and have, by and large, put women back in the kitchen where they belong. Even Mrs Root can now boil an egg as well as any man. Well done!

Not that you recommend a life of unremitting drudgery for the ladies! Far from it! You seem to believe in plenty of relaxation too, as we discover on page 48 of your book, where you announce, with more pride than discretion, perhaps:

'I've just given one to each of the men in my life. They seemed pathetically grateful. I felt almost guilty!'

<u>Good</u> for you, Shirley, I thought, but why feel guilty? Even we senior citizens have to uncorset ourselves from time to time. When I reached the end of the book, however, I did begin to feel that perhaps you had been spreading yourself rather more thinly than a lady mindful of her reputation ought. Here, under the provocative heading 'How to get hold of the men in your life!', you tell us who these favoured fellows are. And a pretty impressive line-up they make! They are, in no particular order, as far as I can tell: your doctor, dentist, insurance broker, taxi driver, bank manager (very sensible!), milkman, vet, decorator, plumber, carpenter, electrician, TV repair man, newspaper boy, florist and various unspecified functionaries at the local police station, station, hospital and town hall.

Wow! Superwoman indeed!

Could you oblige with a photo, Shirley? I believe you reside in France due to your tax situation (nothing wrong with that) so I am enclosing a pound to cover the costs.

Yours admiringly,

Henry Root

Henry Root.

Shirley Conran,

Monte Carlo
4 December 1979

Dear Mr Root,

How very kind of you to write
to me! I was delighted
to get your letter — and how
thoughtful of you to enclose a
pound note. I shall buy
a ~~bottle~~ of wine with it
and drink to the health
of Mr + Mrs. Root!

With best wishes

Shirley Conran

Shirley Conran, author of SUPERWOMAN.
Crown Publishers, Inc.

with best wishes

139 Elm Park Mansions
Park Walk
London, S.W.10.

Mr Cliff Richard,
'Top of the Pops!'
BBC TV,
London, W.12.

5th September 1979.

Dear Cliff,
        You won't mind my calling you Cliff. We must be about the
same age, you and I. You're a credit to the over-forties, Cliff!
Twenty years at the top and still No 1!
        Con-grat-u-laaaaations!
        So they call you the pop of the tops, the father of them all!
That's absurd You never fathered anyone - unlike some. Nor did
you ever do anything unexpected with a chocolate bar (see Tom
Davies's veiled reference in last week's 'Observer' to this practice
vis-à-vis Miss Marianne Faithful.)
        Could you oblige with a photo, Cliff? You're Mrs Root's
favourite crooner. When I mentioned your name to my boy Henry Jr
(15) he observed that you are now working behind the cosmetics
counter in the Chingford branch of Boots the chemist, but it
transpired that he was confusing you with Miss Yana, the blonde
chanteuse of the early '50s. Remember her, Cliff?
        Cheers!

        Henry Root
        Henry Root.

139 Elm Park Mansions
Park Walk
London, S.W.10.

The Rt Reverend Robert Runcie MC,
The Bishop's Palace,
St Albans,
Herts.

9th September 1979.

Your Grace,

So - you made it all the way to the top spot! Well done!
Here's a pound. It's my experience that you chaps with your collars
back to front seldom say no to a little something for the collection.
Nothing wrong with that. You don't do much harm, in my opinion, so
good luck to you!

From what I've read in the papers you sound suitable material
for Canterbury. According to 'The Observer' you are a witty, polished
man who keeps pigs, had a good war, admires P.G. Wodehouse, supports
Luton Town, plays tennis and squash, was once on the wine committee
of the Athenaeum and knows his way around the world. Well done!
Just what's needed in these confusing times!

I read in 'The Evening Standard' that your better half, Mrs
Runcie, can't bear a lot of religious carry-on. "To me it's not
what I believe in," she said. "Too much religion makes me go off
pop". Surely she doesn't include Cliff Richard in this? His work
has always struck me as compatible with God's mysterious ways.
Otherwise I agree with her. Like her, I'm not a conventionally
religious man. I don't go to church or anything like that, but
if I was involved in an accident I think I'd say my prayers. My
daughter Doreen, who's studying philosophy at Essex University (for
all the good it's doing her) says that this is merely a modern
version of Pascal's best bet argument. What's she talking about?
Have you any idea?

I was particularly pleased to read the editorial in 'The Sunday
Telegraph' which said: 'Dr Runcie has never, unlike some other
prelates, seen the role of the priest in terms of a superior welfare officer; never doubted that God's kingdom is not of this world'.
Hear! Hear! My position precisely! I've worked hard for my pile
and I don't want some do-gooder in the pulpit telling me that I
should redistribute it among the weak and lazy. Let's go on gulling
the unfortunate into expecting their share in the hereafter!

Many deep thinkers such as Malcolm Muggeridge, Mary Kenny,
Christopher Booker and Richard West have been much influenced in
arriving at this point of view by the Reith Lectures of a Dr Edward
Norman with their emphasis on the essentially _spiritual_ nature of
Our Lord's message. Did you hear them? My daughter Doreen says
that by putting the hocus-pocus back into Christianity and evacu-
ating it of all ethical content, Dr Norman has performed the useful
function of making religion unintelligible even to sympathetic
humanists - but what can you expect from a slip of a girl reading
philosophy at a red-brick university?

Let's keep ethics out of religion, religion out of politics
and politics out of sport!

Up the Springboks!

Support Mrs Thatcher! (She put you where you are today!)

Yours faithfully,
Henry Root
Henry Root.

The Rt Rev Robert Runcie MC,
The Bishop's Palace,
St Albans,
Herts.

139 Elm Park Mansions
Park Walk
London, S.W.10

21st October 1979.
Trafalgar Day! Let's go!

Your Grace,

To put it mildly ('Blessed are the meek'!) I am astonished
not to have received any acknowledgement from you of my letter of
9th September, in which I was good enough to enclose a pound for
your roof.

This was not much, I realise, but I would not like to think
that you can only be bothered to thank folk who send you more substantial contributions.

May I remind you that it is easier for a rich man to enter
the Kingdom of God than a camel?

You may be rather busy at the moment, but surely you could
have designated a junior (what's the Dean doing?) to help with the
mail?

At least you've had time to issue an edict confirming that
there is no place in the church for homosexualists. Well done!

This is the kind of muscular Chistianity we need. But let's
reply to our letters too!

Support Mrs Thatcher!

Render unto Caesar etc!

Yours sincerely,

Henry Root

Henry Root.

The Bishop of St Albans
Abbey Gate House, St Albans, Hertfordshire AL3 4HD
ST ALBANS 53305

24th October, 1979.

Dear Mr. Root,

I write immediately to apologise unreservedly for my failure
to reply to your letter of the 9th September.

It is no doubt good for my pride since we think that we have
an excellent answer system and have already dealt with several thousands
and had no complaints; but there is no doubt at all that we slipped up
with your donation and your letter. It was in a small pile marked
'for further consideration'. We eliminated that sort of pile after the
first few days but about three letters remained in it.

I still do not quite know what to make of your mixture but you
seem to write with robust good humour so God bless you.

Yours sincerely,

Robert St Albans

Henry Root, Esq.,
139 Elm Park Mansions,
Park Walk,
London. S.W.10.

139 Elm Park Mansions
Park Walk
London, S.W.10.

Mr And Peter Forster,
The Evening Standard,
47 Shoe Lane,
London, E.C.4.   6th September 1979.

Dear Mr And Peter Forster,

      I assume from your name that you come originally from
Sweden, Finland or Norway. Not your fault. Good luck to you.

      You seem to be settling in well and you write agreeably for
a foreigner (if somewhat affectedly - over here we express ourselves
in a rather more masculine prose.)

      I do object most strongly, however, to your suggestion in
yesterday's 'Evening Standard' that we should all carry identity
cards to assist in the easy arrest and deportation of tourists.

      Such invasion of the citizen's right to privacy may be all
right where you come from, but had you lived among us for a little
longer you would know that such practices are contrary to our
hard-won freedoms.

      Writing as you do for a Tory paper, you should know that in
the last war many millions of Tories gave up their lives <u>fighting</u>
such things as the obligatory carriage of identity discs and compulsory finger-printing on the spot.

      I look forward to your correcting this lapse in a future
column.

      Jeres! (as you no doubt say in your country!)

      Henry Root.

Henry Root.

139 Elm Park Mansions
Park Walk
London, S.W.10.

Sir Keith Joseph,   6th September 1979.
23 Mulberry Walk,
London, S.W.3.

Dear Sir Keith,

I was sorry to read in yesterday's evening papers that your
house was recently burglarised while you were elsewhere propounding
the moral virtues of private enterprise.

I'm sure you'll be able to see the funny side of it!

I expect your mistake was to inform the robbery squad at
your local police station that your house would be empty. That's
always asking for trouble (unless, of course, one wants to make a
quick killing on one's over-insured valuables!)

You'd be the last person, of course, to disapprove of the
police's reasonable habit of diversification after dark into more
profitable lines. Market forces naturally compel them to subsidise
their still meagre pay-packets with a little entrepreneurial activity
on their own account.

Here's a pound. Not much, but you're a fine man and if Tories
everywhere sent you a pound you'd soon be able to replace what was
burgled.

I'm rather long in Grand Metropolitan at the moment. Would
you advise me to hang on or get out while I'm ahead? Horse's mouth
and all that.

Support Mrs Thatcher!

Even the police are monetarists now! Let's go!

Yours sincerely,

Henry Root

Henry Root.

DEPARTMENT OF INDUSTRY
ASHDOWN HOUSE
123 VICTORIA STREET
LONDON SWIE 6RB
TELEPHONE DIRECT LINE 01 212 3301
SWITCHBOARD 01 212 7676

Secretary of State for Industry

Henry Root Esq

12 September 1979

Dear Mr Root.

Thank you for your kind letter and your
thoughtful contribution. I am rather puzzled
about the £1 - and shall give it to the next
deserving flag day.

It was particularly quixotic on your part to
send me the £1, since you clearly think that
I am the Joseph of Grand Metropolitan. I am
not. He is no relation whatsoever - and I
am certainly in no position to advise you
whether to hang on to those or any other shares.
But you and I both believe in the market
economy with its choice.

Yours,

Keir Joseph.

139 Elm Park Mansions
Park Walk
London, S.W.10.

Mr Peregrine Worsthorne,
The Sunday Telegraph,
135 Fleet Street,
London, E.C.4.

6th September 1979.

Dear Mr Worsthorne,

My attention has only recently been drawn to an astonishing attack you made some months ago in 'The Sunday Telegraph' on that fine man Lord Longford.

'That Lord Longford should team up with Janie Jones, the convicted procuress', you wrote, 'may not at first glance seem to be a matter meritting much adverse comment. It might even be thought desirable, and a mark of a civilised society, for such a universally execrated wretch to have at least one friend in high places'.

Well! Calling Lord Longford a universally execrated wretch is irresponsible journalism at its worst, in my opinion, and I would strenuously dispute that Miss Janie Jones moves in high places. That she is well-connected I wouldn't deny, but I do not agree that she <u>herself</u> is welcome in the best drawing-rooms, except in her capacity of, as it were, chauffeuse and bunny-mother. It was her custom, when I used to avail myself of her services to supply the 'artistes' at certain local Tory Party functions, to deliver 'the cabaret' at some titled person or cabinet minister's home then leave. I do not recall that she ever hob-nobbed on a social level with those who later, and quite rightly, took it to be their duty to queue up in their pin-stripe suits and Old Etonian ties to give evidence against her.

I await your explanation for this extraordinary outburst.

Yours sincerely,

Henry Root

Henry Root.

SUNDAY TELEGRAPH

135 FLEET STREET LONDON EC4P 4BL TELEPHONE: 01-353 4242 TELEGRAMS: TELESUN LONDON EC4
TELEX: 22874 TELENEWS LONDON

7th September, 1979

Henry Root, Esq.,
139 Elm Park Mansions,
Park Walk,
London S.W.10

Dear Mr Root,

I am afraid you have rather misread that
article. I never called Lord Longford "a
universally execrated wretch" as will become
clear if you study the piece more carefully.

Yours sincerely,

Peregrine "orsthorne
Associate Editor

SUNDAY TELEGRAPH LIMITED REGISTRATION NO 667848 ENGLAND
REGISTERED OFFICE 135 FLEET STREET LONDON EC4P 4BL

139 Elm Park Mansions
Park Walk
London, S.W.10.

Mr Alan Watkins,
The Observer,
8 St Andrews Hill,
London, E.C.4.

10th September 1979.

Dear Watkins,

To be blunt, I don't usually like your stuff. It's too clever by half, in my opinion, and your tone - at once 'superior' and colloquial - often grates.

However, in your obituary for Philip Hope-Wallace this Sunday you hit an appropriate note for once. Well done!

It so happens that I have recently commissioned myself to compile an anthology of modern British prose and I would like your permission to quote two passages from your piece as under:

'Philip Hope-Wallace, opera critic of 'The Guardian', died last week. He was 67. He was an essayist, a linguist, a drinker and a wit.....He was beautifully polite - as much to a West Indian bus conductor as to his host at a party, to whom he would invariably send a thank-you letter.'

Of how many people, in these confusing times, can one say that they are polite to West Indian bus conductors? Precious few, alas! What a great man he must have been!

The other passage I would like to use is:

'He was once discussing the prologue to 'Pagliacci' on the wireless. "When I cease being moved by that music," he said, "I shall know I am dead". It is difficult to think of any young music critic today who could or would make that kind of statement'.

It is indeed.

His anecdote, about Elsie and Doris Waters, which you quote, is certainly hilarious. 'It is a measure of his gifts as a racon-teur,' you wrote, 'that it never failed to bring the house down'. I'm not surprised. I'm still chuckling over it myself.

I look forward to receiving the necessary permissions.

Yours sincerely,

Henry Root

Henry Root.

THE OBSERVER

The Observer Limited Registered number 146482 England
Registered office 8 St. Andrews Hill London EC4V 5JA Telephone 01-236 0202
Telegrams Observer London EC4 Telex 888963

22nd September 1979

Mr H. Root,
139 Elm Park Mansions,
Park Walk,
London SW10

Dear Mr Root,

Thank you for your letter of 10th September.
I apologise for the delay in replying.
Reproduction of my articles is in the hands
of my agent, Giles Gordon, Anthony Sheil
Associates Ltd., 2/3 Morwell Street, London
WC1, with whom I suggest you get in touch.

Yours sincerely,

A. Watkins

<u>Alan Watkins</u>

139 Elm Park Mansions
Park Walk
London, S.W.10.

The Chairman,
Leslie & Godwin,
Dunster House,
Mark Lane,
London, E.C.4.   12th September 1979.

Dear Sir,

     Your name has been given to me as insurance brokers who
are more or less on the up and up, paying their obligations
without demur.

     I am planning to take a late summer holiday with Mrs Root
and my two youngsters, Doreen (20) and Henry Jr (15), on the
sunshine island of Ibiza.

     Having never trusted foreigners since being overcharged in
Llandeilo, I write now to enquire about cover for the trip.

     What would be the cost of insuring myself, Mrs Root and
my two youngsters against seizure from the beach and ransom?

     I would pay generously in the case of myself and reasonably
for my two youngsters, but I would not wish the premiums on Mrs
Root to be too heavy. She's still a handsome woman, but no
longer in her first youth. Don't misunderstand me. It's not
that I wouldn't pay to get her back. It's simply hard to credit
that anyone would snatch her in the first place – so why waste
money on a large premium?

     Perhaps you could send round one of your young operatives
with the kidnap application forms.

     Yours faithfully,

     Henry Root

     Henry Root.

Leslie & Godwin Overseas (Non Marine) Ltd
SUBSIDIARY OF LESLIE & GODWIN LTD.
LLOYD'S INSURANCE BROKERS

Dunster House
Mark Lane
London EC3P 3AD   (Reg. Office)

Telex 888581 LESGO.G
Cables
Twentythree London
Telephone 01 623 4631

Registered No. 1401861 England

Mr.H.Root,
139 Elm Park Mansions,
Park Walk,
LONDON, S.W.10.

19th September 1979

Our Reference JD/CC

Dear Sir,

Thank you for your letter of 12th September enquiring about the
availability of Kidnap and Ransom insurance. We have been
arranging this class of business for clients for several years
and for security reasons we have code named this insurance
'Porters'.

We enclose herewith an application form for 'Porters' insurance
which we would ask you to complete and return to us as soon as
possible. On receipt of the completed form we will endeavour
to obtain a quotation for yourself and your family.

Thank you for your enquiry.

Yours faithfully,

Manager.

Directors
D. W. H. Smith (Chairman)   J. Barson (Managing Director)
E. E. Lawrence

139 Elm Park Mansions
Park Walk
London, S.W.10.

Mr Paul Johnson,
The Evening Standard,   12th September 1979.
47 Shoe Lane,
London, E.C.4.

Dear Johnson,
          Your article in yesterday's 'Evening Standard' about the
proposed tour of this country by a party of South African rugby
players started a right old ding-dong in my lounge-room, I can
tell you!

          I supported you whole-heartedly, of course, in your ringing
denunciation of the notion that the State should ever meddle in
the private arrangements of sportsmen on and off the ball, and I
vehemently seconded your telling point that rent-a-crowd lefties
who would ban all tours of this country by our Springbok friends
should, to be consistent, also oppose sporting engagements with
the Soviet Union, but my daughter Doreen expostulated as follows:

          "Johnson's talking through his hat as usual. An act util-
itarian - which is what most of us are - is not involving himself
in a contradiction (in any formal sense) if he opposes sporting
links with South Africa but not with the Soviet Union. Anyway,
protesting against the South African rugby players is not a political gesture, but a moral one. What old-fashioned deontologists,
like Johnson, are in fact saying is 'keep morality out of sport'.
To be consistent they should campaign for the legalisation of
cock-fighting, bear-baiting and wrestling in mud by naked mountain
ladies, all of which are considered sports by certain people."

          Well, I don't understand what she's talking about, so perhaps
you'd like to answer her. I'm sure she must be mistaken and I'd
like to be able to point out the fallacy in her position. Could
you oblige? I'd be most grateful.

          I look forward to hearing from you.

          Up the Springboks!

          Yours sincerely,

          Henry Root

          Henry Root.

from PAUL JOHNSON, Copthall, Iver, Buckinghamshire. Iver 653350

11 Oct 79

Nothing I can say will have the
slightest influence on a Sociology
student at Essex University - so
I won't try. Someday. No doubt,
your daughter will emerge from
under the carapace of her jargon
a begin to think for herself. P.J.

139 Elm Park Mansions
Park Walk
London, S.W.10.

Mr Ray Cooney,
26 Charing Cross Road,
London, W.C.2.

15th September 1979.

Dear Cooney,

I see you're reviving Carol Channing at Drury Lane. Well done!

She's a game old bat and can always be heard at the back of the hall. Of how many of today's young artistes can that be said?

I was disappointed not to receive an answer from you to my letter of 29th March, in which I suggested that I might become one of your fairies. Perhaps you never received it. In case that is so, I now enclose a copy.

I'd like to bring Mrs Root and my two youngsters, Doreen (20) and Henry Jr (15) to Miss Channing's first night on 25th September. I know you'll want to issue me with complimentary tickets (as a potential fairy), but I wouldn't hear of it. Here's a fiver for yourself. Send me four of your best orchestra stalls.

Are you having a 'do' afterwards? Let me know where it's being held as I'd like Mrs Root to meet Miss Channing.

See you on the 25th!

Good luck!

Henry Root

Henry Root.

P.S. I'd really like to invest in your shows, so send me a prospectus of your up-coming productions. Cheers!

139 Elm Park Mansions
Park Walk
London, S.W.10.

Lord Thorneycroft,
Conservative Party Central Office,
32 Smith Square,
London, S.W.1.   12th September 1979.

Dear Lord Thorneycroft,

Following a most unsatisfactory exchange of letters with two
of your jacks-in-office at HQ - Major-General Wyldbore-Smith and
Mr Alistair McAlpine - I was compelled to write to the Liberal Party
yesterday, informing them that I intended to join their ranks.

Word of this apparent defection will by now have reached you.
Don't worry. I'm only pretending to join the Liberals for the purposes of a life peerage. (Titles, as you no doubt know, come at a
sharper price from them, due to their lack of current wherewithall.)
The purpose of this letter is to emphasise that I will, of course,
remain at heart a Tory, and as soon as I am adequately ennobled will
once more cross the floor.

Meanwhile I can be of use to you as a mole in their midst,
attending confabs wired for sound and reporting back to you on
weirdos bent on direct action and civil disobedience.

For the moment I think we should keep this arrangement confidential between ourselves. Better that our Leader should remain
uncompromised. Were a wheel to come off it would be better that
she was genuinely uncognisant of the fact that her man-on-the-doorstep
had become a 'plumber'.

I enclose a pound for yourself as a token of my essential
loyalty.

Support Mrs Thatcher!

Over and out!

Henry Root

Henry Root.

From

THE CHAIRMAN OF THE PARTY

The Rt. Hon. The Lord Thorneycroft

CONSERVATIVE & UNIONIST CENTRAL OFFICE,
32 SMITH SQUARE,
WESTMINSTER, SW1P 3HH,

Telephone: 01-222 9000

PT/SO   4th October, 1979

Dear Mr Root,

Lord Thorneycroft has asked me to thank
you for your letter of the 12th September,
the contents of which he has noted.

He has asked me to return to you herewith
your £1.

Yours sincerely,

Shirley Oxenbury
Chairman's Office

H. Root, Esq.,

139 Elm Park Mansions
Park Walk
London, S.W.10.

Mr And Peter Forster,
The Evening Standard,
47 Shoe Lane,
London, E.C.4.   21st September 1979.

Dear Mr And Peter Forster,

        In your column yesterday you asked how the expression
'Hampstead intellectual' came into being.

        Had you lived in this country a little longer you would
know that the term dates from the time that Mr Hugh Gaitskill
(who used to be the leader of the Labour Party here) lived in
this part of London. It was his custom to hold early evening
sherry parties in his home for so-called left-wing 'thinkers'
of his stripe. Most had been to Winchester School and had
acquired their leanings through being kicked hard and often
at an impressionable age by the likes of better adjusted Winchester boys such as Mr Willie Whitehouse.

        Had you lived among us for a little longer you would also
know that it is customary in this country to reply to letters.
I have not yet heard from you in response to mine of 6th September.

        Never mind. Here's a stamp. In fact, here are two stamps.
Now you can answer both my letters.

        I hope you are gradually becoming more accustomed to our
ways. We're not a difficult people if treated with respect. Good
luck to you!

        Jeres!

Henry Root

Henry Root.

London, S.W.10.

The President,
The Society of West End Theatre Managers,
19 Charing Cross Road,
London, W.C.2.   27th September 1979.

Mr President,

     I wish to protest in the strongest possible terms about the behaviour of one of your members.

     On the 15th of this month I sent Mr Ray Cooney a fiver and instructed him to send me four front stalls for the revival of Carol Channing at Drury Lane.

     I haven't heard a word from him! I didn't receive my tickets and no doubt the fiver's down the drain!

     I realise that Mr Cooney, being, I take it, a recent immigrant to this country, may not as yet be fully au fait with our way of doing things, but I think you'll agree with me that simply pocketing a fellow's money probably isn't on even where Cooney comes from.

     I may add that I wrote to Cooney originally in April saying that I'd like to be a fairy in one of his shows, and he didn't answer that letter either!

     His kind have delightfully sunny and easy-going temperaments, of course, but I think there is a limit to the allowances one can go on making. I look forward to hearing what action you propose to take against him, Mr President, and to receiving my money back.

     Yours sincerely,

     Henry Root

     He

ray cooney productions limited

SUITE 33, 26 CHARING CROSS ROAD, LONDON WC2H 0DH

Telegraphic Address: RAYCOPRODS LONDON

V.A.T. Regn. No. 239 5344 46

Telephone: 01-240 3747
01-836 9771
01-836 9751

3 October 1979

Henry Root Esq.
139 Elm Park Mansions
Park Walk
LONDON, S.W.10.

Dear Mr. Root,

We are in receipt of your letter dated 15 September which unfortunately only reached this office yesterday. We are therefore returning your £5 which you enclosed as the first night of Miss Channing at Drury Lane has since come and gone.

Yours sincerely,

for Ray Cooney

139 Elm Park Mansions
Park Walk
London, S.W.10.

Lord Rothermere,
Associated Newspapers Ltd,
Carmelite House,
London, E.C.4.

16th September 1979
Battle of Britain Sunday!

Dear Lord Rothermere,

What a day to be writing to you! Battle of Britain Sunday!
I believe you flew Spitfires in the last show. Or was that Sir
Max Atkins? Same difference. Well done!

I read recently that you are being sued for libel by your
scandal writer, Nigel Dempster. It seems you compared the flavour
of his column to that of stale cabbage. That's been obvious to
one and all for years. Why have you only just caught on? Never
mind. You probably don't read 'The Daily Mail' and who shall blame
you?

I see that a friend of Dempster's, the little Jap Mr Taki,
attacks you in this week's 'Spectator' on the grounds that your
father was crackers and ran his affairs from a pigeon loft. So
what? The least said about Dempster's father the better, I imagine,
and no doubt at the time you were flying Spitfires over the White
Cliffs of Dover Mr Taki's father was bombing Pearl Harbour. So
where would they have been on VD Day? Lying low, I wouldn't wonder!

Anyway, I'm glad to see you're defending the action. You'll
win hands down, of course, but I enclose a pound to help with the
costs.

Might I suggest alternative defences?
1.   Nothing said about Dempster could lower him in the estimation
of right-thinking folk on the Clapham omnibus. Or:
B.   'The Daily Mail' is held in such low repute that nothing in
it could be believed, least of all anything said by its proprietor.

Let's go!

Yours sincerely,

Henry Root

Henry Root.

THE CHAIRMAN'S OFFICE

ASSOCIATED NEWSPAPERS GROUP LIMITED

NEW CARMELITE HOUSE,
CARMELITE STREET,
LONDON, EC4Y 0JA

TELEPHONE
01-353 6000
01-353 4000
TELEX 261461/2

4th October, 1979

Mr. Henry Root,
139 Elm Park Mansions,
Park Walk,
London S.W. 10.

Dear Mr. Root,

I have great pleasure in returning
your pound as I am not being sued for libel by Mr.
Nigel Dempster.

From your letter it would seem that you
are addicted to the reading of idle gossip and are foolish
enough to believe all that you read. It is a pity that
apparently an expensive education should have been so wasted.

Yours sincerely,

M White

Lord Rothermere.

Dictated by Lord Rothermere.
Signed in his absence.

Registered Office, Carmelite House, London, EC4Y 0JA Reg. No. 84121 England

139 Eln Park Mansions
Park Walk
London, S.W.10.

Dr John Rae,
Westminster School,
17 Dean's Yard,
London, S.W.1.

17th September 1979.

Dear Dr Rae,

     I would like to congratulate you on the well produced TV
commercial for your school last week. You won't mind my saying,
however, that you yourself came across as a bit of a ponce,
putting yourself about the quad in red robes of a flowing cut
and declaiming your lines like King Rat in a pantomime. Mrs
Root explained that such behaviour comes under the heading of
'tradition' and dates from Uncle Tom's Schooldays. I expect you
know what you're doing.

     Here's the heart of it. I've had a lot of trouble over the
years with my boy, Henry Jr, and I might be interested in seeing
whether you can straighten him out. First I'd have to be satisfied
on certain points arising out of the commercial. On the debit
side we have to put your own performance; the information imparted
that the fat foreign raconteur Peter Ustinov is a former pupil as
are 'Tony' Benn and Philby the Foreign Office mole; the emphasis
on book-learning rather than ball games; the participation of girls
in the curriculum; the fact that an older lad was clearly seen at
one point to be playing the guitar; and the apparent discontinuation
of corporal punishments.

     I was favourably impressed, however, by your firm stand
against the use of drugs obtained from ethnic minorities in the
town and still more by the fact that you encourage the taking of
alcohol so long as the lads are resourceful enough not to get
caught blotto. It seems too that you have already produced six
Prime Ministers. Well done! This suggests that the masters must
be a shade less obviously crackers than they look.

     In the circumstances, and on balance, I'll take a risk with
my boy's future. I gather places are at a premium, so I'm prepared
to pay over the odds to secure him a position at the head of the
queue. I enclose a fiver (this is for you personally, you understand)
and I can tell you that there's a lot more where this came from if
you play your cards right.

     I look forward to hearing from you.

     Yours sincerely,

     Henry Root

     Henry Root.

From

THE HEAD MASTER
WESTMINSTER SCHOOL
17 DEAN'S YARD, SW1P 3PB
01-222 6904

18th September 1979

Dear Mr. Root,

Thank you for your letter of 17th September.

If you would like your son to be registered for Westminster you should write to the Registrar, Mr. Geoffrey Shepherd, Westminster School, Little Dean's Yard, London, S.W.1., or telephone him on 222 5516. The entrance to Westminster is by examination only.

I am returning your £5 note; you will no doubt appreciate that I am not in a position to keep it.

Yours sincerely,

Mr. Henry Root,
139 Elm Park Mansions,
Park Walk,
London, S.W. 10.

139 Elm Park Mansions
Park Walk
London, S.W.10.

The Managing Director,
J. Walter Thompson Ltd,
40 Berkeley Square,
London, W.1.

17th September 1979.

Dear Sir,

No doubt you will have already been tipped off through the 'media' grapevine that Sidgwick & Jackson is shortly to publish Vol 1 in my series SEMINAL IDEAS IN A NUTSHELL, edited by HENRY ROOT with the assistance of Doreen Root (20).

For literary folk they seem to be more or less on the up and up (though a tendency to wear pink shirts, drop names and offer sherry wine at tea-time has to be watched) and doubtless they know how to evaluate a manuscript. Judging by what I've seen, however, (and in spite of the reasonable selling job they did for Shirley Conran, the cook, and Mr Edward Heath) I'm much less happy about their ability to push the product. The head of publicity is a girl (which hardly inspires confidence, I think you'll agree), two of the Directors, Stephen du Sautoy and Rocco Forte, are, as their names suggest, of foreign extraction, and already many of my most valid concepts - such as engaging 'Sir' Robert Mark to endorse the package on TV (television) - have been vetoed by some character who wafts into the office at lunchtime, sugars off moments thereafter for an 'appointment' in the West End and isn't seen again for the rest of the day.

In a word, they don't know how to hood-wink the paying customer into forking out for a product he didn't want in the first place.

This is where you come in. Bamboozling the mugs is your business. I've had my people run you through the computer and I'm glad to be able to tell you that you've come up brand new. Well done! In the circumstances I'm prepared to put the marketing of the series your way. (In fact I was strongly advised to give the job to young Bell of Saatchi and Saatchi, but it seemed unpatriotic to brief a Japanese outfit. Nothing racist, mind - I just don't draw too well with the clever little monkeys.)

When shall we meet to run a few ideas up the flag-pole? What about one day next week? If I hear nothing to the contrary, I'll run through the door of your office at 12.30 on Thursday 27th September.

Perhaps I should emphasise that I expect this account to be handled by you personally. I don't want to be greeted on the 27th by a junior visualiser or the lad who holds up the story-boards at a client's meeting!

Here's a pound. Come up with some solid, viable ideas and you'll find there's plenty more where this came from.

I'm looking for maximum visibility. So spend! Spend! Spend! This could be a valuable account for you.

Yours with a concept,

Henry Root

Henry Root.

J. Walter Thompson Company
LIMITED

40 Berkeley Square, London, W1X 6AD Tel: 01-629 9496
Telegraphic address: Thomertwal, London Telex: 22871

24th September 1979

Mr. H. Root
139 Elm Park Mansions
Park Walk
London SW10

Dear Mr. Root

Thank you so much for your letter.

Michael Cooper-Evans has passed it to me as the Account
Director of J. Walter Thompson's Entertainment Group.
I know that you were most anxious that you dealt with
him personally but he felt that such an exciting project
as yours should be handled by the appropriate department.

One thing I must explain is the way in which we get paid.
Occasionally we have fee payments, particularly on smaller
or development jobs, but mainly we take a commission on
the media expenditure. This is 15%. As an example I'm
returning 85p of your pound.

I'm looking forward to meeting you on Thursday, and perhaps
even Doreen.

Yours sincerely

SEAN O'CONNOR
Story-board Holder

DIRECTORS: J. J. D. Bullmore (*Chairman*), P. H. Miles, A. R. G. Morrison (*Deputy Chairmen*); M. Cooper-Evans, (*Managing Director*);
P. W. Bostock, I. N. E. Bruce, L. A. Carter, D. R. Cawston, M. W. M. Colebrook, D. R. M. Curling, G. W. Effer, J. B. H. Goble, T. S. Hamaton,
R. P. Hornby, B. H. C. Johnson, S. H. M. King, D. G. Lanigan, J. M. Lannon, G. J. Lawrence, G. J. S. Ogden, J. R. Page, J. A. Paine,
D. J. L. Richardson, D. E. A. Rousell, A. J. Scouller, A. W. Stead.

Registered Office: 40 Berkeley Square, London, W1. Registered in England No. 1190652.

139 Elm Park Mansions
Park Walk
London, S.W.10.

Mrs Deborah Owen,
78 Marrow Street,   19th September 1979.
Limehouse,
London, E.14.

Dear Mrs Owen,
        I enclose for your evaluation a copy of my humorous play
THE ENGLISH WAY OF DOING THINGS by HENRY ROOT. It's an amusing
romp in two acts with only enough unnecessary nudity to attract
the mugs.
        As you will quickly perceive, it concerns the antics of a
Police Commissioner from the north who is impeded in the course
of his duty by the fact that he is always socially out of his
depth with those whom he sets out to apprehend. I have based it
on the famous 'Spaghetti House Siege Situation', which, as you
will remember, dragged on for several days because when Sir Robert
Mark turned up with his handcuffs and a megaphone he was denied
entry on the grounds that he hadn't booked a table and was un-
suitably dressed for Knightsbridge.
        In fact Sir Robert himself has already turned down the part
of the Police Commissioner on the grounds that he doesn't really
want to be an actor, but I will shortly be offering the part of
Lady Mark to Miss Hylda Baker. Miss Glenda Jackson might be
suitable for the part of the rough old boiler who 'takes an early
bath' in Act 1.
        My friend Jeffrey Archer speaks most highly of your capacities,
endorsing you as an agent on the up-and-up with editorial expertise
and separate client account. Well done! In the circumstances I'm
prepared to put the representation of my play in your hands for
a trial period.
        I'm a trifle concerned by your address. I myself was born
in the East End, but I made it my business to swim clear as soon
as I could. Never mind. Your corner of THE ENGLISH WAY OF DOING
THINGS by HENRY ROOT should enable you to make the move to a more
literary neck of the woods. Perhaps when we meet you should come
to me. There are quite a few folk in your part of the world still
nursing bruised ribs from the days when I was elbowing my way up
the ladder in wet fish. I wouldn't want to embarrass those with
whom I once hob-nobbed as equals by passing among them now in my
Rolls HR1 without a nod. I'm sure you'll understand.
        I trust your husband, so-called Dr Owen, isn't in charge of
your foreign rights department! No, I'm only joking! He did his
best.
        Yours sincerely,
        Henry Root
        Henry Root.

DEBORAH OWEN
LITERARY AGENT · 78 NARROW STREET
LIMEHOUSE · LONDON E14 8BP
TEL: 01-987 5119 CABLES: DEBOWEN LONDON E14

21st September 1979

Henry Root Esq
139 Elm Park Mansions
Park Walk
London SW10

Dear Mr Root,

Thank you for your letter of September the 19th enclosing
your play entitled THE ENGLISH WAY OF DOING THINGS.

I fear that I do not handle plays as they require quite a
different appraisal to fiction and this is not an art in
which I feel well-educated.

You may find it helpful to look at the list of agents in
the CASSELL AND PUBLISHERS ASSOCIATION DIRECTORY OF PUBLISHING.
This will tell you which agencies will consider plays and also
those that specialise in plays.

I am returning your play to you with this letter and thank
you for enclosing an s.a.e.

Yours sincerely,

Deborah Owen

ncl.

Deborah Owen Limited
Registered in England at the above address No. 1009342

139 Elm Park Mansions
Park Walk
London, S.W.10.

Miss Harriet Harman,
The National Council for so-called Civil Liberties,
186 Charing Cross Road,
London, W.C.1.

24th September 1979.

Dear Miss Harman,
        I saw you on TV the other night arguing the matter of jury-
fixing with that foreign boffin from London University, Professor
Zander.
        Why should an attractive lass like you want to confuse her
pretty little head with complicated matters of politics, juris-
prudence, sociology and the so-called rights of citizens? Leave
such weighty considerations to us men, that's my advice to you!
        A pretty girl like you should have settled down by now with
a husband and a couple of kiddies. Or, if you must earn a living,
why do you not pursue a career suitable to women such as that of
model, actress, ballroom-dancing instructress or newsreader? You
certainly have the looks! (You will agree, I think, that the
outstanding success achieved by the misses Rippon and Ford has
amply demonstrated that reading the news is far too trivial an
occupation for grown men.)
        Here's a pound. Go out and buy a pretty dress and then give
my friend Lord Delfont a phone call. Mention my name and say you'd
like to drop in for some advice about a career in entertainment or
ATV.
        Good luck!
        Yours sincerely,

        Henry Root

        Henry Root.

139 Elm Park Mansions
Park Walk
London, S.W.10.

His Honour Judge King-Hamilton Q.C.
The Old Bailey,
London, E.C.4.   24th September 1979.

Your Honour,

So! Amid the predictable and orchestrated cries of outrage
from the so-called liberal press, 'The Guardian' has let the cat out
of the bag re the sensible practice of 'jury fixing'!

You were right to give 'The Guardian' a tongue-lashing from
the bench, but you might, in my opinion, have gone further. Did not
such outrageous irresponsibility warrant a night or two in the
sneezer for the Editor? I'm sure Mr Justice Cantley or Mr Justice
Melford Stevenson as was would have taken more drastic steps.

What, after all, is wrong with jury rigging? Only those who
have broken the law have anything to fear from this practice. And
what would be the point of the police taking endless trouble to
rig the evidence unless the jury had been tampered with too? Months
of valuable police work would go down the drain. This is what that
fine man Sir Robert Mark understood so well. <u>He</u> knew that the whole
point of a criminal trial is to get the defendant into what we call
'a no-win situation'.

Good luck with the anarchists trial which has given rise to
all the brouhaha. Is it too late for me to be appointed to the
new rigged jury? With me on the panel you'd have one vote of guilty
in your pocket before you started.

Might I congratulate you (better late than never!) on the fine
showing you put up while presiding last year at the so-called Gay
News blasphemy trial? Lemon should have gone to the slammer, but
otherwise you shaped up well and I trust your client Mrs Whitehouse
was appropriately grateful.

How about a signed photo? You've got the sort of head that
might put the wind up my boy, Henry Jr. The lad's badly off the
rails and your features on his bedroom wall might stop his thoughts
and hands straying whither they'd be better not to stray till later.

Tell me something. Are you merely Judge King-Hamilton rather
than <u>Mr Justice</u> King-Hamilton because you're no good at it, or is
there another reason?

Keep up the good work!

I look forward to hearing from you.

Yours sincerely,

Henry Root

Henry Root.

CENTRAL CRIMINAL COURT
Old Bailey London EC4M 7EH

Telephone 01-248 3277

Your reference

Our reference
MM/MJG
Date

25 September 1979

Dear Mr. Root,

    I write on behalf of His Honour Judge King-
Hamilton to acknowledge receipt of your letter
dated 24th September, addressed to him.

    As I am sure you are aware, Her Majesty's
Judges are not permitted to enter into personal
correspondence relating to cases which they are
trying nor, indeed, to make comments publicly
about them but the Judge has asked me to thank
you for your interest in writing to him.

            Yours sincerely,

Michael McKenzie
Courts Administrator

H. Root Esq.,
139 Elm Park Mansions,
Park Walk,
London, S.W.10.

139 Elm Park Mansions
Park Walk
London, S.W.10.

The Senior Treasury Counsel,
The Old Bailey,
London, E.C.4.

24th September 1979.

Dear Sir,

Now that the sensible practice of 'jury fixing' is out in
the open thanks to the irresponsible behaviour of 'The Guardian',
I would like to nominate myself as 'a rigged juryman' in certain
trials.

In cases involving pornographers, blasphemers and those prone
to civil agitation and disorder you'd have at least one vote under
your belt even before the curtain had gone up.

I am 45, a householder, a man of means and not without associates, including Sir James Goldsmith.

You can rely on me!

Here's a pound! Put my name at the top of the list if you
want a conviction!

I look forward to hearing from you.

Yours sincerely,

Henry Root

Henry Root.

Copies to: The Lord Chancellor.
             The Attorney-General.
             The DPP.

CENTRAL CRIMINAL COURT
Old Bailey London EC4M 7EH

Telephone 01-248 3277

Your reference

Our reference 01?/MS/

Date
28 September 1979

Dear Sir,

Thank you for your letter of 24th September,
the contents of which have been noted.

I am returning your £1 note.

Yours faithfully,

for Courts Administrator

Mr. Henry Root,
139 Elm Park Mansions,
Park Walk,
London.
S.W.10

139 Elm Park Mansions
Park Walk
London, S.W.10.

Mr Malcolm Muggeridge,
c/o The Parkinson Show,
BBC TV,   4th October 1979.
London, W.12.

Dear Mr Muggeridge,

Congratulations on your performance last night in 'The
Parkinson Show'! For once Parky met his intellectual equal.
Well done!

That said, I must admit that my daughter Doreen (20) took
exception to some of your remarks. She found you particularly
unsound on the concept of progress. "It is an illusion", you
averred.

"In denying the possibility of progress," my Doreen proclaimed, "Muggeridge seems to be using the word in a rather
unusual way. Perhaps he is confusing it with the notion of
perfectability. If he is merely arguing for fallibilism, then
of course I'd agree with him. However, if he's using the word
'progress' as it's generally used, then he would seem to be
talking nonsense – and not for the first time. For instance,
would he want to argue that he has made no progress as a writer
in the last sixty years? Does he deny the possibility of
improvement? If he thinks he's improved, then he must believe
in 'progress' as the word is commonly used. If he doesn't think
he's progressed at all, then I would suggest he doesn't understand
what the term means. If he would merely admit that while he
has made some progress he's still no bloody good and his entire
writing career has been a total waste of time, then of course
I'd agree in his case, while making greater claims for serious
writers".

What do you say to that?

I left the lounge-room to make tea at a certain point in the
show, so I missed the introduction of the third lady with mauve
hair swept up and rather too much personal jewellery here and there.
Surely this couldn't have been your wife, referred to by Parkinson
in the course of the show as beautiful and by yourself as delightful? If she is your wife, can't you stop her wearing gents' suits
in public? If she isn't your wife why on earth did you bring her
with you?

Could I trouble you for a photo? I know you don't favour
personality cults and have testified to this in your many 'media'
appearances, but you are Mrs Root's favourite celebrity after
Terry Wogan and a photo of you would make her day. I enclose
the postage!

Yours sincerely,

Henry Root

Henry Root.

NO REPLY!

139 Elm Park Mansions
Park Walk
London, S.W.10.

Derek F.S. Clogg Esq,
Theodore Goddard & Co,
16 St Martin's-le-Grand,
London, E.C.1.

4th October 1979.

Dear Mr Clogg,

Women are sentimental creatures, are they not? When they leave you, they like to hang on to something of yours they've grown attached to. Your money, your house, your cars, your children.

I write to you thus because, following an unfortunate lapse at 'The Talk of the Town' about which I'd rather talk in detail only in conference, I'm thinking of dumping Mrs Root. The mishap was occasioned by the fact that Mrs Root had recently seen a film of a wine-tasting festival on TV (BBC2) in which the participants had, after sampling for bouquet and after-taste, hit a spittoon from three yards. Taking this to be the done thing, Mrs Root took aim and hit the wine-waiter in the eye over the same distance. The fact is I'm after a peerage, and whoever's at my side as Lady Root must measure up.

I'm told that you're the top divorce lawyer in town, acting smartly for such as the Duchess of Argyle and the 'headless' Cabinet Minister who waited at table in a suspender-belt. Well done!

My concern is that I'm a very well-to-do man, duly alarmed by stories in the media of the large sums folk of substance now have to hand over to their wives on parting. Only this week I read that the wife of the cowboy Clint Eastwood is tearing into him to the tune of ten million!

Can we fix things so that Mrs Root only manages to pull away a few thousand? Do you have a scheme? She's welcome to the children.

When can we meet? What about Monday 15th October at noon? Perhaps we can discuss tactics over lunch.

I look forward to our first conference.

Yours sincerely,

Henry Root.

Henry Root.

THEODORE GODDARD & CO.

16 ST. MARTIN'S-LE-GRAND

LONDON EC1A 4EJ

D. DUDLEY MORGAN
PETER A. J. MORLEY
J. R. FISHER
R. DEREK FOX
BLANCHE H. M. A. LUCAS
MARK N STACEY
MICHAEL Q WALTERS
F. J. CALDERAN
R. R. SHUTE
M. J. W. TOD
EDWIN A. JONES
WILLIAM S. ROGERS
M. A. CROFT BAKER
N. J. HARRIS
ANTONY HEALD

CHRISTOPHER CLOGG
W. M. STUART MAY
ANDREW BINGHAM
MARTIN G. CHESTER
P. GRAFTON GREEN
DIANA GUY
DAVID S. WILKINSON
R. N. PRESTON
DEREK W. LEWIS
SIMON STUBBINGS
MARTIN KRAMER
GUY I. F. LEIGH
C. J. J. NAPLES
DIANA SHEEZUM

R. DEREK WISE C.B.E (RESIDENT IN PARIS)
EDWARD WILTSHIRE (RESIDENT IN MADRID)

CONSULTANT
DEREK F. S. CLOGG

ASSOCIATES   BRUCE S. WALTER

E. A. CLARKE
NICHOLAS WHITNEY

Telephone: 01-606 8855
Cables: Assumpsit London E.C.1
Telex: 884678
Telegrams: Assumpsit London Telex
Telecopier Extension 208
L.D.E. and C.D.E. Box Number 47
Stock Exchange Number STX 2346

Associate Offices.

167 RUE DE L'UNIVERSITE
PARIS 75007
Telephone (010 331) 705 88 45
Telex: 280861

LAGASCA 108
MADRID 6
Telephone (010 34 I) 275 03 34
Telegrams: Interlex

OSPREY HOUSE
5 OLD STREET
ST. HELIER, JERSEY C.I
Telephone (0534) 76086
Telex 4192269

Our Ref   5.
Your Ref

8th October 1979.

Dear Mr. Root,

Thank you for your letter of the 4th October.

I should be very happy to see you to discuss your case, but I am starting an action today which will last about three weeks and I should not be able to see you except at 4.30 or thereabouts in the afternoon. Perhaps you could kindly telephone my secretary and make an appointment.

Perhaps I ought to tell you our terms of business. My time is charged out at £50 an hour. My assistants at about £35, and before starting any litigation we have to be put in funds to the extent of £500 generally on account of our costs and disbursements such as Counsel's fees etc.

Yours sincerely,

Derek F. S. Clogg.

Derek F.S. Clogg.

Henry Root, Esq.,
139 Elm Park Mansions,
Park Walk,
London SW10.

139 Elm Park Mansions
Park Walk
London, S.W.10.

Derek F.S. Clogg Esq,
Theodore Goddard & Co,
16 St Martin's-le-Grand,
London, E.C.1.

9th October 1979.

Dear Mr Clogg,

Thank you for your letter of 8th October in the matter of
dumping Mrs Root. I note your charges and those of your assistant
and would say that both seem reasonable.

It so happens that since I wrote to you on 4th October I
have had a slight change of heart. This has been brought about
by my sudden realisation that Mrs Root is, after all, a solid wife
and mother, who has often held up adequately in public bearing in
mind her background (cocktail waitress) and the fact that two
nights ago she carried out a random spot check of my personal parts
(you know what women are like) and came across some photographs
of an 'artistic' bent of some 'models' posing at a price. Though
these photographs were legitimately taken in the course of my
researches for a book commissioned by Jonathan Cape Ltd, Mrs Root
has most sensibly persuaded me that they could be misconstrued in
the wrong hands.

In the circumstances I judge it best to reconsider the marriage
situation for the time being, though if matters deteriorate I will
get in touch with your 'personal' secretary for a conference.

Meanwhile I compute that I have taken up, say, ten minutes
of your valuable time and I accordingly enclose as per your tariff
a fiver (cash! No problem with our friends at the Revenue!)

Yours sincerely,

Henry Root

Henry Root.

139 Elm Park Mansions
Park Walk
London, S.W.10.

Miss Mary Kenny,
The Sunday Telegraph,
135 Fleet Street,
London, E.C.4.

8th October 1979.

Dear Miss Kenny,

So! You have at last made the big leap from the obscurity of
the Women's Section to the centre pages where men of affairs like
Peregrine Worsthorne write!

Well done!

A small step for man. But a giant step for an Agony Aunt!

Your article this Sunday about the effeminacy of the Pope
was most interesting.

'The true man,' you wrote, 'is not permanently tough, agg-
ressive, granite-faced and unassailable; the true man is someone
who has the courage to be a whole individual, which means developin
his "feminine", emotional, spiritual side too.'

This is well said, but I wonder where you'd draw the line.
Take the case of my boy, Henry Jr (15). He has developed his feminine side to such an extent that it's difficult, in my opinion,
to know which sex he is.

He wears eye make-up and girl's hats, he pouts and sulks if
reprimanded, he sleeps in his earrings and shows no interest at al
in such normal masculine pursuits as pin-ups and sport.

Should one let **him develop** in his own way, or should one
thrash the lad?

I very much look forward to receiving your advice in this
matter.

Yours sincerely,

Henry Root.

Henry Root.

FROM: MARY KENNY

Dear Mr Root,   13.10.79.
         Thank you for your kind letter.
I suppose I should have said in
my piece that the "true man"
also develops his masculine
side - I rather took that for
granted: wrongly, actually. I
certainly would draw the line at
exaggerated behaviour in either

sex - especially behaviour exaggerat-
ing the characteristics of the other
sex. I think one should put
one's foot down, gently but
firmly — he probably would
react badly to an over-
tough approach.
        Wishing you the best of
luck : my old Irish mother
still says "spare the rod"... Regards,
                              Mary K.

139 Elm Park Mansions
Park Walk
London, S.W.10.

Miss Marjorie Proops,   5th October 1979.
The Daily Mirror,
Holborn Circus,
London, E.C.1.

Dear Marje,
        Mrs Root recently drew my attention to a back number of
'The Guardian' (left behind by a house-painter with a degree in
Psychiatry from Sussex University who was doing our lounge-room
in over-all muffin) in which a Miss Polly Twaddle argued that
wives should be paid a good wage for cleaning, hoovering, dusting,
making beds, cooking, shopping, sewing, darning, taking the
kiddies to school and spending long hours at the hair-dresser.
        Good heavens! If I had to pay to have such trivial tasks
performed, I'd hire a man and have them done properly.
        You look like a wise old bird. Do you agree?
        Yours,

        Henry Root

        Henry Root.

Mirror Group Newspapers Lim
Holborn Circus London EC1P 1l
Switchboard: 01-353 0246

Telegrams: Mirror London EC1
Telex: 27286

Please Quote:-GM/62009/RL

From Marjorie Proops

Mr. H. Root,
139, Elm Park Mansions,
Park Walk,
London.S.W.10.

19th October,1979.

Dear Mr. Root,

Thank you for your letter which I read with interest.

Arguments both for and against payment to wives for housework can be very persuasive but looking at things from a purely practical point of view I don't think it is really feasible. After all - a man's wage provides the economic base of maintaining the family unit and only an eccentric sort of man would insist on spending his income solely on himself. Likewise, a housewife who insisted on a " wage" for herself is not being very sensible because surely a good and loving marriage is based on sharing everything and not upon cold and hard financial bargaining.

I hope that my comments have answered your question.

With all good wishes to you and your wife.

Yours sincerely,

S. Tra

ARJORIE PROOPS.

Marje Proops is away
so this letter is being
signed in her absence

Registered Office: Holborn Circus London EC1
A Company registered in England (No 168 660)
and a subsidiary of Reed International Limited

139 Elm Park Mansions,
Park Walk,
London, S.W.10

From: Lord Root
Chairman & Chief Executive
Henry Root Wet Fish

9th October 1979.

George Gale Esq,
The Daily Express,
Fleet Street,
London, E.C.4.

Dear Mr Gale,

I expect to be raised to the peerage in the near future and have therefore taken the precaution of having my new stationary printed in good time.

You will notice almost at once that I have utilised at the foot of the page one of your most telling pronouncements - a slogan which, if I may say so, encapsulates Tory thinking in a nutshell.

Well done!

It has been drawn to my attention, however, by my lawyers, Theodore Goddard & Co, that the use and publication of this without your permission could be considered a breach of copyright. They have suggested, therefore, that to be on the safe side I should write to you seeking the necessary permissions.

I should be most grateful to know that such permissions will be forthcoming.

Might I take this opportunity to congratulate you on your many fine polemical articles in 'The Daily Express'? You must be making quite a reputation for yourself and will no doubt soon be in a position to move on to a 'quality' paper such as 'The Daily Mail'. In the meantime 'The Express' can boast that in you and Jean Rook it has the two best writers in Fleet Street on the staff.

Well done!

Yours sincerely,

Henry Root

Henry Root.

Copy to Derek F.S. Clogg Esq, Theodore Goddard & Co.

"Common sense is a sturdy plant and self-interest a great fertiliser". George Gale

December 14 1979

Dear Henry Root,

Many thanks for the down-payment. I decided it was neither bribery nor corruption so spent it on champagne at [E] house.

By all means use the quote. I hope it sells well, just like hot cakes.

Yours ever,

[signature]

139 Elm Park Mansions
Park Walk
London, S.W.10.

Mr Francis King,
The Spectator,
56 Doughty Street,
London, W.C.1.

9th October 1979.

Dear Mr King,

I am presently compiling an anthology of great modern British
prose and I would like permission to include in it the opening paragraph of your book review in 'The Spectator' of 22nd September as
under:

'We all have lists of things that, though there is nothing
intrinsically wrong with them, just happen not to be to our tastes.
My own list would include restaurants in which the service is
better than the food and the decor than either; cars, however
large or powerful, with only two doors; ocean cruises; and literary
fantasies. The last of these aversions makes it impossible for
me fully to enjoy 'Orlando', 'Lady into Fox' or 'The Master and
Margarita', much though I admire Virginia Woolf, David Garnett and
Mikhail Bulgakov; and it also makes it difficult for me to be sure
of being fair to 'Wild Nights', much though I admire Emma Tennant
too'.

This is how criticism should be, and so rarely is. Poised,
urbane, civilised and always hinting at interests outside the
musty world of books. Well done! As my daughter Doreen (20) said
when she read it:

"Literary journalism of this distinction makes one realise
that Dr Leavis died in vain".

I enclose a stamped addressed envelope for the courtesy of
your permission or for the name and address of your accredited
representative should you prefer to be handled by others.

I look forward to hearing from you.

Yours sincerely,

Henry Root

Henry Root.

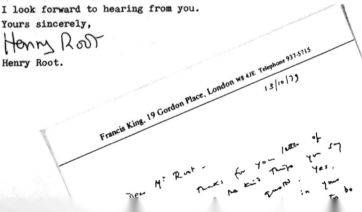

Francis King, 19 Gordon Place, London W8 4JE Telephone 937-5715

13/10/79

Dear Mr Root -

Thanks for your letter of
the kind things you
quoted. Yes,
in your
To be

139 Elm Park Mansions
Park Walk
London, S.W.10.

Mr Victor Matthews,
Trafalgar House Investments Ltd,
1 Berkeley Street,
London, W.1.   16th October 1979.

Dear Mr Matthews,

I gather you own 'The Evening Standard'. Well done! It makes a vital contribution to the artistic life of London — or so it always claims. Nothing wrong with that.

It surprises me, however, that you don't encourage your jounalists to reply to letters from ordinary folk on pertinent issues. Surely intercourse between journalist and reader is the life-blood of a popular newspaper?

On 6th September I wrote to your occasional columnist from Norway, Mr And Peter Forster, congratulating him on the way he has settled in among us, but chiding him for his suggestion that we should all carry identity cards so that the police might more easily distinguish between residents and tourists.

It's not in my nature to get anyone into trouble, but I have to tell you that he didn't reply. So, on 21st September I wrote to him again, gently pointing out that in this country it was considered polite to reply to letters. And, to encourage him, as it were, I enclosed <u>two</u> 10p stamps.

These he seems to have pocketed! One must make allowances for newcomers, of course, but I doubt whether pocketing a fellow's stamps is on even where Forster comes from.

As I say, I don't want to get the poor chap into trouble, but could you take him to one side and mark his card?

I look forward to hearing from you and to receiving a reply from Mr And Peter Forster on the burden of my two letters.

Yours sincerely,

Henry Root

Henry Root.

TRAFALGAR HOUSE LIMITED

1 BERKELEY STREET · LONDON · W1X 6NN

TELEPHONE 01 499 9020
CABLES TRALON G

TELEX: 21341

23rd October, 1979

H. Root, Esq.,
139 Elm Park Mansions,
Park Walk,
London, S.W.10.

Dear Mr. Root,

Thank you for your letter of the 16th instant the contents of which I have noted, and I am passing this on to the Editor of the EVENING STANDARD so that he may look into this.

Yours sincerely,

Victor Matthews,
Group Chief Executive
and Deputy Chairman.

Directors: Nigel Broackes (Chairman)   Victor Matthews (Deputy Chairman and Chief Executive)
G. C. D'Arcy Biss   Sir Francis Sandilands, CBE   G. H. B. Carter   E. W. Parker (Managing Director)
V. A. Grundy   P. R. Howell   H. W. A. Francis, CBE   W. B. Slater, VRD   The Marquess of Tavistock
Registered Office: 1 Berkeley Street, London, W1X 6NN.   Company No. 867281   D. J. Groom   D. M. Taylor
Registered in England.

Evening STANDARD

P.O. Box 136 47 Shoe Lane LONDON EC4P 4DD

Telephone 01-353 8000 Telex 21909

From the Editor

26 October 1979

Dear Mr Root,

Mr Victor Matthews has sent me your letter of 16 October. I agree with you that nothing is more infuriating than to write a letter to someone requiring a reply and to get nothing back, particularly when you've enclosed stamps.

Mr Forster is a freelance who is not on my staff, but I have written asking him to reply to your letter.

Yours sincerely,

CHARLES WINTOUR

H Root Esq.,
139 Elm Park Mansions,
Park Walk,
London SW10.

EVENING STANDARD CO., LTD.

Registered Office 47 SHOE LANE LONDON EC4P 4DD   Registered London No 193452

139 Elm Park Mansions
Park Walk
London, S.W.10.

Mr Denis Thatcher,
10 Downing Street,
London, S.W.1.   18th September 1979.

Dear Thatcher,

As you will know, I have kept in close touch with the Prime
Minister, your wife, over the past few months, advising her as to
door-step opinion. She's a very busy woman, of course, so generally
some fellow called Ryder replies, but he seems a civil enough sort
of chap.

Anyway, it occurred to me today that she probably gets a lot
of letters and that it would make a nice change for you to find one
on your breakfast tray.

Incidentally, I'm much enjoying your correspondence now appearing in 'Private Eye', but one thing puzzles me. How do the letters
come into their possession? I can't believe that you've sold them
first serialisation rights, particularly since many of them seem to
touch on confidential matters. Surely there's a 'D' notice on all
the tippling that goes on at No 10, not least your own? Is there a
mole at HQ? Or have 'Private Eye' an operative who makes it his
business to introduce himself via a drain-pipe into your quarters
at a late hour for the purpose of going through your files? I'd
put little beyond them. My friend Sir James Goldsmith had a lot of
trouble with them. Did you know that at the time of his courageous
court case against them last year it was their custom to rummage
through his dustbins in search of discreditable scraps and droppings.

Perhaps you could advise me on a small matter. I'm of a mind
to join Deal Golf Club, of which I gather you're a member. In your
letter to your pal Bill published in the current 'Eye' you refer to
an incident involving a homosexualist treasurer who had his finger
in the till and elsewhere too I wouldn't wonder. Has this been sorted
out, and is the club now on a sound moral and financial footing? I
certainly don't want to enrol myself if there are still irregularities
upstairs at the 19th.

Keep up the good work! Your wife, Mrs Thatcher, is an inspirational leader and though you must sometimes tire of playing Yvonne
to her General de Gaulle, I'm sure your support is priceless.

I look forward to hearing from you, Denis.

Yours sincerely,

Henry Root

Henry Root.

1O DOWNING STREET

5th October 1979

Dear Mr. Root,

Mr Thatcher has asked me to reply to your letter of
18th September.

As an assiduous observer of and listener to
"door step opinion",which must necessarily occupy
a great deal of time, it may have escaped your
notice that "Private Eye" magazine has over
the years published several features (eg Mrs
Wilson's Diary and Heathco) which purported to
be authentic.   My researches have revealed
that they were simply imaginative figments
of journalistic enterprise.   The present
"correspondence" in the pillar of the publishing
establishment merely follows that tradition.

It therefore follows that your enquiry concerning
potential membership of a particular golf club might
more appropriately be made to the officers of the
club.

Yours sincerely

Derek Howe

Derek Howe
Political Office

H Root Esq

139 Elm Park Mansions
Park Walk
London, S.W.10.

The Secretary,
Deal Golf Club,
Deal,
Kent.   10th October 1979.

Dear Sir,

    I hereby nominate myself for membership of your well-run club on the personal recommendation of Mr Denis Thatcher.

    He tells me that you have managed to clear up the unpleasantness you had involving a homosexualist treasurer with his hand where it shouldn't have been and that a gentleman can now associate himself publicly with your club without qualms.

    Well done!

    I gather that your greens are of the best and your bunkers an adequate hazard off the tee. However, I should like to try them out for myself and to this end I shall be arriving with Mrs Root and my two youngsters, Doreen (20) and Henry Jr (15), for a round before lunch on Sunday 28th October. Kindly ensure that there is a space in your car park for my Rolls Royce HR1.

    Neither Mrs Root nor I have essayed the game before, but we are expensively equipped as to clubs and wardrobe. Do you hire motorised buggies by the hour? Mrs Root has a leg, you understand, and humping my new Gary Player specials round the course might prove too much for her. (Don't worry! Whatever she may lack in expertise out on the links, she'll more than compensate for by her performance at the 19th! She was a cocktail waitress in her younger days and can still sing twelve verses of 'Get off the Table, Mabel, the Money's for the Beer!' with little prompting.)

    Thatcher tells me that there's a queue of folk eager to join your club in spite of the unfortunate publicity, so to encourage you to leap-frog me up the waiting-list I now enclose a fiver for yourself. No need to tell the rest of the Committee about your windfall. They'll all want a 'drink'!

    I look forward to meeting you on Sunday 28th October. Perhaps you'd care to lunch with us? Bring your good lady, by all means, but let's go dutch. I don't want to kick off with a large mess bill!

    Yours to the 19th!

Henry Root

Henry Root.

Royal Cinque Ports Golf Club Ltd.
Deal

22nd October, 1979

H.Root, Esq.,
139, Elm Park Mansions,
Park Walk,
LONDON.S.W.10.

Dear Sir,

    The Secretary of the Royal Cinque Ports Golf Club has passed to
me your letter of 10th October.

    I enclose herewith a cheque for £5.00 in return for the
cash enclosed with your letter, which you sent as an inducement
in order to enhance the possibility of being elected a Member
of the Royal Cinque Ports Golf Club. The Secretary never has
and never will be a party to this sort of financial inducement.

Yours faithfully,

GORDON C. TAYLOR
CAPTAIN

The Company is registered in England. No. 475915.
Registered Office: Royal Cinque Ports Golf Club, Golf Road, Deal, Kent CT14 6RF

139 Elm Park Mansions
Park Walk
London, S.W.10.

Mr Denis Thatcher,   24th October 1979.
10 Downing Street,
London, S.W.1.

Dear Thatcher,

Oh dear oh dear! I applied for membership of Deal Golf Club as you suggested, and today I received this daft letter (copy enclosed) from some silly old fool telling me that they can't accept financial inducements!

Could you have a word with the old buffer next time you're down there? Obviously the Secretary's got the stick by the wrong end and I'm sending him a snorter today, but a stiff word from you might clear the air.

Sorry to trouble you with this. Anything I can do for you, just let me know.

Guess who I saw at 'The Bristol Suite' the other night? Old 'Tubby' Walton! I'd been first to the Embassy Club, where I'd had the shock of my life. Remember it in the old days? Davy Kaye and dancing partners who'd accept credit cards? Well, the place seems to be under new management and the bunnies are now men! That's right! I hadn't been there two minutes when some little fairy in satin trunks asked me if I'd care to dance! Sign of the times, no doubt. Anyway, I beat a hasty retreat and took myself off to 'The Bristol Suite', where I saw old 'Tubby' Walton. He was as smashed as a rat and under the table with a coloured 'hostess' who had a ring through her nose. He'd just made her his sole beneficiary under a new will he'd scribbled on a table-cloth. Should we tell Peggy, do you think? Anyway, I told him about my experience at 'The Embassy' and he said:

"The Embassy, eh? That puts me in mind of a rum thing that happened to me during the war. I had to go to Cairo on a diplomatic mission and when I arrived at the airport I hailed a taxi and said 'Take me to the Embassy, Abdul.' Well, the confounded fellow took me to some evil back-street establishment full of half-naked girls smoking things through pipes and Guardsmen sodomising everything that moved. 'No, no, no, Abdul!' I said. 'Not the British Embassy, man, 'The Embassy Night Club'!! You have to watch these Arabs."

Rather odd, don't you think?

All the best,

Yours,

Henry Root

Henry Root.

139 Elm Park Mansions
Park Walk
London, S.W.10.

The Secretary,
The Royal Cinq Ports Golf Club,
Deal,
Kent.

24th October 1979.

Dear Mullin,

What's going on? I sent you a fiver to pop me to the top of
your waiting-list and now I've received an extraordinary letter
from some fellow called Taylor (who claims to be a Captain, though
whether Army or Royal Navy he doesn't say) returning the fiver and
pointing out that financial inducements aren't acceptable!

What's it got to do with him? I suppose he wants a fiver too.
Well that won't wash with me and I may say that Denis Thatcher, on
whose express recommendation I applied for membership, will not
be at all pleased by this development.

I now return the five pounds together with a copy of a letter
I have today sent Thatcher. He's got better things to do than be
troubled by this sort of cock-up, so pull your finger out, there's
a good fellow.

I look forward to receiving the membership application forms
by return.

See you at the 19th!
Yours sincerely,

Henry Root

Henry Root.

139 Elm Park Mansions
Park Walk
London, S.W.10.

Lord Snowdon,
22 Launceston Place,   15th October 1979.
London, W.8.

Dear Lord Snowdon,

Here's a concept which could do us both a bit of good!

Some months ago I was commissioned by Jonathan Cape Ltd to produce a book entitled WOMAN WATCHING by HENRY ROOT. Far from being a mere stroke of publishing opportunism, cashing in on the rather dubious 'popular' success of 'Manwatching' by Desmond Morris, this was to be a serious study of how women comport themselves in private places when supposing themselves to be unobserved.

I went to work with Hasselblad and strobe, introducing myself incognito when least expected, and, as you will see from the enclosed photographs, obtained many telling angles before ejaculation.

Imagine my surprise when, after an eternity of editorial shadow-boxing and feminine dithering, Debra Byron (my editor at Cape) withdrew from the project!

Here's the scheme. It occurs to me that were the book to have an Introduction by yourself one would be at an advantage when closing a deal with another publisher, and the book on publication would have a better chance of attracting the mugs to boot.

I have in mind approximately 2000 well-chosen words by yourself for which I would pay handsomely. Perhaps you would prefer me to tie up the details with your agent, if you have one. I myself, being a businessman of various experiences not all to do with fish, represent myself to advantage, but you may prefer to be handled by others. Nothing wrong with that.

Might I congratulate you on your excellently designed monkey-house at London Zoo? I was there on Saturday with my young nephew Bruce (5) and was quite impressed. You couldn't see the monkeys, but no doubt that was just as well. Not your fault.

I look forward to hearing from you and I enclose a stamped addressed envelope for the return of my prints after due scrutiny. I wouldn't want to see them in 'Playboy' magazine under your name!

Yours sincerely,

Henry Root

Henry Root.

23rd October, 1979.

Dear Mr. Root,

I am writing on behalf of
Lord Snowdon to thank you for your
letter of 15th October.

Although he appreciates the thought
which prompted you to write it is with
regret he is unable to take advantage
of your suggestion.

I enclose the photographs you kindly
sent with your letter.

Yours very sincerely,

Dorothy Everard

Personal Assistant to
The Earl of Snowdon.

Henry Root, Esq.

139 Elm Park Mansions
Park Walk
London, S.W.10.

Mrs Deborah Owen,
78 Marrow Street,
Limehouse,
London, E.14.

16th October 1979.

Dear Mrs Owen,

I'm so sorry I haven't replied sooner to your sensible
letter of 21st September in which you were honest enough to point
out that you knew nothing at all about the live theatre. Never
mind. Your suggestion that you should represent me merely in
the world of books suits me excellently, and I now enclose a
synopsis of my work in progress - SEMINAL THINKERS IN A NUTSHELL,
edited by HENRY ROOT - together with correspondence relating
thereto between myself and the house of Sidgwick & Jackson.

From Lord Longford's letter you will see that his firm
teetered on the very brink of buying the concept, only to gather
up their skirts and draw back nervously like a silly girl startled
by a mouse.

Before nominating another publisher, I thought I might pick
your brains (you might as well earn your 5%!) What about Weidenfeld
and Nicolson? Are you familiar with Lord Weidenfeld himself? I
have always suspected that he might be my sort of person, but are
they serious publishers? Or are they primarily in the catering
business, occasionally celebrating a party by bringing out a book
by a ballet critic, a titled pop historian or a dizzy Irish lady
novelist with her head in the literary clouds and her mind on
matters below the belt?

I look forward to hearing your reaction and I would like you
to know how much more secure I feel about my literary future now
that my affairs are to be responsibly represented.

Yours sincerely,

Henry Root

Henry Root.

DEBORAH OWEN
LITERARY AGENT · 78 NARROW STREET
LIMEHOUSE · LONDON E14 8BP
TEL: 01-987 5119 CABLES: DEBOWEN LONDON E14

22nd October 1979

Henry Root Esq
139 Elm Park Mansions
Park Walk
London SW10

Dear Mr Root,

I fear that you misunderstood my letter to you of September the 21st.

I did write to you primarily to tell you that I do not represent theatrical works but in fact I should also have said that I am not taking on any new writers at the present time. This is a very small agency and one of the realities of staying small is that I have to accept the limitations that this involves - ie: sticking to the number of authors that I know I will have time to look after.

Therefore, I must thank you for your s.a.e. once again and return to you your synopsis and letters.

Yours sincerely,

M. J. Dooling

Encls.

Deborah Owen Limited
Registered in England at the above address No. 1009342

139 Elm Park Mansions
Park Walk
London, S.W.10.

The Managing Director,
Robson Books,
28 Poland Street,
London, W.1.   25th October 1979.

Dear Sir,

        I have just returned from Selfridges department store where
I and Mrs Root attended a signing session held for 'David Jacobs's
Book of Celebrities' Jokes and Anecdotes', and I want you to know
that we're both still roaring with laughter at the amusing antics
of Mr Jacobs himself, Reggie Bosanquet, Arthur Mullard and Ernie
Wise! (Reggie seemed to have had a very good lunch! Let's hope
he's not reading the news tonight!)

        The book itself is a splendid rib-tickler and should do very
well as a stocking-filler for undemanding folk this Christmas. Well
done!

        What's more, it's given me this solid idea! Might not 'The
Book of Celebrities' Most Embarrassing Incidents' do even better?
I have in mind all those hilarious anecdotes 'personalities' recount
on 'chat' shows, usually involving matters appertaining to the
water-works in the case of men and, in the case of female celebrities, the collapse of their knicker elastic on formal occasions!

        Since the best of these anecdotes tend to be told on 'The
Parkinson Show', I think it might be a sharp idea to rope in
Michael as co-Editor. What do you think?

        I now enclose for your consideration a suggested list of
anecdotes and some of the celebrities we should invite to participate.

        I look forward to receiving the go-ahead to use your name.

        Yours sincerely,

        Henry Root

        Henry Root.

The hilarious story recounted by Esther Rantzen on 'The Michael arkinson Show' about the time she was drying her hair (stark naked!) n front of the gas fire in theatrical digs (this was when she was still a member of the general public). Someone (a man!) entered the room unexpectedly and was brought face to face with the sight of Esther's backside! (I can't remember all the hilarious details, but I'm writing to Esther today asking her to furnish me with same.)

2. The incident involving that urbane actor Rex Harrison and the loose toilet seat! Harrison was at a smart showbiz party and had occasion to visit the loo! (It happens to all of us - even to celebrities!) Unbeknown to Rex, the loo seat was new and had not been properly fixed! He aimed a kick at the cat (which had accompanied him uninvited into the smallest room!) and shot feet first through the door (he'd forgotten to lock it!) and down the stairs, arriving like a man on a toboggan among the other celebrities in the lounge-room!

3. The hilarious incident concerning David Niven and the missing Mess sherry! This occurred before Niven became a celebrity. He was still in the army at the time and was stationed in India. One evening the Colonel of Niven's regiment noticed that some of the best sherry was 'disappearing' and suspicion naturally fell on the darky mess-wallah. At Niven's suggestion, the bottle of sherry was passed round the table and the officers relieved themselves into it in turn! The next day more of the sherry had gone! So once again the irrepressible young officers filled it up by 'natural means'! This went on for a week or so. Then, concerned for the mess-wallah's health, they called him in and confronted him with the matter. It transpired that each evening he'd been putting a drop into the officers' soup!!

4. The celebrated occasion when Diana 'Revolving' Dors went to a fancy-dress party as a hula-hula dancer from Hawaii and won first prize as a thatched cottage!

5. The anecdote recounted by the lovely (and abrasively intelligent!) actress Diana Rigg (again on 'The Parkinson Show') about the first time she appeared nude on stage! She stepped nervously out of her clothes, whereupon a fellow in the front row of the stalls cried: "Get off! My girlfriend's got better boobs than that! Bring back the comic!"

6. The hilarious occasion when that witty writer Katherine White-horn lost her knickers at Royal Ascot just as she was being presented to Her Majesty the Queen!

7. The time when that exuberant, larger-than-life character, Oliver Reed went into a Turkish bath in the Fulham Road. He took off his clothes, piled them neatly in a corner and groped his way through

THE CELEBRITIES' BOOK OF EMBARRASSING INCIDENTS (cont.)

the steam to join the queue of men waiting to have a massage. Then
the steam cleared and he discovered he was in a fish and chip shop!
"What's it to be, madam?" enquired the proprietor, "cod or hake?"

9.   The incident when Joan Collins stepped out of the bath, trod on
her son's skate-board and shot out of the front-door and down the
drive! If her money-belt hadn't got caught in the gate-post she'd
have skated (nude!) down Old Church Street and into Kensington High
Street, putting 2p onto the rates!

10. The incident involving Anna Raeburn and the Peeping Tom who gave
himself up to the police!

11. The anecdote recounted by Terry Wogan about the men's relay race
at the nudist camp! There was a mix-up with the baton at a change-
over and one of the contestants was dragged half-way round the track!!

And many many more!

                                        © HENRY ROOT
                                          139 Elm Park Mansions
                                          Park Walk
                                          London, S.W.10.

ROBSON BOOKS LIMITED
PUBLISHERS
28 Poland Street   London   W1V 3DB
Telephone   01-734 1052/3
Cables   Robsobook London W1

2nd November 1979

Mr Henry Root
139 Elm Park Mansions
Parl Walk
LONDON SW10

Dear Mr Root,

Than you for your letter and suggestion. Was Reggie Bosanquet really
present at Selfridges? If so, perhaps it was I who had the very good
lunch...........

On the face of it, it is a good idea but how would it differ from the
<u>Book of Bricks</u>? If it is really on a different tack, and Mr Parkinson
would agree to participate, then we could be interested. I see you
have his name on the top of the outline. Does this mean you have already
approached him? Perhaps you would be good enough to let me have your
thoughts —— and, also, it would be helpful to have some information
on your good self. At this stage, naturally we cannot give the go—ahead
to use our name.

I'll look forward to hearing from you.

Yours sincerely,

JEREMY ROBSON

Registered in England 1097826. Registered office as above. Directors Jeremy Robson (Managing)

139 Elm Park Mansions
Park Walk
London, S.W.10.

Sir James Goldsmith,
Now!
161-189 City Road,
London, E.C.1.

21st October 1979.
Trafalgar Day! Let's Go!

Dear Sir James,

May I be the first to congratulate you on your excellent new
publication, NOW!? We needed a bang-up-to-the-minute _news_ magazine
and NOW! fills the gap superbly. Your exclusive this week on the
sinking of the Titanic was especially timely. Well done!

I would also like to congratulate you on your balanced review
of 'Goldenballs', so-called Richard Ingrams's book about yourself.
That it is an ill-considered hotch-potch of lies, sneers and innu-
endoes comes as no surprise.

I gather the publishing trade is furious with you for reviewing
the book before its official publication day. How absurd! Why
should one wait - entirely to oblige a publisher - till publication
date to nail a slur? I believe, in fact, that you may have started
a viable new trend, which is to review books at _any_ time, possibly
even before they are written. This would serve two purposes. An
adverse review might disuade an author from writing a worthless
work, whereas a rave notice would encourage him to go to his typewriter.

It so happens that for some months I have been trying to
arrange publication of my own first novel - DAY OF RECKONING by
HENRY ROOT. From the enclosed copies of correspondence with the
house of Cape, together with the synopsis of the work, you will
see that it is a book of substance and that Cape were on the point
of publishing it when an attack of editorial cold feet caused them
to withdraw.

It occurs to me that were you (or someone else better qualified, nominated by your Literary Editor) to give the book a favourable review at this stage, another publisher might be persuaded to
take the book on.

I look forward to hearing from you.

Yours against conspirators in the media!

Henry Root

Henry Root.

TELEPHONE 01-480 5676

65-68, LEADENHALL STREET.

LONDON.

EC3A 2BA.

26th October, 1979.

H. Root Esq.,
139 Elm Park Mansions,
Park Walk,
<u>LONDON S.W.10</u>.

Dear Mr. Root,

Thank you very much for your letter. *(of books)*
Unfortunately we are not in the publishing
business, so we cannot be of any direct help
to you but I am sending your letter onto the
Chief Executive of W. H. Allen to see whether
he has any interest in your project.   No
doubt he will be in touch with you.

Yours sincerely,

<u>James Goldsmith</u>

139 Elm Park Mansions
Park Walk
London, S.W.10.

Mr Bruce Page,
The New Statesman,
10 Great Turnstile,
London, W.C.1.

23rd October 1979.

Dear Mr Page,

I hereby nominate myself for the post of Assistant Literary Editor as advertised in recent issues.

Let me specify at once that I am not a regular reader of your paper. However, my daughter Doreen (20) takes it for her sins, so I have glanced through it often enough to see why you are eager to make a clean sweep of your reviewing staff. The mistake of the present incumbents is to review exclusively the work of so-called experts and self-appointed cranks.

As was recently pointed out in a letter in your correspondence columns by no less an authority than Alan Bennett (who, as you may remember, was one of the four clever young dentists who took the town by storm some years ago in the spoof review 'Beyond the Fringe'), the only readable bits in your paper are now written by that comical old party, Arthur Marshall. Hear! Hear!

It will be my policy as Deputy Literary Editor to recapture readers lost to your more urbane competitor, 'The Spectator'. Like the Literary Editor of that excellently civilised journal, I shall select my reviewers for their knowledge of wine, haute cuisine, gaming, cricket, blood sports and fisticuffs, and I will ensure that only books of general interest — such as 'David Jacobs's Book of Celebrities' Jokes and Anecdotes' — are covered. (Arthur Marshall would write hilariously on this, but it's a smoked sprat to a porpoise that under your present literary staff it won't even be reviewed.)

You'll want to know a little about me. Educated (like you, I imagine) at the University of Real Life, I went early into the wet fish business and, by keeping wages low and refusing to recognise the unions, so flourished that I was able to retire to my corner a few years ago. On the advice of my friend Jeffrey Archer (do you know him, Bruce? Nice little man, bright as a button), I have now turned my considerable energies to literary matters and my work in progress includes: DAY OF RECKONING by HENRY ROOT, a novel rejected by Cape; WOMAN WATCHING by HENRY ROOT, a psychological study of women and madness (with an introduction by Lord Snowdon), commissioned by Cape, but then rejected after much editorial dithering (photos enclosed); and SEMINAL THINKERS IN A NUTSHELL, edited by HENRY ROOT.

I enclose synopses of these plus correspondence appertaining, and I would be grateful if you would return them to me after due scrutiny.

Let's smoke out the wet left and recapture the middle ground from 'The Spectator'!

I look forward to meeting you, Bruce, and to discussing the terms of my employment.

Yours sincerely,

Henry Root

Henry Root.

NEW STATESMAN

Registered Office:
10 Great Turnstile, London WC1V 7HJ
01-405 8471   Telex 28449
Cables: Newstat, London WC1

23 October 1979

Henry Root,

ew of the large number of applications for
post, I apologise for sending you a standard
informing you that unfortunately your
cation was not successful. The new Deputy
ary Editor will be Paul Binding.

sincerely,

Caute
ry Editor

The Statesman
Reg
rd Hoggart. Directors:
ce Page, E. F. Peacock,

Mr David Caute,
The New Statesman,
10 Great Turnstile,
London, W.C.1.

139 Elm Park Mansions
Park Walk
London, S.W.10.

30th October 1979.

Dear Caute,

Thank you for your roneod reply to my letter of 23rd October,
applying for the post of Assistant Literary Editor under you.

'I apologise for sending you a standard reply', you wrote.

Your apologies are not accepted. I thought you left-wingers
were all for brotherly love and the small man (not that I'm a small
man, you understand. Merely a novice in the world of letters.)

In applying for the job I took the trouble of sending exampl
of my work in progress, to show I was qualified for the job. The
least you could have done was cast your eye over these and append
your valuable assessment. Raymond Mortimer must be turning in his
grave at such high-handedness from one of his successors.

I now return my work in progress and look forward to receivi
your comments.

Yours sincerely,

Henry Root

Henry Root.

PS. Sorry to see Julian Barnes is back. I thought you'd got rid
of him. Why don't you employ a TV critic with something to say l
Richard Ingrams?

Copy to Bruce Page.

Dear Mr Root,
Your stuff has no interest for me
Anything further from you will go into the
wastepaper basket.
David Caute

139 Elm Park Mansions
Park Walk
London, S.W.10.

Mrs Mary Whitehouse,
National Viewers and Listeners Association,
Ardleigh,
Colchester,
Essex.   24th October 1979.

Dear Mrs Whitehouse,

So! According to your doctor you've lost your voice because you talk too much.

This blow comes at a time when we can ill afford your vocal absence from the 'media' scene. Who else is to speak out against the pornographers, left-wing subversives and gay Christians coming out of the toilet? Wherever one looks, the family is being threatened.

Couldn't we get a second opinion?

Please God your voice will soon return. Meanwhile here's an amusing anecdote which may help to cheer you up. Miss Sally Ann Voak, 'The Sun's' expert on health, diet, yoga, astrology, levitation, foreplay, transcendental meditation and related difficulties wrote an article recently explaining how top Hollywood lovelies live longer and lead an active sex life well into old age ('Ginger Rogers! And She's 76!') by observing strict eating habits. In the course of her reseraches for the article, Miss Voak spoke to several top Hollywood lovelies on the telephone, including Telly Savalas (TV's Kojak!) He admitted that he often forgot his diet, stuffing himself instead with unhealthy junk foods.

"I have this problem," he growled. "I've got this sweet tooth. I can't resist ice-cream with lashings of chocolate sauce."

"Crushed nuts?" asked Sally.

"No," said Telly. "Just a touch of laryngitis."

Eh? Not bad? It helps to have a good laugh, don't you think?

How about a signed photo, Mary? If you're to be 'off the scene' for a while, it would be nice to have a really good picture to remember you by. Being a retiring sort of person, only allowing yourself to be dragged into the limelight by your sense of duty to the community, you may not keep a stack of photos handy, but I'm sure you must have an old snap-shot somewhere you could let me have. I enclose a pound to cover your expenses.

Get well soon!

Yours sincerely,

Henry Root

Henry Root.

NATIONAL VIEWERS' AND LISTENERS' ASSOCIATION

Hon. General Secretary :
Mrs. MARY WHITEHOUSE
Ardleigh, Colchester
Essex CO7 7RH
Tel. Colchester 230123

26th October 1979

Mr. Henry Root,
139 Elm Park Mansions,
Park Walk,
London SW10.

Dear Mr. Root,

Thank you very much for your very kind letter to Mrs. Whitehouse
and most generous contribution towards expenses.

I'm afraid she really does have to cut down the amount of public
speaking she undertakes, but as requested I have pleasure in enclosing
a photograph.

Yours sincerely,

Anne Boyle
Mrs. A. Boyle
Secretary to Mrs. Whitehouse

139 Elm Park Mansions
Park Walk
London, S.W.10.

P.C. Jim Jardine,
The Police Federation,
15-17 Langley Road,
Surbiton,
Surrey KT6 6LP.   26th October 1979.

Dear Constable Jardine,

Your recent letter in 'The Guardian' (my chauffeur takes it),
in which you pointed out that the unfortunate murder of Blair Peach
was retaliation by the Police for the killing of P.C. Kellam, had
my whole-hearted support. As you said, this made the score, in a
sense, one all.

However, a recent letter in 'The New Statesman' (my daughter
Doreen (20) takes it) from Mr Michael Meacher MP suggests that the
Police are in fact winning this particular contest, and by a
commendably wide margin. Mr Meacher pointed out that between 1970
and 1976 45 people died from non-natural causes while helping the
police with their enquiries, excluding suicide.

Even with the recent murder of a detective in Gloucester, that
makes the score:

The Police 46 - The General Public 2.

Not bad, and a clear refutation of the view being put about
that the police are losing the fight against lawlessness. Well done!

While I have your attention, might I point out that you never
answered my letter of 23rd April 1979, in which I asked you whether
my local candidate at the General Election, Mr Nicholas Scott, was
an officially approved Law and Order Candidate, supported by the
Police Federation.

I would have thought that law and order started with answering
letters!

Let's hope you answer this one!

Yours sincerely,

Henry Root

Henry Root.

Police Federation OF ENGLAND AND WALES

15-17 Langley Road Surbiton Surrey KT6 6LP Tel: 01-399 2224 (4 Lines)

Established by Act of Parliament

Our Ref: JTJ/MF

Your Ref:

31st October, 1979

Mr.Henry Root,
139, Elm Park Mansions,
Park Walk,
London, S.W.10.

Dear Mr.Root,

The short answer to your letters of 23rd April and 26th October 1979 is that I am far too busy with matters of real importance to bandy words with you on facetious comments. I note, however, that you choose to ignore the murder of five police officers in the period 1970-1976, which is a good indication of your general attitude.

On points of fact; I never said that the death of Blair Peach could be regarded as police retaliation for the murder of P.C.Kellam. As Mr.Peach died in April and Mr.Kellam in October, you will see that you were talking nonsense in attributing such a statement to me.

Two, there has been no 'recent murder of a detective in Gloucester'.

Three, the Police Federation does not, and never has, supported a political party or candidate. At the General Election we wrote to every candidate setting out our views on the question of the rule of law.

I am sorry to have to spoil your fantasies with facts.

Yours sincerely,

J.T.JARDINE
Chairman

Please reply to the Secretary

139 Elm Park Mansions
Park Walk
London, S.W.10.

P.C. Jim Jardine,
The Police Federation,
15-17 Langley Road,
Surbiton,
Surrey.

3rd November 1979.

Dear Constable,

I have before me your discourteous letter of 31st October in reply to mine of 26th October.

If this is the manner in which you write to those who support the work the police do, how on earth do you write to those who, in the words of that fine man, Mr James Anderton, are engaged in an orchestrated attempt to bring the police (and therefore democracy itself) into disrepute?

Goats and monkeys, man, I'm on your side! I was merely congratulating you for having the courage in these sentimental times to draw the public's attention to the fact that the Police do a very dangerous job which they can only prosecute effectively by occasionally resorting to over-robust methods. What's controversial about that?

I'm sorry I got the score wrong and I'm grateful to you for pointing out that it should read:

The Police 46 - The General Public 7.

Thank you for correcting the two other errors in my letter. I am of course delighted that there has been no recent murder of a detective in Gloucester. And I quite see that you couldn't have said that the Blair Peach murder was in retaliation for the murder of P.C. Kellam. I must have misread your letter in 'The Guardian'. Perhaps you could let me know whose murder it was that triggered off the Blair Peach killing?

I look forward to hearing from you.

Yours sincerely,

Henry Root

Henry Root.

Copy to Sir David McNee.

Police Federation OF ENGLAND AND WALES

15·17 Langley Road Surbiton Surrey KT6 6LP Tel: 01·399 2224 (4 Lines)

Established by Act of Parliament

Our Ref: JTJ/MF

Your Ref:

9th November, 1979

Mr.H.Root,
139, Elm Park Mansions,
Park Walk,
London, S.W.10.

Dear Mr.Root,

I have read again your original letter, in the light of your second one. I may well have mistaken your ironical style and misjudged your intentions, in which case I am quite happy to apologise.

Let me make it clear, however, that I am not going to accept all the premises in your letters.   I must reject the idea that there is a 'score' to be kept; those "killed by the police" and "police killed by the public".   In the latter, there is no doubt of the cause of death.   In the former, except for a number of cases where police officers have been forced to shoot armed criminals or deranged persons who were threatening others with firearms, the cause of death is inconclusive.   Mr.Meacher's references to 42 people who have died in police custody from other than natural causes or suicide is gravely misleading.   Inquests are held in such circumstances and my information suggests that in only two cases in recent years have inquests recorded verdicts which blame the police for the deaths.

Nor do I accept that people have been killed by the police in acts of vengeance.   I must repeat, I have never suggested that the death of Blair Peach was in retaliation for the death of any police officer.   All that I said was that people who raised an outcry over his death remained silent when a police officer was killed.   The Police Federation would never support a criminal action by a police officer.   We are not in the business of revenge.   Our concern is with the maintenance of the rule of law and the certainty of justice.

If my first reply was couched in rather peremptory terms, I should explain that I received a large number of 'pro' and 'anti' letters about the Peach case. Some of the 'anti' letters made the point about deaths in police custody, so I may have formed a wrong idea of your point of view.

Yours sincerely,

J.T.JARDINE
Chairman

139 Elm Park Mansions
Park Walk
London, S.W.I0.

Mr Michael Parkinson,
The BBC,
Television Centre,
London, W.I2.   26th October I979.

Dear Michael,

    Following the great success of 'David Jacobs's Book of
Celebrities' Jokes and Anecdotes', I have been commissioned by
Robson Books to produce 'The Celebrities' Book of Embarrassing
Incidents!'.

    In compiling a draft list of humiliating incidents showing
that celebrities are human like the rest of us but more so, I have
discovered that many of the most hilarious anecdotes were first
aired publicly on your lively 'chat' show. I have therefore
managed to persuade Robson Books to let me rope you in as co-Editor
on the grounds that having your name on the writing-paper will
make it easier for us to collect a fund of good stories from well-
known 'personalities'.

    I hope you'll agree with this arrangement. The concept
strikes me as very solid - not least because the 'celebrities' will
do all the work! All we'll have to do is listen to their anecdotes.
And we won't have to pay them much, if anything! A fiver an
anecdote should keep them quiet and we can cop all the royalties!

    Since the concept's mine, I suggest that you and I split
the take 70/30 in my favour. Let me know if this suits you and
I'll instruct Robsons to draw up the contracts.

    I look forward to hearing from you. We could make a lot of
easy money on this one, Michael!

    Keep pitching 'em on middle-and-leg!

    Yours sincerely,

Henry Root

Henry Root.

139 Elm Park Mansions
Park Walk
London, S.W.10.

The Commanding Officer,
The Royal Marines School of Music,
Deal,
Kent.   29th October 1979.

Dear General,

        I should like to enlist my boy Henry Jr under your firm
command as soon as possible.

        The lad's just turned 16 and frankly he's in shocking shape.
He sits around in his room all day, trying on his sister's clothes,
painting his finger nails and dreaming of life as a rock and roll
crooner.

        Short of sending him to one of Mr Willie Whitehouse's 'short,
sharp shock detention camps' (I've applied for a place at one of these,
but have so far received no reply from Mr Whitehouse) I see nothing
for it but a career in the services on the musical side of things.

        I gather he plays the trumpet, though his repertoire at the
moment is restricted to a version of Miss Channing Pollock's hit
tune 'Hullo Dolly'. I suppose that's a start.

        It so happens that I have just joined the Royal Cinq Ports
Golf Club at Deal and will be driving down with Mrs Root to inspect
the links on Sunday November 11th, so if it will be convenient for
you, Mrs Root and I will drop in on you in the afternoon of that
day to discuss the arrangements.

        I gather that 'a bit goes on' after lights-out in a military
atmosphere and (since Henry Jr needs little encouragement in this
area in my judgement) I wonder whether he could have a private room?
I'm told that you don't have to get up very early in the morning
to catch the Royal Marines with their trousers down these days.
Sign of the times.

        I look forward to hearing from you, General.

        Tell it to the Marines! Let's go!

        Yours sincerely,

        Henry Root

        Henry Root.

139 Elm Park Mansions
Park Walk
London, S.W.10.

The Commanding Officer,
The Royal Marines,
State House,
High Holborn,
London, W.C.1.   11th November 1979.

Dear General,

     My boy Henry Jr wears tights and plays the trumpet so, calcu-
lating that a career in the Marines might straigten him out, I wrote
to the Commanding Officer of the Royal Marines School of Music on
29th October, saying that Mrs Root and I would drop in on him on Sunday
11th November to chat things over.

     Receiving no reply, I sent him a telegram a few days later asking
him whether he was expecting us. To my amazement I received no reply
to this either!

     What's going on? Aren't you keen to recruit? I'd be most
grateful, General, if you'd look into this on my behalf, signalling
a rocket, if you deem it appropriate, to your fellow at Deal.

     Support the Iron Lady!

     Yours sincerely,

Henry Root

Henry Root.

FROM: Commander A W P KELVE Royal Navy

**Royal Navy, Royal Marines and
Women's Royal Naval Service**
State House High Holborn London WC1R 4TG

Telephone 01-405 9951 ext 53

H Root Esq	**Your reference**
139 Elm Park Mansions	**Our reference** LON 713/2
Park Walk	
London SW10	**Date** 13 November 1979

Dear Mr Root,

Thank you for your letter dated 11 November 1979.

I well appreciate the concern you must feel regarding your son, and his ambition to join the Royal Marines as a Musician.

At this stage I have no idea why your letter and telegram to the Commanding Officer RM School of Music were unanswered, but I can say that your letter to me, will be forwarded through the appropriate channels.

If Henry would make a formal application to the Careers Information Office State House (Reply card enclosed) then we will be delighted to see him, and I wish him luck in his application.

I am sorry that you have been caused any inconvenience, and hope that Henry will achieve his ambition.

Yours sincerely

Andrew Lewis

Royal Marines School of Music
Deal
Kent
Deal 62121 **Ext** 296

20/12/1

H ROOT
9 Elm Park Mansions
ark Walk
ondon SW10

29 Nov 79

AREER COUNSELLING

Reference:

A. Letter dated 29 Oct 79

¶. Thank you for the letter concerning possible enlistment for your son, Reference A.

2. It is requested that all detail be passed to:

Department of Naval Recruiting
Ministry of Defence
Old Admiralty Building
Spring Gardens
London SW1A 2BE.

S Down

S DOWN

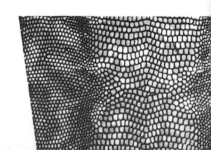

139 Elm Park Mansions
Park Walk
London, S.W.10.

Mr Michael Ivens,
40 Doughty Street,
London, W.C.1.

5th November 1979.

Dear Mr Ivens,

You will have been as shocked as I was to discover that in spite of two humiliating defeats in the courts, the vendetta conducted by 'Private Eye' against Sir James Goldsmith continues apace.

As you will have seen, an appeal to finance further cowardly assaults has just been set up by 'Private Eye' under the lamentably crude title of The Gillardballs Fund, but after four weeks of distraught pleading they have only been able to raise the paltry sum of £515.50.

To counter this, I and a few of Sir James's closest associates have formed 'The Friends of Sir James Goldsmith Against Moles in the Media Fund'. Various money-raising activities are planned and you may wish to show your solidity by joining a counter-revolutionary march which Paul Johnson has organised for Sunday 25th November.

Capitalists will muster at noon outside the Bank of England to participate in a programme of traditional right-wing, two-nations activities, the funds from which will go to the Sir James Goldsmith Appeal. Carrying banners proclaiming such divisive Tory messages as 'Greed is a Moral Responsibility!', 'Freedom to Rob under the Law!', 'Asset-Strippers Lib!', 'Support the Opaque Society!', "Winning is Good Business!' and 'It's All About Profits!', we will march first to Transport House, where we will burn stuffed effigies of Lenin, Benn, Vanessa Redgrave and Moss Hart on the steps outside and then make our presence known through the letter-box.

To demonstrate that elitism has an acceptable face, we shall then distribute food hampers from Fortnums among the low-paid workers of St George's Hospital before taking a party of miners' kiddies on a conducted tour of Westminster School (by arrangement with my friend Sir John Rae) so that they will discover the advantages they are missing because of their parents' lamentable lack of drive and prudence. First they will be confused by having Latin insults bellowed at them by the scholars of the sixth form; then they will be debagged and tossed into the Thames by the rowing eight; finally they will be flogged off the premises with damp towels and sent home whimpering to their parents.

Tired but satisfied, we will then respond to the Chelsea area, sneering at liberals, social security scroungers, boat-persons and kid-glove pansies on the way. Here we'll duff up a couple of lame ducks outside Sir Keith Joseph's delightful house in Mulberry Walk, where sherry wine will be purveyed in his charming lounge-room prior to an address on the virtues of monetarism.

I know Johnson will be most upset if you can't make it, and Sir James himself, needless to say, would take a very dim view of your failure to attend!

I look forward to hearing from you.

Yours sincerely,

Henry Root

Henry Root.

139 Elm Park Mansions
Park Walk
London, S.W.10.

The Commissioner,
The City of London Police,
26 Old Jewry,
London, E.C.2.

5th November 1979.

Dear Commissioner,

I enclose a copy of a letter which is being sent out to various leading capitalists concerning a monetarist demonstration planned for Sunday 25th November.

Since the march sets forth from a spot on your territory, I imagine that your permission for assemble might be necessary.

I take it that this will be immediately forthcoming since it is hardly to be conceived that a group of City gentlemen will comport themselves except with due regard for the requirements of law and order. Banners will be carried, but chanting will be kept to a minimum.

I look forward to hearing from you with the necessary permissions, and I would like to say that you would be more than welcome on the march yourself, albeit you're only a policeman. I imagine that you will be sympathetic with its aims.

Yours sincerely,

Henry Root.

Henry Root.

TELEPHONE 01-606 8866
EXT 226
TELEGRAMS ADJUTOR LONDON TELEX

OFFICIAL LETTERS TO BE ADDRESSED
THE COMMISSIONER OF POLICE
FOR THE CITY OF LONDON

PLEASE QUOTE REF
YOUR REF
M2/1617/79

CITY OF LONDON
"A" Department
37 Wood Street
London EC2V 7H

Dear Mr. Root,

8th November, 1979

I am directed by the Commissioner of Police for the City of London to acknowledge your letter of the 5th November, 1979, referring to a proposed demonstration on Sunday, 25th November, 1979.

In order to discuss your proposals and arrange police coverage for the event I should be grateful if you would telephone this office so that an appointment can be made.

Yours sincerely,

Chief Superintendent

Mr. H. Root,
139, Elm Park Mansions,
Park Walk,
London, S.W.10.

THE FREE ENTERPRISE ORGANISATION

Henry Root Esq   14th November 1979
139 Elm Park Mansions
Park Walk
LONDON S W 10

Dear Mr (   ) Root

    Many thanks for your kind invitation to march.
But I am afraid I must decline to walk behind deathbed
converts. Moreover, Private Eye is the only paper
that has ever carried the word "nice" about me, even
though it was quoted from somebody.

    My regards to Mrs Root, whom I seem to remember
once having met under curious circumstances in the
Levant.

Yours

Michael Ivens

40 Doughty Street, London WC1N 2LF   Tel: 01-405 5195

139 Elm Park Mansions
Park Walk
London, S.W.10.

The General Secretary,
The National Union of Journalists,
Acorn House,
314 Gray's Inn Road,
London, W.C.1.

5th November 1979.

Sir,
        I wish to complain about the behaviour of one of your members,
Mr Geoffrey Wheatcroft.
        I am presently engaged on the compilation of an Anthology of
Great Modern British Prose, and I wrote to him on 23rd August seeking
his permission to incorporate passages by himself, Mr Richard Ingrams,
Mr Taki, Mr George Gale and Dr Patrick Cosgrave, all of which first
appeared in 'The Spectator', of which periodical Mr Wheatcroft is,
as you may know, temporarily the Literary Editor.
        Receiving no reply, I wrote to him again on 15th September.
To this letter I got a note from his 'personal' secretary, Miss
Clare Asquith, apologising for Wheatcroft's general slackness and
high-handedness (part and parcel of being well-born and working
for a Tory magazine, no doubt) and saying that she'd be only too
happy to put a squib up him.
        Since I heard nothing further, I wrote again on 21st October,
asking what was going on. To my utter amazement, I have received
no reply to this letter at all!
        What can   do? Can you drum him out of the union, so that
he is no longer in a position (arrived at, no doubt, by the in-born
ability to skip with the agility of a mountain goat up the sturdy
mesh of the old-boy network) to obstruct the serious work of those
with a less dilettante attitude to the world of letters?
        I look forward to hearing from you.
        Yours sincerely,

        Henry Root

        Henry Root.
Copy to Geoffrey Wheatcroft.

NATIONAL UNION OF JOURNALISTS

Acorn House, 314/320 Gray's Inn Road, London WC1X 8DP
Telephone: 01-278 7916

Dictated 10th December 1979

c.c. General Secretary

CCM/G

12th December 1979,

Mr. Henry Root,
139 Elm Park Mansions,
Park Walk,
London S.W.10.

Dear Mr. Root,

Thank you for your letter to the General Secretary of November 5th. I must apologise for the delay in replying but I took my annual holiday in a lump this year and it has taken some time to catch up on back correspondence which had been passed over to me to handle.

Frankly I do not think there is anything that I can do to help you over your problem about getting Mr. Wheatcroft to give his permission to use passages by himself in your anthology of Great Modern British Prose. I am surprised that he is reluctant to give you permission unless he thinks that his work only qualifies for an anthology of Superb Modern British Prose, but his actions are not really ones that fall within the general requirements of the Union's Code of Conduct.

The only action the Union could take is if another Union member laid a complaint against Mr. Wheatcroft that he was guilty of a breach of our Code of Conduct, but I am afraid the behaviour about which you complain does not really fall within the terms of that Code of Conduct.

The only practical suggestion that I can offer is that you might perhaps write a tongue-in-cheek letter for publication in the Spectator saying that you are writing an anthology of Great Modern British Prose and you are somewhat staggered at the modesty of some people who are unwilling to give permission to have their prose appear in such an anthology.

Such reluctance perhaps maybe attributed to excessive modesty or an incredible lack of self-confidence in the prose itself.

A letter along those lines appearing in the Spectator might perhaps flush Mr. Wheatcroft out, I don't know?

The other flash of inspiration which has just occurred to me is that if the prose appeared in the Spectator the copyright therefore may belong really to the magazine itself since Mr. Wheatcroft as an employee gives up that copyright to the publication which employs him. You could therefore perhaps write to the Editor of the Spectator and seek his permission as Editor to reproduce work that has appeared in the magazine. Beyond that all I can suggest is that the preface to the anthology might say that work by certain people would have appeared but for their failure to give permission for it to appear. It is not unknown for prefaces to both thank people for their help and sometimes not thank people for their lack of help!

Yours sincerely,

CHARLES HARKNESS, DEPUTY GENERAL SECRETARY.

General Secretary: Kenneth Ashton   Deputy General Secretary: Charles Harkness

139 Elm Park Mansions
Park Walk
London, S.W.10.

Mr Malcolm Muggeridge,
c/o The BBC,
Television Centre,
London, W.12.   5th November 1979.

Dear Mr Muggeridge,

    I am naturally most disappointed not to have received the
courtesy of a reply to my letter of 4th October, particularly
since I enclosed the postage.

    I suppose you want money too for the cost of the photo. Sorry!
I should have thought of that. I now enclose a pound, which I
trust covers your expenses adequately in the matter.

    I look forward to hearing from you.

    Yours sincerely,

    Henry Root.

    Henry Root.

        This letter is extremely insolent. I have been
    abroad and only lately returned, and have no trace
    of your previous letter in a large accumulation of
    mail.

Mr Malcolm Muggeridge,
c/o The BBC,
Television Centre,
London, W.12.

139 Elm Park Mansions
Park Walk
London, S.W.10.

Dear Mr Muggeridge,

10th November 1979.

Congratulations on your recent performance on the TV Show, 'Friday, Saturday Morning'!

Your massive intellect soon reduced those so-called zany young men from Monty Python to quivering jelly and your awesome moral authority threw a cruel spotlight on their cheap, blasphemous jests. Well done! I found your performance inspirational, but my daughter Doreen, with whom I was watching, had her usual silly quibbles.

At one point you averred that you had once asked Sister Teresa what was the difference between her and a social worker. She had replied, you said, that a social worker was inspired by an idea, whereas _she_ was inspired by Christ. Were Christ to be revealed as not being who he claimed to be, she said, her work would be over. To which my daughter Doreen exclaimed:

"How disgraceful! If that is truly Sister Teresa's position, then her work has no ethical foundation whatsoever. If she does good work merely because she imagines herself to be commanded to do so by Christ, her position is morally symmetrical to that of a person who does evil work because he imagines himself charged to do so by the Devil. Albeit her work has good consequences, no more credit should be given to her than blame should attach to the man who is commanded by the Devil. If her explanation is that she recognises Christ's teachings as good, then, like the social worker, she is inspired by an idea. If she doesn't recognise Christ's teachings as good (by some other yardstick) why does she follow them? Either Sister Teresa's position is incoherent or, which is more likely, Muggeridge's account of it is."

Well, that's all gibberish to me, Malcolm, but I would be very grateful if you could explain the fallacy in her argument so that I can confound the irreverend young chit.

Later she took exception to your saying that were a blasphemous film to be made about Mohammad 'all the anti-racialists would be up in arms'. "Is not Muggeridge an anti-racialist?" she asked. So what if you're not!

Sorry you haven't replied yet to my letter of 4th October, nor to the follow-up with which I enclosed a pound. Don't worry. I expect you're a very busy man. Incidentally, ignore the PS to my first letter. It seems that the lady I mistook for your wife was in fact Mr Quentin Crisp, the male model. Sorry!

Yours sincerely,

Henry Root

Henry Root.

139 Elm Park Mansions
Park Walk
London, S.W.10.

22nd November 1979.

Mr Malcolm Muggeridge,
The BBC,
Television Centre,
London, W.12.

Dear Mr Muggeridge,

Frankly I'm baffled. On 5th November I wrote to you in the most civil terms, enquiring as to whether you had yet had time to digest the contents of, and formulate a reply to, an earlier and equally civil letter. To boot, I enclosed a pound to cover your expenses in the matter.

To my astonishment you returned my letter of 5th November, on which you had appendixed an unsigned note to the effect that it was extremely insolent!

In what consists the insolence? I do not accept your thinking on this, and now return the pound, pending an explanation.

All I want is a photograph of yourself (pulling, if possible, one of your funny faces) to add to Mrs Root's collection of media celebrities. What's wrong with that? You are reacting, if I may say so, like some immature crooner or association football player bleating about the invasion of his privacy consequent upon his becoming a 'personality'. If you don't like the heat in the kitchen I suggest you repair forthwith to the loungeroom. You should have thought of the pressures at the top before aiming yourself thither with such singleness of purpose.

Let's have a little Christian humility, Malcolm!

Yours sincerely,

Henry Root

Henry Root.

139 Elm Park Mansions
Park Walk
London, S.W.10.

Professor Sir A.J. Ayer,
10 Regents Park Terrace,
London, N.W.1.

17th November 1979.

Dear Sir Alfred,

I'm told you're qualified to settle two disputes - on the subjects of football and philosophy - currently raging in my loungeroom.

1. Last night the BBC News featured a football match between Ipswich and England.

"This isn't a game of football," expostulated my daughter Doreen (20), "it's a category mistake."

What was she talking about? It looked like a game of football to me.

B. Last weekend we were watching the TV show 'Friday Night, Saturday Morning', in which that eminent thinker Mr Malcolm Muggeridge was putting two zany young upstarts from 'Monty Python' through the threshing machine of his massive intellect. Discussing blasphemy, Muggeridge observed that he had once asked that saintly woman Mother Teresa to define the difference between herself and a mere social worker. She had replied that a social worker was inspired by nothing more than an idea, whereas she was inspired by a person, namely Christ. Were Christ to be revealed as not being who he claimed to be, she has said to Muggeridge, her work would be over. She would have no further interest in doing good. At this point my daughter Doreen declaimed:

"If that is a true account of Mother Teresa's position, her work has no ethical foundation at all. If she does good work merely because she imagines herself to be commanded to do so by Christ, her position is morally symmetrical to that of a person who does evil work because he imagines himself to be commanded to do so by the devil. Albeit her work is good, no more credit should accrue to her than blame to the man who is commanded by the devil. If then, like the social worker, she recognises Christ's teachings as good, her explanation is that she _is_ inspired by an idea. If she doesn't recognise them as good (by some independent criterion) why does she follow them? Either her position, or Muggeridge's account of it, is utterly incoherent. I suspect the latter. Poor old fool".

I'm sure my Doreen's talking nonsense and I think it important in the interests of law and order that the young chit be confounded. Could you pronounce her mistaken in a few crisp, well-chosen sentences? I'd be obliged.

Yours sincerely,

Henry Root

Henry Root.

IO REGENTS PARK TERRACE

LONDON NWI 7EE

01- 485 4655

28 November 1979.

Dear Mr. Root:

The term "category mistake" was introduced
into philosophy by my old tutor, Gilbert Ryle.
You will find that he makes considerable use of
it in his famous book, <u>The Concept of Mind</u>.
The point of your daughter's joke was presumably
that since the England team is a national football
side and Ipswich Town only a club side, they
belong to different categories.

On your second point your daughter is simply
right.   Many philosophers, including Leibniz and
Russell, have pointed out that morals cannot be
founded on authority.

Yours sincerely,

A. J Ay~

Professor Sir Alfred Ayer.

139 Elm Park Mansions
Park Walk
London, S.W.10.

Gay Noel Music Ltd,   21st November 1979.
24 Denmark Street,
London, W.C.2.

Dear gay Noel,
        Having occasion just now to look up the telephone number of
Gay Nites Women's Lingerie (Mrs Root's birthday looming, alas!) my
eye caught your entry in the directory – Gay Noel Music Co Ltd.
        Well done! I admire a man who admits of his proclivities pub-
licly, and what could be more public than the telephone directory?
It so happens that you might be in a position to help me. It is
becoming increasingly obvious to me that my boy Henry Jr (15), insofar as he wears tights and paints his fingernails, is of your
stripe. Nothing wrong with that. The fact is too that the lad
plays the guitar and pens songs of a protest nature, so I'm wondering whether you'd like to take him on?
        Of course you'll want to see the lad and hear his stuff before
committing yourself to representation, so I'll bring him in plus
tapes at 3pm next Tuesday week, 4th December. Let me know if this
won't suit. I'd hate to run through the door of your office to
find you were being attended to by your masseur in another part.
        I look forward to meeting you on the 4th!
        Yours sincerely,

        Henry Root

        Henry Root.

THE RICHARD ARMITAGE—NOEL GAY ORGANISATION LTD

NOEL GAY ARTISTS LIMITED

Registered Office: 24 DENMARK STREET . LONDON . WC2H 8NJ
Telephone: 01-836 3941/5 · 01-240 0451/4
Grams: Noelgay London WC2H 8NJ · Cables: Noelgay London Telex · Telex No: 21760

30th November, 1979

Henry Root, Esq.,
139 Elm Park Mansions,
Park Walk,
LONDON. SW10.

Dear Mr. Root,

Your letter dated November 21st.

I am afraid the Company can in no circumstances audition composers
in the first instance. Should you wish to send tapes they will be carefully
listened to.

Yours sincerely,

Lorraine Hamilton

R N M Armitage . R C Walker . G X Constantinidi . R Germains
in accordance with the Employment Agencies Act 1973-No. SE(A) 613
of the Agents Association Ltd. Registered in England No. 610415
this letter does not constitute a contract

139 Elm Park Mansions
Park Walk
London, S.W.10.

Michael Rubinstein Esq,
6 Raymond Buildings,
Grays Inn,
London, W.C.1.

3rd December 1979.

Dear Mr Rubinstein,

I'm told you know a certain amount of law, being commendably quick to act against those who commit a slur or slander.

Well done!

I'd like you to represent me in a matter of some delicacy but with a high profit potential. From the enclosed correspondence, you will immediately see that I had occasion some weeks ago to to invite certain well-positioned folk to join a monetarist march, organised by my friend Paul Johnson. One such receiving an invitation was Mr Michael Ivens of the Free Enterprise Organisation, AIMS.

Imagine my surprise when I received his reply, a copy of which I now enclose! I have quizzed Mrs Root most vigorously re the thrust of his accusation and I am satisfied that she has never been near the Levant (indeed she has never even heard of it) and that she has never met Mr Ivens under curious or any other circumstances.

This being so, you will agree with me, I take it, that Mr Ivens's letter constitutes a libel of a most disagreeable kind and insofar as my 'personal' secretary has read it, damage has already been caused, with many jokes of an off-colour nature being promulgated in the typing-pool.

I imagine that upon institution of proceedings recompense of an unusually punitive weight would be awarded to me in the High Court, and since I am eager to get this action under way as soon as possible, I would welcome the opportunity of an early conference.

Might I, incidentally, congratulate you on the way you have handled yourself in your many media appearances re the recent 'Professor' Blunt revelations? Being a plain man who has worked his way to the top of the pile in wet fish by the sweat of his brow and of those under him, I have little time for antique dealers, art historians of a Neopolitan bent, thirties pansies and full Colonels in the KGB who infiltrate her Majesty's household. But you were only doing your job. Nothing wrong with that.

I look forward to your providing me with the same excellent service.

Let's make money here!

Yours sincerely,

Henry Root

Henry Root.

MICHAEL RUBINSTEIN A. J. HUCKER JOAN RUBINSTEIN ANTHONY RUBINSTEIN
C. FOWLER   RICHARD H. BAX   T. R. H. ROBERTSON   H. ALEXANDER
R. I. YONGE   THOMAS HALL   MARGARET A. BROWN
CONSULTANT: R. A. H. CLARK

6, RAYMOND BUILDINGS,
GRAYS INN, LONDON, WCIR 5BZ.
TELEGRAMS: RUBINSTEIN LONDON W C I
TELEX NO. 21145 WHANDW G
TELEPHONE 01-242 8404

7th December, 1979

OUR REF   MR/AS

YOUR REF

Henry Root, Esq.,
139 Elm Park Mansions,
Park Walk,
London, S.W.10.

Dear Mr. Root,

Thank you for your letter of the 3rd December. I very much appreciate your kind remarks about my handling of the "Professor" Blunt revelations". (There is no need to put 'Professor' into quotation marks since he still has the right to be called by that title.)

Mr. Michael Ivens' letter does not appear to be headed "Confidential" but I gather that it was addressed only to you, presumably on the envelope as well as on the letter itself. The mysterious reference to your wife in the second paragraph if it were deemed defamatory of her, which is by no means certain, might entitle her to claim damages for libel in view of the publication of the letter to a third party, namely yourself, but would not, on the face of it, entitle you to succeed in such a claim. That your 'personal' secretary has seen Mr. Ivens' letter and as a result jokes, holding you or your wife up to ridicule, may be told in the typing-pool causing you damage, as you say, will not necessarily affect the interests of Mrs. Root in any possible claim against Mr. Ivens nor, of itself, entitle <u>you</u> to make such a claim.

The first question, therefore, is whether your wife would wish to make a claim against Mr. Ivens in respect of what you and perhaps she believed to be a defamatory innuendo in the last paragraph of his letter of the 14th November, which she would have to claim libels her to you and probably to you alone. I do not know myself whether the reference to a meeting "under curious circumstances in the Levant" would be recognised by anyone as necessarily involving a defamatory innuendo. This might be possible or it might be hard to prove. I think it more likely, however, that it would be defensible by Mr. Ivens if he chose to defend any claim made against him, as would be almost certain, as only intended as a harmless joke in the context of a friendly reply to your letter to him of the 9th November which, I am bound to say, reads to me as deliberately light-hearted although I appreciate that you may have intended it as politically serious. If I am right about the way that a jury would be inclined or persuaded to interpret this exchange of correspondence then I must tell you (and Mrs. Root through you) that there would be no prospect at all of either of you making money out of a claim against Mr. Ivens. You would have to place a substantial sum at stake before deciding to initiate proceedings and a sum well into five figures might be at risk should the action proceed to trial – in some two or three years time. Meanwhile, I am sure you would find that any possible damage done to either of you in the typing-pool would have been dissipated by the normal respect expected of those who work there and you might well recognise the disadvantages to you both of the prospect of being made to look ridiculous for having brought the action if the Plaintiff were to lose it or to be awarded only nominal or contemptuous damages at the end of the day.

You will understand from what I have written above that my advice is to ignore Mr. Ivens' letter and to put the whole incident behind you – and Mrs. Root too, of course.

2.

If you are dissatisfied with the above advice then I shall be glad to see you by appointment and would ask you to let me have a sum of £50.00 on account for costs incurred and to be incurred. Should you decide to take the matter no further, in accordance with my advice, I would appreciate your notifying me of that decision and would then propose to make no charge whatsoever for my advice in this letter.

Yours sincerely,

139 Elm Park Mansions
Park Walk
London, S.W.10.

Ms Jean Rook,
The Daily Express,
Fleet Street,
London, E.C.4.   5th December 1979.

Dear Jean,
        So - they call you the biggest bitch in Fleet Street! Nothing
wrong with that. Well done!

        I have read your column with interest for many years. You see
like a sensible old trout and you write with unusual flair. More t
the point, you always take a healthily pragmatic attitude to life's
many problems, and that is why I now address you.

        Frankly, Jean, I have for some time been casting round for an
excuse to dump Mrs Root. She's been a good mother to my two childr
Doreen (20) and Henry Jr (15), but she doesn't shape up too well on
all occasions and since, after many years of striving, I am at long
last getting somewhere in cafe society I would welcome upon my arm
occasions involving the boulevardier Norman St John Stevas and othe
of that ilk a somewhat younger woman.

        It so happens that the opportunity I've been waiting for seems
to have come my way. I have just received an extraordinary letter
from Mr Michael Ivens of the Free Enterprise Organisation, AIMS, in
which he alleges that he was familiar with Mrs Root 'under curious
circumstances in the Levant'.

        Whether this allegation is true or not, it seems that I have
two possible courses of action open to me. I can either line my
pocket by bringing (via Rubinstein) an action for libel against th
fellow Ivens (by no means a man of straw from all I hear), or I ca
take this opportunity of showing Mrs Root the door on the grounds
that she has cuckolded me with the aforesaid Ivens.

        Which should I do, Jean? To assist you in framing your advic
I enclose a typical picture of Mrs Root. It was taken on an occas
when, unmindful of the fact that we had guests of some consequence
in our loungeroom, she suddenly removed her clothes, put some Russ
music on the gramaphone and danced the mazurka with a rabbit on he
head. Albeit we're a musical household (it is not unusual for us
after dinner to entertain our guests with the cast album of 'Olive
or 'Hullo Dolly') this was going too far.

        I realise that you don't purport to be a kind of thinking man
Anna Raeburn, so I enclose a stamped addressed envelope for the
courtesy of your advice in the matter and for the safe return of
the snap of Mrs Root, which Rubinstein will no doubt need as evidence in such proceedings as I may decide to bring.

        I look forward to hearing from you, Jean!

        Yours,
        Henry Root
        Henry Root.

DAILY EXPRESS

Express
Newspapers
Limited

121 Fleet Street
London EC4P 4JT
Telephone
01-353 8000
Telex No 21841
Cable Address
Express London

11 December 1979

Mr H Root
139 Elm Park Mansions
Park Walk
LONDON
SW10

Dear Mr Root

Thank you for your letter.

I am certainly not a thinking man's Anna Raeburn,
so you must solve your own problems.

Yours sincerely

Jean Rook
Assistant Editor

Enc

Registered in London No 141748.
Registered office: 121 Fleet St London EC4P 4JT

139 Elm Park Mansions
Park Walk
London, S.W.10.

Lord Hugh Scanlon,
The House of Lords,
London, S.W.1.   6th December 1979.

Dear Lord Scanlon,

    In spite of your politics, you have always struck me as a pla:
man who shoots straight from the shoulder and no monkey-business.
For this reason, I now seek your advice on a matter of some relevan
to myself.

    For some time now I have been contributing steadily to both
Tory and Liberal Party funds with, frankly, the intention of being
elevated to the peerage on the recommendation of one or the other.
All is going according to the book and 'discussions' of a confid-
ential nature are now taking place between myself and, on behalf o
the Tories, an agreeable old stick called Major-General Wyldbore-
Smith (I expect you know him) and, on behalf of the Liberals, Miss
Edna McGregor of Flat K8, Sloane Avenue Mansions, London, S.W.3.

    However - the recent revelations re moles, pansies and Marxis
in the Establishment have caused me to reconsider my position. I'
a simple, self-taught man, your Lordship, born, like yourself, bel
the salt, and nothing wrong with that, I think you'll agree. A ma
worth is not to be judged by his knowledge of so-called 'art', muc
less 'art' of a Neopolitan slant. Here's the nub of it. Have you
since being raised to the upper house, ever been obliged to mingle
with antique dealers and homosexualists? Is the Establishment rif
with such and is one frequently obliged to take lunch with Rees-Mo
in Printing House Square with Mr Rubinstein on hand in case of all
ations?

    I am prepared to pay a heavy price (financial) to be elevated
to the peerage, but if the price includes eating smoked trout with
Thirties pansies and full Colonels in the KGB I might have to esch
the honour after all.

    Your valuable advise would be esteemed, my Lord, and since yo
don't hold yourself out as some sort of Marje Proops of the Upper
House, I enclose a pound to cover your costs in the matter.

    Yours sincerely,

    Henry Root

    Henry Root.

ENGINEERING INDUSTRY TRAINING BOARD

ST MARTINS HOUSE

140 TOTTENHAM COURT ROAD

LONDON W1P 9LN

01 387 0501

LORD SCANLON
CHAIRMAN

HS/TG

18th December 1979

Henry Root Esq
139 Elm Park Mansions
Park Walk
London SW10

Dear Mr. Root,

Please forgive the delay in replying to your letter of 6th December but in addition to being absent from London, I could not really make up my mind whether I should reply. However, I give you my advice not only freely, but in returning your pound note, I must emphasize that any official advice would be much more costly than you can afford.

If you had been more particular in the choice of your parents you could now have been in the House of Lords and one or all of the persons you describe, and this could not affect your right to take your seat and all the privileges the House confers. Because you were not so indulgent, there is nothing else I can suggest.

Yours sincerely,

139 Elm Park Mansions
Park Walk
London, S.W.10.

The Editor,
The Times Educational Supplement,
New Printing House Square,
London, W.C.1.   10th December 1979.

Dear Sir,

My chauffeur has just drawn my attention to an avertisement
for your journal in last week's 'New Statesman' mentioning an
article by someone called Anthony Quinton entitled 'Philosophy
in Small Doses'.

It's clear to me that either you or the aforesaid Quinton
'borrowed' this concept from my own proposed series SEMINAL
THINKERS IN A NUTSHELL Edited by HENRY ROOT, though how my
synopsis happened to fall into your hands I don't entirely
understand. I can only suppose that a mole within Sidgwick and
Jackson Ltd (the only publishing house yet to have seen it) leaked
a copy to you or Mr Quinton.

In case you think I'm testing the wind (as we used to say in
the Navy) I now enclose a copy of my submitted synopsis together
with correspondence applying thereto between myself and Lord
Longford. I think you will agree that the similarity between
'Philosophy in Small Doses' and SEMINAL THINKERS IN A NUTSHELL
Edited by HENRY ROOT is too pronounced to be fortuitous.

I trust this matter can be resolved to my advantage without
recourse to law, Mr Editor, so I look forward to hearing what action
you propose to take to repair some of the damage you have inevitably inflicted on my concept.

I enclose a stamped addressed envelope for the safe return of
my papers after you and your legal advisers have perused them.

Yours faithfully,

Henry Root

Henry Root.

Copy to Michael Rubinstein.

THE TIMES
Higher Education
SUPPLEMENT

Times Newspapers Limited, P.O. Box no. 7, New Printing House Square,
Gray's Inn Road, London WC1X 8EZ (registered office)
Telephone 01-837 1234 Telex 264971 Registered no. 894646 England

From the Editor   December 12, 1979

Dear Mr Root,

   Thank you for your letter of December
10.

   I can see no possible resemblance
between the headline chosen for the
article by Mr Quinton and your
"seminal thinkers in a nutshell"
synopsis.

             Yours sincerely,

             Pere Scott

             Peter Scott

Mr Henry Root,
139 Elm Park Mansions,
Park Walk,
London SW 10

139 Elm Park Mansions
Park Walk
London, S.W.10.

Sir Reginald Murley,
The President,
The Royal College of Surgeons,
35 Lincoln's Inn Fields,
London, W.C.2.

15th December 1979.

Dear Sir Reginald,

So - at last someone has had the courage to prescribe publicly
the correct treatment for heartless pickets! Your recent comments
as reported in the papers were an inspiration!

"Debag the cads!" you cried, "and daub them with brightly-
coloured dyes!"

Hear! Hear!

I should like to volunteer as a leading dauber in one of your
debagging squads and to this end I now enclose a pound towards your
initial expenses. These could be heavy, if we're to be as well
organised and quickly on the scene as Sir David McNee's flying
Special Patrol Groups. Might I suggest that, with the exception
of you and me, we recruit for the most-part public schoolboys?
They have most experience of the debagging and application of boot
polish to the water-works of those under them.

I await your instructions, Mr President! I can be ready at
the drop of a scalpel to debag within a radius of fifteen miles
of the above address.

Let's daub the parts of pickets first and ask questions later!

Yours sincerely,

Henry Root

Henry Root.

35-43 LINCOLN'S INN FIELDS, LONDON WC2A 3PN

Telephone 01 405 3474   Cables COLLSURG LONDON WC2

19th December, 1979

OFFICE OF THE PRESIDENT
Sir Reginald Murley, KBE,TD,MSMPRCS.

Dear Mr. Root,

Thank you for your kind letter and the enclosed pound note which I presume is a donation towards supply of gentian violet or other suitable dyes. My letter has evoked an extraordinary number of enthusiastic supporters who have contacted me in various ways. Strangely enough, I have not had any abusive letters nor indeed any reprimands from N.U.P.E. and C.O.H.S.E!

Yours sincerely,

Reginald Murley

President.

H. Root Esq.,
139 Elm Park Mansions,
Park Walk,
London, SW10.

JOHN HUNTER 1728-1793

139 Elm Park Mansions
Park Walk
London, S.W.10.

Lord Hailsham,
The House of Lords,
London, S.W.1.

23rd December 1979.

Dear Lord Hailsham,

I have been much disturbed recently by stories in the press about 'Operation Countryman', the so-called investigation into alleged police corruption in the Metropolitan and City of London forces.

Re-reading that fine man Sir Robert Mark's excellent book 'In The Office of Constable', I came across on page 230 a categorical statement to the effect that he had completely rid the Met of all corruption and wrongdoing (not that there had ever been very much in the first place). With characteristic humility he gives much of the credit for this achievement to those under him. 'Kellend and his men,' he writes, 'and, perhaps, more than anyone else, Jim Starritt, deserve an honoured place in Metropolitan Police history for putting and end to malpractice which had done the force incalculable harm for many year' (italics mine.)

So there we have it in black and white and from the horse's mouth. Since we can assume that Sir Robert is neither ignorant nor dishonest (we have his own word on that), we can conclude that 'Operation Countryman' is a shocking waste of public money and can only have been set up by those engaged on an orchestrated attempt to bring the police into disrepute.

Can you, my Lord, as head of Law and Order inform me why you have not put a stop to this expensive smear campaign?

I should like also to seek your advice on a more purely literary matter. Your opinion seems relevant because I gather you write rhymes and prose yourself and I see from the back of Sir Robert's book that you reviewed it favourably in 'The Sunday Telegraph'. I notice that Sir Robert has frequent recourse to quotation from Shakespeare, not least from Hamlet, the moody Dane.

'I might have been forgiven for thinking with Hamlet,' Sir Robert declaims at one point, 'that "The time is out of joint: O cursed spite/That ever I was born to set it right"'

In other parts he uses quotations from the Bard as chapter headings, comparing himself to such as Coriolanus and Mark Anthony (Othello and Bottom the Weaver nowhere get a mention.)

I myself have aspirations as a writer and I would be very grateful if you could inform me as an expert whether frequent references to such as Shakespeare are stylistically desirable, adding ballast to one's manuscript.

Since it is not your function, my Lord, to run a literary or legal advisory service, I enclose a pound to cover the cost of your trouble in these two matters.

Support the Met!

Yours sincerely,

Henry Root

Henry Root.

139 Elm Park Mansions
Park Walk
London, S.W.10.

Mr Robin Day,
'Ask Me Another!!',
The BBC,   7th January 1980.
Television Centre,
London, W.12.

Dear Robin,
    I'm prepared to participate as a member of the viewing public
in your popular TV panel show 'Ask Me Another!!' If nominated, I
shall put the following question to the team:
    "Do the celebrities think that Mrs Thatcher is the ordinary
man's answer to le vice anglais?"
    In the ensuing discussion I shall play a prominent part, elab-
orating my own thoughts on the matter.
    There'll be some demand to appear on your show, I expect, so,
being a man of the world like yourself, I now enclose a pound to oil
the wheels of my nomination. I enclose too a photo of my head.
As you will see, I am square-built like yourself with a forceful
personality which would show to effect on camera.
    See you in the studio, Robin!
    Yours sincerely,

    Henry Root

    Henry Root.

BRITISH BROADCASTING CORPORATION
LIME GROVE STUDIOS LONDON W12 7RJ
TELEPHONE 01-743 8000 TELEX: 265781
TELEGRAMS AND CABLES: TELECASTS LONDON TELEX

15th January 1980

Mr H Root
139 Elm Park Mansions
Park Walk
London S.W.10

Dear Mr Root

Thank you for your letter to Robin Day of 7th January.

You look a lovely fellow - not, I think, a picture of "head" so much as a portrait of hat and torso! Much as I would like to retain the wheel-oiling green-back, I am unfortunately an employee of the BBC, not a man of the world like yourself!

If you would seriously like to join the audience for "Question Time" one night, I would be only too happy to send you a ticket, or tickets, for the show. I cannot, however, guarantee that you would get a chance to put a question as the subjects debated are chosen on the night from the questions submitted by our audience on arrival - and decided by merit and newsworthiness. However, the opportunity is equal - so if you would like to come please write again or ring me on 01-743-8000 Ext. 3422/3 so we can agree a suitable date.

Thanks again for writing.

Yours sincerely

Barbara Maxwell

Barbara Maxwell
Producer, "Question Time"

Encs.

139 Elm Park Mansions
Park Walk
London, S.W.10.

Miss Barbara Maxwell,
'Question Time',
The BBC,
Lime Grove Studios,
London, W.12.

28th January 1980.

Dear Miss Maxwell,

Thank you for your letter of 15th January in reply to mine of
7th January to Robin Day.

I would indeed be prepared to appear on your excellent quiz
show on a date nominated by yourself, and look forward to receiving
an entry pass. (One would be sufficient, since I haven't appeared
publicly with Mrs Root following a disagreeable incident backstage
at the first night of Mr Ray Cooney's spoof musical 'Hullo Dolly').

I look forward to placing many apt questions and trust that
Miss Bel Mooney will not be among the celebrities on the panel. I
realise that you are now bound by statute to have a token woman on
the team, but I suggest that one with rather less to say for herself
than Miss Mooney might prove more acceptable. Might it not be a
good thing too (with regard to the ratings) to go for a 'looker'?
I have in mind such as Miss Fiona Richmond or Miss Vickie Hodge? It's
up to you, of course. You know what you're doing.

Please advise me in good time as to my wardrobe.

I look forward to hearing from you.

Yours sincerely,

Henry Root

Henry Root.

139 Elm Park Mansions
Park Walk
London S.W.10.

The Prime Minister,
10 Downing Street,
London, S.W.1

1st January 1980,

Dear Prime Minister,

So - it's honours for big business! Nothing wrong with that!
You were voted into office to promote the interests of your own
class - the lower-middles on their way up - and this is what you're
doing. Well done! The wets and have-nots may bleat, but they have
no one to blame but themselves. They were stupid enough to vote
for you!

How inspiringly your list reads compared to the last one,
which could best have been described as honours for tap dancers
and international criminals! (I gather that 50% of those recognised
were unable to bend the knee at the Palace due to the fact that
they were on Interpol's missing list! No, I'm only chaffing!)

I think the honours that will be greeted with most enthusiasm
by ordinary folk everywhere (apart from those so deservedly con-
ferred on various high street provisioners and drapers) are the
CBE for Norris McWhirter (the runner), the OBE for Emlyn 'The Flying
Pig' Hughes (he can't play for pussy, but he motivates the lads on
and off the ball), the OBE for Cliff Richard for his services to
music (he never did anything discreditable with a chocolate bar)
and the knighthood for John 'What I'm looking for is mediocrity,
laddie!' Junor. I don't normally approve of honours for intellectuals,
but I'm prepared to make an exception in Sir John's case. I'm only
sorry that, if you were going to include thinkers on your list,
you didn't find room for Malcolm Muggeridge, Philip Wrack and
Anna Raeburn. Next year perhaps!

Let's feel the lash of stern government in 1980! Roll back
the nanny state!

Your Man on the Door-Step!

Henry Root

Henry Root.

10 DOWNING STREET

8 January 1980

Dear Mr. Root,

The Prime Minister has asked me to thank you for your letter of 1 January. She was grateful to you for writing as you did.

The views which you expressed have been noted.

Yours sincerely,

J.B. Edmunds

Henry Root Esq

139 Elm Park Mansions
Park Walk
London, S.W.10.

The Editor,
The Daily Express.   ('The Voice of Britain'. Well done!)
Fleet Street,
London, E.C.4.
                                          21st January 1980.

Sir,

Like Mrs Patricia M. Edwards, a mother of Westo-super-Mare,
I too read with anger and concern the news in 'The Daily Express'
that Myra Hindley has gained an Open University degree in the
Humanities and is now a BA.

It is an outrage that she should be able to do this while the
unfortunate Mrs Edwards's son has been compelled to discontinue his
own studies due to the retirement of his teacher.

'If my son was in prison,' wrote Mrs Edwards, 'perhaps he
would have that misguided eccentric Lord Longford to compaign for him'.

Precisely! Recently Mrs Root's sister Beryl fell off her
bicycle and broke her pump. This couldn't have happened to Myra
Hindley for the simple reason that bicycles aren't allowed in
Holloway. What has the eccentric Lord Longford got to say to that?

Yours faithfully,

Henry Root

Henry Root.

c.c.   Lord Longford.

SIDGWICK & JACKSON
Limited
PUBLISHERS

Registered Office:

Telegrams: Watergate, London
Telephones: 01-242 6081 2 3

1 Tavistock Chambers

Place of Registration: London, England
Registered Number of Company: 100126

Bloomsbury Way, London W.C.1A 2SG

7th February 1980

Dear Mr. Root.

Thank you for sending me the letter
that you have written to the Daily Express.

To be quite honest, I wonder if you
are being serious or pulling my leg? You
can't really mean that some one in prison
for fourteen years should be denied educational opportunities, so I assume that you
feel I need a bit of teasing - which may
be true.

Please don't hesitate to telephone
me if you felt that we could make any progress that way.

Yours sincerely,

Lazzar

Henry Root, Esq
139 Elm Park Mansions
Park Walk
S.W.10

Managing Director: WILLIAM ARMSTRONG
Chairman: THE EARL OF LONGFORD, K.G., P.C.
Deputy Managing Directors: W.D. PROCTER, S. du SAUTOY
DAVID KARR (U.S.A.), R.A. SHADBOLT

139 Elm Park Mansions
Park Walk
London, S.W.10.

Lord Hailsham,
The House of Lords,
London, S.W.1.

4th February 1980.

Dear Lord Hailsham,

　　Congratulations on your recent ruling that, as head of the judiciary, various legal controversies (I refer to the jury rigging debate and the behaviour of judges not least old King-Hamilton) are none of your business. Well done! You've got better things to do than interpose your oar in legal matters.

　　Not so well done, however, re your failure to reply to my letter of 23rd December 1979 about the shocking waste of public funds involved in so-called 'Operation Countryman'. In the light of Sir Robert Mark's categorical assurance in his excellently written book 'In The Office of Constable' (good title!) that he left the Met as clean as the Aegean stables, I'd aver that 'Operation Countryman' constitutes a slander upon Sir Robert's person.

　　If you have no intention, my Lord, of replying to my points both as to Law and Order and writing style (see my references to Sir Robert's frequent resorting as to Shakespeare and the stylistic desirability thereof) I'd trouble you for my pound back which I appended to my letter of 23rd December.

　　Thanking you.

　　Yours sincerely,

　　Henry Root

　　Henry Root.

139 Elm Park Mansions
Park Walk
London, S.W.10.

Mr Michael Parkinson,
The BBC,
Television Centre,
London, W.12.

14th January 1980.

Dear Michael,
    I am disappointed not to have heard from you in reply to my letter of 26th October re 'The Celebrities' Book of Embarrassing Incidents' and my suggestion that you should co-edit this book under me.

    Never mind. Such is the viability of the concept that Robson Books Ltd are keen to proceed with or without your assistance, but I would still appreciate any 'near-the-knuckle' anecdotes you might be able to put my way. You must have at your finger-tips a greater fund of embarrassing (but harmless!) anecdotes than even Niven or Ustinov.

    So let's hear from you Michael! Remember - it's a fiver an anecdote and I never met a Yorkshireman who could let pounds sterling slip down the drain! So get your mind off all that top-drawer crumpet that I expect comes your way up at the BBC and start recalling some of the titillating anecdotes you've heard in your time as a professional celebrity!

    Incidentally, might I congratulate you on your excellent 'chat' with Miss Twiggy the singing mannequin last week? Many of the 'flat-chested' cracks were new to me. Well done! And when she spoke of Fred Astaire the talented old hoofer, your interjection - "They say he was incapable of a graceless movement!" - was most apt. Are such off-the-cuff ejaculations scripted or impromptu? You chat show hosts certainly have to be on your toes!

    I look forward to hearing from you, Michael.
    Yours sincerely,

Henry Root

Henry Root.

BBC tv

BRITISH BROADCASTING CORPORATION

TELEVISION CENTRE WOOD LANE LONDON W12 7RJ

TELEPHONE 01-743 8000   TELEX: 265781

TELEGRAMS AND CABLES: TELECASTS LONDON TELEX

4th February, 1980.

Mr. H. Root,
139 Elm Park Mansions,
Park Walk,
LONDON.
SW10

Dear Mr. Root,

My idea is that the kind of book you suggest should
be done for charity and no individual should profit
because the real work in the book is done by the stars
you quote. Therefore, if you are willing to donate
all of your royalties - as I am mine - I might consider
helping, otherwise you are on your own.

Yours sincerely,

Kim O'Mahony

pp

Michael Parkinson

BBC tv

BRITISH BROADCASTING CORPORATION

TELEVISION CENTRE WOOD LANE LONDON W12 7RJ

TELEPHONE 01-743 8000   TELEX 265781

TELEGRAMS AND CABLES: TELECASTS LONDON TELEX

5th February, 1980.

Mr. Henry Root,
139 Elm Park Mansions,.
Park Walk,
LONDON.
SW10

Dear Mr. Root,

I return your £1.

I frankly find your letter offensive.
You can rest assured you will get no
co-operation from either myself or any
member of my team.

Yours sincerely,

Kim O'Mahony

pp · Michael Parkinson

Enc.

139 Elm Park Mansions
Park Walk
London, S.W.10.

Mr John Field,
The News of the World,
30 Bouverie Street,   22nd January 1980.
London, E.C.4.

Dear Mr Field,
        'The Column With The Sunday Punch' has lost nothing since you
took over its authorship from Phillip Wrack. You write crisply and
to the point. Well done!
        I particularly liked your item last Sunday re the crooner Paul
McCartney's arrest in Japan on marijuana charges. Perhaps you could
have pointed out that if this silly young man had landed in Iran he
would have found himself playing the banjo in future with one hand!
        'It is time,' you wrote 'that he learned to live under the same
laws that apply to the rest of us.'
        Hear! Hear!
        Being, like your predecessor and indeed like all the excellent
journalists on your fine newspaper, a stern moralist, you are of the
view, I take it, that we are obliged to obey to the letter even those
laws of which we disapprove. (Leaving aside, of course, the absurd
drink/driving laws which all men of the world ignore). I ask you
this because I find myself clapped in something of a moral paradox.
It seems to me that not only are we obliged to obey all laws (save
the aforementioned), we are also obliged to inform the authorities
when we suspect that a law is being broken. Are you of the opinion
John, that a citizen failing to do such is aiding and abetting in
the commission of a crime? The fact is that my boy Henry Jr is a
persistent wrong-doer as to the wearing of tights and the smoking of
substances. Despite remonstrances and frequent biffings (spare the
rod etc) he refuses to kick the evil habit in favour of alcohol. Am
I - and here's the crutch of my dilemma - legally obliged to grass
the lad to the local constabulary? And if I don't am I myself breaking the law in that I'm harbouring a wrong-doer? Much as I'd like
to get him into trouble there are those to the left of centre who'd
rule that blowing the whistle on one's own son wasn't cricket. What
would Ritchie Benaud, your cricket correspondent, say?
        I realise that you don't purport to run a drug abuse advice
service, so I enclose a stamped addressed envelope for the courtesy
of your thinking in this matter.
        Yours sincerely,
        Henry Root
        Henry Root. A father.

Mr John Field,
The News of the World,
30 Bouverie Street,
London, E.C.4.

139 Elm Park Mansions
Park Walk
London, S.W.10.

25th February 1980.

Dear Mr Field,

I am disappointed that you haven't yet replied to my letter
of 22nd January in the matter of Henry Jr's persistent wearing of
tights and smoking of substances, even though I enclosed a stamped
addressed envelope for your convenience. I would point out that
your predecessor as composer of 'The Column With The Sunday Punch!',
Mr Philip Wrack, always answered my letters with dispatch.

Never mind. I expect you've been flat to the boards suing
so-called 'Bron' Waugh for his defamatory observations about yourself
and Mr Shrimsley. (I gather he designated the latter 'illiterate'.
How absurd! A careful perusal of the 'News of the World' shows this
to be by no means <u>literally</u> true, so where's Waugh's defence?)

That said, it must be admitted that suing for libel is a
costly business and since Waugh and 'Private Eye' will no doubt
soon be launching some such childish appeal as 'The Shrimsleyballs
Fund' to defray their expenses, I would like to contribute to your
side of the dispute. Here's a pound, John. Use it to silence
cowardly bullies in the media.

I look forward to hearing from you re the thrust of my letter
of 22nd January.

Yours sincerely,

Henry Root

Henry Root.

26 February 1980

Mr H Root
139 Elm Park Mansions
Park Walk
London SW10

Dear Mr Root

Thank you for your letter.   Technically I
suppose it is a citizen's duty to report
law breaking but in practice I am sure that
this will not apply in your case.   Your
problem with your son is very difficult and
really you must make your own decision.
All I can say that in the similar position
I would not go to the police, but instead
I would seek the advise and help of a doctor.

With best wishes.

Yours

John Field

28 February 1980

Mr H Root
139 Elm Park Mansions
Park Walk
London SW10

Dear Mr Root

Thank you for your second letter.   I am
sorry about the delay in replying to your
earlier letter which occurred because I
have been involved in another project.
However, I had belatedly replied and this
must have crossed with your second letter.

Mr Shrimsley is very touched by your offer
of £1 towards any possible legal costs.
But he prefers to finance any litigation
with his own funds.   I therefore return
your money with thanks and best wishes.

Yours

John Field

139 Elm Park Mansions
Park Walk
London, S.W.10.

Mr Phil Harris,
PO Equipment Development Division,
93 Ebury Bridge Road,
London, S.W.1.

2nd February 1980.

Dear Mr Harris,

So! Amid the usual orchestrated cries of outrage as the wet left breaks wind and lobbies the so-called NCCL, 'The New Statesman' has blown the whistle on phone-tapping! Big deal! Men of the world such as you and I have known of this sensible practice all along of course. How can you control folk in a free society unless you keep on file their indiscretions?

I should like to take the unusual step of requesting a tap on my own phone (352 9689) unless, that is, I am already on your 'hot target list' as one of the country's top folk of consequence. My reason for making this request is that I'm trying to dump Mrs Root. (She doesn't measure up, you understand, in all respects.) I have been advised by my lawyer Rubinstein that ditching her without good cause might be expensive (I am not without means) and that it is therefore of the essence that I 'get something on her'. It so happens that I have in my possession a letter from a Mr Michael Ivens (head of AIMS, a right-wing pressure group) in which he alleges that Mrs Root was 'known to him' some years ago in the Levant. Alas, all efforts to make this claim stick have proved empty and Rubinstein states that were I to go into court with nothing but this allegement I'd catch a cold.

So there it is. Please tap my phone as from today's date, ignoring my own private calls to such as my 'masseuse', but transcribing all calls between Mrs Root and such of a male tone of voice with whom she may be of a mind to cuckold me, not least the aforesaid Ivens.

I am unsure of the charge for this excellent service, so I enclose a pound on account.

I have marked this letter 'private and confidential' because it occurs to me that, unbeknown to you, your mail may be being 'intercepted' by Mr Brinley Jones of the Post Office Investigation Division. Nothing wrong with that. Quis custodet in corpore sano etc etc.

I await the first transcript.

Yours sincerely,

Henry Root.

Henry Root.

Dear Sir

Reference your letter dated 2 February 1980. I r[...]
that the Post Office cannot supply the information
you require and accordingly I return the £1 enclose[...]
with your letter.

13 February 1980

Yours faithfully

J. S.

Mr H Root
139 Elm Park Mansions
Park Walk
LONDON SW10

139 Elm Park Mansions
Park Walk
London, S.W.10.

Mrs Thatcher,
10 Downing Street,
London, S.W.1.

4th February 1980.

Dear Mrs Thatcher,

In taking retaliatory action against the Soviets re the wa
situation post Afghanistan, may I say you have my full support?
the various threatened sanctions - the severing of trade agreemen
the cut-back in exchanges at ballet dancer level, the refusal to
our lads and lassies run and hurdle vis a vis theirs at the Mosco
games and the dispatch of old Lord Carrington on initiatives here
and there (why not swop them Australia for Afghanistan - then the
have to cope Kerry Packer?) - the most effective, I think, will b
your intention to drastically step up the broadcasting in their d
ection of BBC shows. Several evenings on the trot of seeing noth
on their screens save mimes awarding one another trophies, 'male'
skaters gaining six out of six for 'artistic impression' and hors
jumping over obstacles at Olympia in the presence of the Queen sh
soon have them on their knees pleading for mercy in the matter.
haps the sending back to Moscow of Elton John, the bald little wa
from Weybridge, would put the lid on it.

Mention of horses jumping over things reminds me of a good
Princess Anne joke I heard the other day and which you might care
utilise in an up-coming speech. (There are those who think your
various pronouncements on this and that sometimes lack for the li
touch and while I appreciate you would normally eschew royal joke
I imagine that you'll agree with me that Princess Anne jokes have
become all right since she lost all status by marrying down). An
here's the joke. At a recent literary luncheon, Miss Jean Rook,
self-alleged 'Biggest Bitch in Fleet Street', was apprised by her
neighbour of the fact that Princess Anne was looking years younge
these days.

"That's because she's riding older horses," snapped La Roo
she likes to be called.

What do you think? Not bad? Use it by all means in a spe
but perhaps you'd like to credit me along the lines of 'additiona
wise-cracks by Henry Root' - something like that.

Here's a pound! Use it to fund the fight against Soviet
adventurism!

Let's dump the doves and rout the wets! (By which I don't
<u>necessarily</u> mean old Willie Wethouse, though he is beginning to w
somewhat as to the chops.)

Your man on the doorstep,

Henry Root

Henry Root.

10 DOWNING STREET

30th April 1980

Dear Mr Root,

I am writing on the Prime Minister's behalf
to thank you for your recent letter,
together with the enclosed £1, which I am
returning with this reply.

The contents of your correspondence have
been carefully noted.

With best wishes as always,

Yours Sincerely,

Richard Ryder
Political Office

Henry Root Esq

139 Elm Park Mansions
Park Walk
London, S.W.10.

Miss Deirdre McSharry,
'Cosmopolitan',
72 Broadwick Street,
London W1V 2BP.

1st February 1980.

Dear DMcS!,

You won't mind my addressing you as 'DMcS!' since this is how you always end your own lively editorials, a way of signing off which together with the nearby photo of your cheery mug gives your pronouncements a jolly, unpretentious flavour at odds with the 'heavy' feminism of such as Miss Polly Twaddle of 'The Guardian'. Well done! Might I also say, as a mere man, that your magazine is always sharp and caring, dealing in a concerned way with such relevant matters as self-abuse among women and the madness consequent thereon?

Mention of self-abuse and madness brings me to your star 'performer', viable Anna Raeburn. She may be crackers but she's good! It so happens that Robson Books Ltd have recently commissioned me to edit 'The Celebrities' Book of Embarrassing Incidents!' and from the many embarrassing articles contributed by your Miss Raeburn I'd like to quote an extract from her latest emission, which can be taken, I think, as a paradigm of humour. She refers in this article to a recent speaking engagement at a boys' school (lucky lads - as were the lesbians whom Anna recently addressed and who were unable to control themselves! As Anna reported at the time: "They found me a very sexy lady!"), in the course of which the lads asked her as to the differences between her and Jane Lucas, the character in Anna's compassionate documentary 'Agony'. (Incidentally, I wonder if it's occurred to Anna or anyone else to turn this excellent programme into a comedy? Re-written it could be very funny.) In replying, Anna said (and this is the passage I'd like to quote in my upcoming book of celebrities' gags):

'Well, Jane is Jewish. I wish I were but I'm not. Her mother is actually nothing like my mother. Jane drinks coffee - I can't. Actually I think she's a lot nicer than me but she makes the mistake I try not to make. She's on call to the world 24 hours a day. I mean, if my husband had started to make love to me and somebody rang up and told me he was miserable and he had to see me, you wouldn't catch me leaping out of bed, pulling on my clothes and saying "Sorry, honey, got to go, keep - (and I gestured!) warm for me" and rushing for the door!!! Two hundred adolescent boys yelled with mirth and I felt jubilant. Keep the Nobel Prize, the medals, wealth and beauty. I'll settle for being funny every time!"

I'm still chuckling over this, as is Mrs Root, and I'd be most grateful if you'd grant me permission to utilise it in my up-coming humorous book. Thanks DMcS!

One small quibble while I have your ear. At the foot of page 22 it says 'Unfortunately 'Cosmopolitan' cannot accept unsolicited articles and short stories for publication'. I don't get this. If this state of affairs is unfortunate why don't you alter your policy? If, on the other hand, your policy's correct, why do you term it unfortunate? You'd do better to say '<u>Fortunately</u> Cosmopolitan cannot accept unsolicited articles and short stories for publication.'

All the best DMcS!

Henry Root

Henry Root.

NO REPLY!

139 Elm Park Mansions
Park Walk
London, S.W.10.

Mr Alan Thompson,
The Daily Express,
Fleet Street,
London, E.C.4.

26th February 1980.

Dear Alan,

So they call you 'The Voice of Sport'. Well done!

Since I have plans to enter the writing game myself (though on a rather more serious level than you, I must admit), I wonder whether I could seek your expert advice on a literary matter?

I notice that you often make your comments under the bye-line 'Thommo'. Do you sign yourself thus for the purposes of acquiring a bluff, down-to-earth, man-on-the-terraces image?

Would you advise me to sign my own stuff Rooto? To date I've rendered my work here and there (novels, anthologies, plays etc) as WOMAN WATCHING by HENRY ROOT, SEMINAL THINKERS IN A NUTSHELL edited by HENRY ROOT and THE ENGLISH WAY OF DOING THINGS by HENRY ROOT. Would I have better luck, do you think, were I to submit them as:

WOMAN WATCHING by ROOTO.
SEMINAL THINKERS IN A NUTSHELL edited by ROOTO.
THE ENGLISH WAY OF DOING THINGS by ROOTO.

I'd greatly appreciate your ruling on this point, and I enclose a stamped addressed envelope for the courtesy of your reply.

Yours sincerely,

Henry Root

Henry Root. (Rooto).

DAILY EXPRESS

Express
Newspapers
Limited

121 Fleet Street
London EC4P 4JT
Telephone
01-353 8000
Telex No 21841
Cable Address
Express London

6 March 1980

Mr Henry Root
139 Elm Park Mansions
Park Walk
London
S W 10

Dear Rooto

I am in receipt of your letter and the answer
is yes.

Yours sincerely

Alan Thompson

Alan Thompson

Registered in London No 141748.
Registered office: 121 Fleet St London EC4P 4JT